From Both Sides of the Desk

Publisher's Cataloging-in-Publishing
(Provided by Quality Books, Inc.)

Melchior, Tom
    From Both Sides of the Desk / Tom Melchior.--1st
ed.
    p. cm
    ISBN 0-9661613-1-9

    1. Melchior, Tom. 2. High school teachers--Minnesota
--Biography. 3. English teachers--Minnesota--Biography.
4. Students--Minnesota--Biography. 5. Teaching--
Anecdotes.   I. Title.

    LA2317.M386A3 2003   373.11'009776
                   QBI03-700055

To my teachers, students, and teaching colleagues

Close to Home by John Mc Pherson

The year the SAT creators decided to mess with students' minds.

Permission granted by John Mc Pherson

Contents

From Both Sides of the Desk

MINNESOTA SCHOOL BOARDS ASSOCIATION
TEACHER CONTRACT
FOR MINNESOTA PUBLIC SCHOOL DISTRICTS

The School Board of ....**Independent**........ School District No. ....**191**... of the State of Minnesota, ...**Savage**............, Minnesota, at a meeting called for that purpose on the ....**15**.... day of ...**March**..........., 19...**62**... enters into this agreement with ....
........**Thomas Melchoir**........ of ....**Montgomery, Minnesota**........,
(name of teacher)
........................., a legally qualified teacher who agrees to serve in the following position:
........**High School Teacher — English**........
(Elementary Teacher or High School Teacher)

WITNESS, that beginning on or about ....**August 28, 1962**..........,
(month and date)
for the school year 19...**62**.. - 19...**63**..
the above named teacher shall faithfully perform the services prescribed by the school board or its designated representative, and abide by the rules and regulations as established by the school board during the life of this contract for the annual salary indicated below; and that said teacher agrees to teach in the schools of said district in such places, grades, and subjects as shall be designated by said school board subject to reasonable conditions of employment and certification of said teacher legally qualified by the Minnesota State Department of Education.

Pursuant to M. S. 125.12 this contract shall remain in full force and effect except as modified by mutual consent of the school board and teacher or unless terminated as provided by said statute; it being understood that this contract is subject to all state laws relevant in any way to the qualification and employment of teachers and to the power and right of a school board to discharge for cause pursuant to statutory authority.

TEACHER'S SALARY ....**$5640**.......... payable as authorized.

IN WITNESS WHEREOF, We have hereunto subscribed our signatures, dated this ....
day of ...March 15.............., 19...**62**..

Thomas E. Melchior
(Teacher)

....**Independent**.... School District No. ....**191**..
STATE OF MINNESOTA
By _Pat J. Connelly_
(Chairman)
H M Lundberg
(Clerk)

1959: Puerto Rico: Four "gringo" teachers take a break from Colegio San Antonio Abad to tour the island.

c. 1970: Nicollet Junior High School: Making the set for an animated film.

Introduction

I WALKED INTO SCHOOL FOR THE FIRST TIME IN 1942 WHEN I was six. I walked out for the last time in 1993 when I was fifty-eight. I spent fifty-one years walking in and walking out of various temples of learning. For approximately 66,400 hours I was either student or teacher. Very often I was both. Pete Seeger wrote a satirical song which asked, "What did you learn in school today, dear little child of mine?" My mother was singing those words long before Pete got his first banjo.

I asked my grandson the same question recently when I picked him up at kindergarten. "Well, Sam, what did you learn today?"

"I can't remember," he replied.

"Sure you can," I said. "What did you do in reading? Did you learn more about animals?"

"I forgot," he said emphatically. "I can't remember."

His answer sounded familiar. During my first year of teaching, I had asked myself similar questions: "What did I teach in school today and what did my students learn today? I always knew the answer to the first question, but I had no idea what my students had learned.

When I told a few colleagues that I wanted to write a book about my teaching experiences, they said, "Go for it. Write a book about how to teach and what you learned about the art of teaching. Tell people who want to teach what methods work. Tell them how to maintain discipline. A book like that would be a great help for people who want to teach. Write about what you learned. Tell the truth. Tell them what you know for certain."

I spent months thinking about their suggestions. I finally decided I could not write the book they described because there was little about which I was absolutely certain. I poured my "truths" into a bucket and they leaked all over me. What a presumptuous old bucket to think it could hold so much water!

The best answers I could give began with "I believe—" and "I think that—." Those introductory words made what followed conditional. I equivocated when they asked for absolutes.

Had my fifty-one years in school taught me no absolutes about teaching? Nothing to which I could exclaim, "And that's the truth!" What had I learned? The process of induction taught me several things of which I'm certain, well, almost certain. I believe Macbeth spoke the truth when he said, "Come what come may, time and the hour runs through the roughest day." Whether I was student or teacher, every day began and every day ended, though some seemed to be never ending. I also know that as time passes, things change.

In graduate school at St. Thomas, Professor Slusser asked one of the students if he believed that life is paradoxical. "Absolutely," William replied. I had never been schooled about paradox. Did I know this? I was embarrassed and began the usual psychic flogging when I deemed myself inadequate.

"So do I," said Professor Slusser. "It is the universal archetype of truth. Perhaps the most pervasive paradox is 'What is, isn't and what isn't is.' Ask Don Quixote, Oedipus and Huck Finn if you don't believe me." Professor Slusser talked about the death-rebirth paradox as the heart of the rites of passage. "Living is dying and dying is living," he said. "The paradox of possession beats in all of us. Owning is being owned. Ask Ishmael, Madame Bovary, and Macbeth about this.

"You can only draw people to you if you give them freedom. These paradoxes are the heart of literature because they are the heart of life," he proclaimed. Perhaps his understanding of these ideas explains why he was so fascinated with Tolkien's *The Hobbit* and *The Lord of the Rings.* I, too, became a believer.

I tried to imagine Education to be a person. Perhaps it was Education's personality that made it impossible for me to write a list of absolutes about what should be taught, why it should be taught, and how it should be taught. For years I paid no attention to Education's personality. Throughout elementary, junior high, and high school I accepted his words as gospel. Except for a few minor quirks, he seemed quite sure of himself.

During my college years Education began to look and act like one of Escher's drawings, the stairs tangled and never leading anywhere but to other stairs or solid walls. At times he melted in front of me like Salvador Dali's clocks.

During my first four years of teaching, I realized that Education was a paranoid schizophrenic. He acted as if everyone was out to "get him." He was distracted by anyone who whispered in his ear. He had just a vague notion of who he was. He couldn't tell me exactly what to do or why I should do it.

Education suffered from mandate overdose. Federal, state, and local governments as well as teacher organizations diagnosed his condition and prescribed varying therapies and medication to help Education become a whole person. Amateurs and professionals examined him but threw up their hands and proclaimed, "Education, cure thyself."

For thirty-four years I rode Education's roller coaster of psychotherapy. While Education wandered about in his labyrinth, seeking to find his center point, he sent my colleagues and me up and down and down and up his roller coaster. Several teachers jumped off whenever Education became momentarily catatonic, but many of us rode for years. Some like me have retired, but many are still riding despite Education's continuing illness. What brave hearts they are!

"Why would anyone choose to ride Education's roller coaster for a career," you may ask. I'm not certain. I believe that many people do not choose teaching; teaching chooses them. It would be similar to asking Gandhi to be CEO of an arms factory or asking Mother Theresa to sell diamond earrings and fur coats. My daughter once told me, "Dad, if I can't teach, I'll have to walk the streets." Fortunately, she's teaching.

What about those who are not called? I interviewed 175 former Minnesota country schoolteachers who ranged in age from 102 to 60. Some taught during World War I. Some are still teaching. I asked each of them, "Why did you become a teacher?" and "When did you realize that you truly loved children?"

The answers to the first question were usually, "There were really only three choices: get married or become a nurse or a teacher. No one responded that a driving altruism was the cause. The answers to the second question were, "I have always loved children. I grew up taking care of my brothers and sisters." Only one person admitted, "I never did learn to love the little buggers." These teachers were all elementary teachers. Many admitted that love might be too strong a word to describe their feelings for the older children, especially the ones who threw gophers into the attic of the school, hid a whiskey bottle in the school tree, or threatened the teacher.

Elementary teachers are more likely to say they love their students, who are flushed with innocence and enthusiasm. I have never asked secondary teachers, "When did you realize that you truly love children?" or "Did you become a teacher because you love teenagers?"

One year I was hired by the school district to screen teaching applicants for the secondary schools. The screening process was the brainchild of an educational company that observed hundreds of teachers and determined the qualities that excellent teachers had in common. They conducted extensive interviews with the teachers and asked each many questions about teaching. Then they observed the teachers to examine how their responses compared to their classroom performance. Based on their observations, they established questions and the appropriate responses. They concluded they could accurately predict which candidates had the potential to become excellent teachers and which did not.

I asked the first level of questions. My job was to record the responses accurately, not to ask other leading questions, or let my intuition influence my data. The professional researchers had developed a list of possible responses and placed them in hierarchical order.

The first question was, "What are the three main reasons you want to become a teacher?" Answers varied from "I was inspired by one of my high school teachers," I love mathematics and want to pass on my passion and knowledge," to various other answers, including "The summers are free."

The researchers had concluded there was only one primary reason and the first response should be, "I want to become a teacher because I love, like, care for, value children" or some similar response that implied they loved young people of all ages. Any other answer diminished the chances of candidates ever moving to the second round of interviews.

As I interviewed each candidate, I tried to picture myself being asked the same questions when I interviewed for my first job. Dirt was richer than I was. I owned nothing but my clothes. I probably would have said, "I need to earn a living, eat, rent a room, buy a car, buy some clothes, and pay off my college bills."

I didn't think about my students-to-be very often, and when I did, my heart beat erratically, not from love but from fear and anxiety. Did I want to teach because I was passionate about literature and the thousands of compositions waiting to be read and corrected? To tell the truth, I wasn't that in love with Samuel Pepys and his diary and I found the novels of Thomas Hardy depressing as hell.

I wondered how my journey to the classroom compared to those of my interviewees. In the eighth grade I decided I wanted to be a coach when I grew up. I knew that to become a coach I had to become a teacher. I applied to St. John's University in Collegeville because two guys I had played baseball against in high school were playing for the Johnnies, and I thought I was just as good as they were. So much for lofty academic ideals!

I took my coaching credits and flip-flopped between majoring in social studies or English. I enjoyed studying the material, but I seldom thought about teaching it. The only literature I studied which I would later teach was British literature and American Literature I. I taught British literature my first year and never taught it again. I taught little of what I had studied in American literature.

I completed all the required education courses and never once did any professor ask me why I wanted to teach. I never asked myself why I wanted to teach English. I liked it, but was that reason enough? How did I feel about teenagers? I had paid no attention to them for four years. My brother was in high school, and I knew I certainly didn't want to teach him.

I student taught one eighth-grade class for two weeks and one sophomore class for a month. No one observed me. My education professor left the monastery, took off for the Southwest, and got married. The entire business was shrouded in mystery. The supervising teachers hung out in the teachers' lounge. They all gave me wonderful recommendations.

During my interview the superintendent and principal never asked, "Tom, why do you want to teach?" or "Why do you want to teach in our school?" At the end of our first and only meeting, Superintendent Schmidt said, "If you would like the job, sign here." The principal shook my hand, gave me my grade book, and showed me my room. Bam! Just like that I was a teacher.

I signed a contract to teach four sections of senior English for $3600 and to coach B squad basketball for $300. During those first four years I taught in three different schools. For four years no one observed what was going on in my classroom. I taught what was in the book. I never asked myself if I was teaching Beowulf, Shakespeare, and the romantic poets because I "loved," "liked," or "cared for" my students. I was too busy trying to save myself from the maelstrom to ask any questions like that. I had to stay a day ahead of my students. I soon discovered the students I liked and didn't like, but that had little to do with the big questions.

My passion for teaching baseball and English never wavered. My spark of love for baseball kindled within me when I was in grade school and the fire has burned ever since. Eventually, however, I gave up my home on the baseball diamond and moved all my energy to my classroom.

I had to wait longer for the sparks of literature and writing to blaze. For years I waited for the answers to "What's truly worth knowing? Am I teaching content or students? Is there a better way to teach this material? How do I feel about my students?"

My English methods instructors lectured about our obligations and opportunities to teach the works of the great writers to our students. "Ignite the spark!" they cried. "Fill their minds with the ideas of the great novelists and poets. Pass on your passion for words. Teach them to write. Teach them to think."

At twenty-one I could identify a crackling fastball and an intimidating curve ball. I could throw them and I could teach others how to do it. I could also give persuasive arguments about why everyone should play the game.

When I entered the classroom as a rookie teacher, however, I had no idea how to "throw" literature or composition. My coaches had taught me how to throw a curve. "Put your thumb here, your fingers here, throw and snap your wrist." We didn't read about it; we did it.

We read and analyzed literature but we didn't teach it. Only once in my English methods class, was I required to teach a poem—Robert Frost's "Birches." Another day I was required to diagram a compound-complex sentence. We never talked about how to write a composition or teach the writing process. We wrote seldom, certainly nothing narrative.

When the bell rang to begin the first period on that first day of school in September 1958, I taught the way my high school English teacher and my college teachers had taught. I mixed me together with Mr. Albrecht, my high school teacher; the good monks, Father Dunstan Tucker, Father Conrad Diekman, and Father Alfred Deutsch, as well as my master mentor, Mr. Steve Humphrey.

The years passed and I continued to ask, "What's worth knowing?" I was a prisoner to that question. Voices plagued me when I slept. My nightmare was a scene right out of a Kafka novel. I sat naked in the center of a bare cubicle. A light bulb burned above me. Water dripped erratically from a faucet, each drop hitting the top of an overturned milk pail. The concrete ceiling and walls were sheetrocked and wallpapered. The ceiling was decorated with thousands of my worksheets and corrected compositions, dripping blood-red ink.

One wall was covered with sheet after sheet of educational philosophies and mission statements such as the following: "The Personal Development and Communications area will provide students with the opportunity to experience a variety of life styles and cultures (1) through vicarious participation such as literature and socio-drama, ESP and all forms of media, and (2) through direct participation such as travel, exchange programs, and technological displacement through time and space." *Education for the Futures, A Learning Path*, Independent School District 191, June 1974. One of the guiding ideas of the document was that there is always more than one possible future. All items in the document were placed in rank order and *prioritized*, a word I came to hate and will not utter to this day.

Another wall was papered with language arts goals, listed in order of importance. Sheets of luminescent gold, blue, green, pink, and yellow glowed on the third wall. Each page was a Xerox copy of required course content accompanied by the suggested methods of instruction.

The fourth wall groaned from the reams of pages that dictated behavioral objectives such as "A minimum of ninety-five percent of the students will correctly identify seventy-five percent of the direct objects in the following sentences. Eight-five percent of the ninth-grade students will construct a five-page expository composition, using complete sentences with correct grammar and usage. Seventy-five percent of all students will identify the rising action, conflicts, climax, and falling action of Jack London's short story 'To Build a Fire.'"

The Harpies' voices seeped out of the walls. "We know you're teaching, Tom," they whined, "so tell us what you have decided is worth knowing." At the mention of my name the walls slid forward.

"Speak," the Harpies wailed, "or we'll squeeze the answer out of you. Surely what you're teaching now can't get a person a job at MacDonalds or Target. Who cares about Melville's silent scrivener? What about your unit on restrictive and nonrestrictive adjective clauses? Do you think a college application will require a person to name the nominative and objective personal pronouns? Who but you cares if your students say, 'Me and my friend seen that movie'?"

When I screamed my answers, the walls paused. "Speak with more conviction," screeched the Harpies. Each night the walls closed in, stopping just as I awoke.

While I struggled for answers to silence the walls, "experts" wrote their versions of the academic gospels and published their current editions of "the truths." Every few years the absolutes changed. Academicians pontificated and the publishing companies provided us with "new math," "new English," or whatever was fashionable. Life went on in the classrooms and Education continued his monthly therapy sessions.

I can't remember when and how I escaped the Harpies. I cannot remember what ignited my flame or when it burst into heat. I never noticed when all those words like *love*, *like*, and *care for* melted together and formed a feeling I could not label. I felt it, but I could not give it sound. The feeling was a symphony that played me for the rest of my teaching career.

Like any symphonic orchestra, secondary education is departmentalized and each subject is taught by a specialist (at least in the ideal world). The first violinist doesn't play the clarinet. The calculus teacher seldom conducts the band and the band instructor will probably never teach the circulatory system of a frog. In larger schools these specialists may never see the works of student artists or examine their vision of the world. Specialists who dissect the words of poets may never enter the maze where technology teachers and their students feast with gigabytes. Nevertheless, we all give our gifts to help our students find their center points and follow their bliss.

Magic begins in the classroom when our parts become whole. When passion for our subjects and commitment to our students play the music the way it can be played, teaching is Beethoven's Fifth Symphony.

Idealism, however, is tempered by reality every hour of our teaching careers. Tony Bousa, former Minneapolis police chief and education advocate, spoke to our high school staff and used a different metaphor to describe teaching. "You are standing in a stream with a rushing current," he said. "The river is running out of control. Your job is to dam the river. Your tool is a #2 shovel. Scoop the sand from the bottom of the river and pitch it upstream to build your dam. Teaching is that difficult, but it's the best thing we have to save the youth of our nation."

My first reaction to the invitation to tell what I know about teaching is to tell a story, so that's what I'm going to do in the remainder of this book.

One of the jewels of stories is metaphor. One thing is something else. For example one might say, "Teaching is a three-ring circus" or "Teaching is a family vacation."

I can't remember when or how it happened, but one day teaching became delicious. Those questions I was asking,—"What's most important? How shall I do it? Will I make a difference?"—became a deluxe root beer float.

Now to make this float you need wonderful ice cream and the best root beer. You also need a scoop, a strong hand, and a frosty mug. You must know how to mix the float. Will you scoop the ice cream, put it into the mug, and then pour in the root beer, or will you pour the root beer into the mug and then drop in the ice cream? Or does it make a difference? Yes, of course it does. Everything makes a difference.

I have called this book *From Both Sides of the Desk* because many of the stories happened while I sat at my elementary, junior high, and high school desks. Many happened as I sat at my teacher desk. Others happened while I sat at life's desk.

About Stories

At any moment in our lives, we can look back and discover that the stories of our lives are following us. At first glance they seem to be scattered haphazardly, bouncing along the ground, dancing like kites in the summer breeze, or tangling themselves in thorny bushes.

Our stories seem detached, disjointed pieces from unrecognizable puzzles. Some look like realistic paintings while others are shimmering mirages. When we move, they follow us, these stories of our lives. Some are tied with silk threads, love stories that reach out to touch the rainbow. Others hook us with log chains, tragic memories that weigh us down like lead. Some are as mesmerizing as yesterday's sunrise. Some are shrouded in the mist of time and pain.   from *They Called Me Teacher*

We are our stories. When we hear the stories of others, they become part of our story, part of us. To discover who I am, I must know the stories of my mother and father and their mothers and fathers and their mothers and fathers and all the stories that are the genes of my story. Every told and untold story changes us.

We do not possess the power to become part of our untold stories, but we do possess the power to tell or not tell our stories. Our choices define who we want to believe we are. Buried stories may fool us into thinking we are someone else, someone incomplete, someone disillusioned. Buried stories, however, speak in dreams and remind us that we are human.

Stories born from imagination speak truth to us through metaphor. We become the falcon circling the sky, the whale gasping for air, the tree grasping the cliff, and the wheelbarrow pelted by rain. We are the teller of tales, the singer of songs, and the quencher of thirst. We are the blind and the beggars. We are the seeing and the gift-givers. We fly toward the light and plunge into the darkness. We are Siddhartha and Huckleberry Finn lost to the river. We are Babba Yaga and Vasalisa. We are those who seek to pass through the eye of the needle, and those who try to prevent the passing through. We are the chosen and the castoffs. We are the ones who can name and the ones who cannot name. We are the one whose heart bleeds and the one whose heart turns to stone.

I Am the Man in the Elevator

My wife went to the hospital on the first day of workshop. I noticed him that Monday night when I went back to visit her. He was standing at the nurses' station holding his pack of Marlboros. He smoked incessantly. I smiled at him, nodded, and he nodded in return. I saw him every time I visited the hospital.

The rooms in that section of the hospital are arranged in a circle. The nurses' station and the visitors' lounge are located in the inner circle. He paced within the circle, moving from chair to chair, sitting only long enough to finish his cigarette. He stubbed it out in the ashtray, lit another, and paced again. He seldom said "yes" or "no" to the nurses or other patients and said nothing to the rest of us. His eyes wandered impatiently from one person to another.

He was about sixty or sixty-five. He had a sharp, angular nose and granite-gray hair, heavily oiled and combed back flat on his head. He slouched when he walked, concealing his height in a loosely fitting, maroon terry cloth bathrobe. He wore brown slippers that flapped when he walked and sounded like someone sanding a terrazzo floor.

His hands were huge. Perhaps their size was distorted because his arms extended so far past the sleeves of his robe. One hand engulfed the Marlboro package while the other fidgeted with the cigarette.

When he did sit, he sat on the very edge of the chair, leaned forward, and rested his elbows on his knees. He held his head in his hands and his long fingers jailed him from the rest of the world.

I often read in the lounge when my wife was sleeping. Time after time I found myself staring at him. When he glanced my way, I tried to hide behind the magazine, the way I did in junior high when I tried to avoid the teacher's scolding eyes.

I saw only one person make him laugh, a young black nurses's aide who treated the solemn hospital atmosphere with delightful irreverence. She put her hand on his shoulder, joked about her hair or her boyfriend, and enveloped him in laughter.

I said good-bye to my wife on Thursday evening and walked down the hall to the elevator. I turned the corner and saw him waiting for the same elevator.

Again we nodded at each other. The elevator doors opened and I followed him in. He looked at me and in a desperate attempt to break the silence, I said, "Going down, huh?" I cringed at the inane question, but he nodded politely. We were on the fifth floor and he punched the button for the fourth floor.

The door shut and he turned to me and said, "Yes, I'm going to visit an old girlfriend."

I laughed at the thought of that strange rendezvous. I thought he was joking. The elevator stopped at the fourth floor. He took one step out the door, turned, and held the door.

He looked at me and began to cry. "My wife died on this floor three weeks ago," he said, "and I'm going down to visit her roommate. Last week I developed a bleeding ulcer, and they brought me to this hospital, and I said, 'For God's sake, don't put me on this floor.'"

He took his hand off the door and it slid shut. The next day my wife moved off the fifth floor. I never saw him again.

Minneapolis Star Tribune, 1978

I believe stories must speak for themselves, but I also know that no story exists in a vacuum. Throughout this book, I will let the other stories speak for themselves (with a few exceptions). In my classes the day I met the man in the elevator, I had lectured my students about the power of stories. I told them that stories and myths speak a universal language. I told them that stories and myths speak about that which cannot be explained.

I never felt the elevator move to the first floor. The door opened and I stood there, dumbfounded. I had just heard the music of life and it was filled with pain. For days the story haunted me. Why had the man told his story to me, a stranger? Was it because I nodded or spoke to him? Did telling the story ease his pain? Was this a story that had a life of its own and demanded to be told?

I knew the only way I could stop being owned by the story was to write it and so I did. The story, the man, and I are one. He touched me with his suffering and that is what it means to be human.

The jump from the literal to the metaphorical is an enlightening leap. We may discover truths about ourselves and others where we least expect to find them.

The Whales

In late October of 1988, three gray whales surfaced for air in a fast-freezing ice hole somewhere near Barrow, Alaska. The Eskimos named the whales Putu, (Ice hole), Siku, (Ice), and Kanik, (Snowflake). The rescue effort involved more than one hundred people, as well as support vehicles and several helicopters. Many questions were raised about the money, time, and effort spent to rescue the whales.

Why We Must Teach: A Parable

The rescue of the whales affected me deeply. I saw a magnificent drama being enacted in a bleak theater. Leviathans surfaced within the touch of man and struggled for survival. The drama began with no watchers and played itself out before the eyes of the world.

Today I'm certain the holes have frozen shut and arctic winds again haunt the ice, but the drama still lingers in my mind's eye.

The ocean beckoned the whales to freedom, but they trapped themselves under an entombing sheet of ice. In that small area three of the ocean's most marvelous creatures gasped for life. Again and again they surfaced in a life-death ritualistic dance.

At first the entire production looked like an act from the theater of the absurd. With death imminent, the whales' archenemies appeared, a most incongruous menagerie: Eskimos wielding chainsaws, dancing on ice blocks and snacking on stew made from bowhead whales, an even more endangered species; the Minnesota entrepreneurs lugging generators and humming machines; the media converging en masse to document the drama; and the Russian ice breaker, sent by the "villains of the evil empire," arriving at the eleventh hour.

Rescuers struggled to free three whales while moralists questioned the ethics of such an effort. For a moment I cringed at the absurdity of the scene and weighed the $600,000 cost of the rescue attempt against the need to house the homeless and feed the hungry.

Now I know my first reaction was wrong. Whether we recognized it or not, we were witnessing the most rational of acts. What was happening was not absurd at all. The way we usually act is absurd. In the world away from that hole in the ice, we separate ourselves into fragments of humanity, arming ourselves to inflict fear and pain on one another; we subject the innocent to tyrannical acts that shatter our most hardened sensibilities; we indulge ourselves in seventeenth-rate ideas and consume them as nurturing pabulum; and we assassinate the environment in acts we label as politically correct and economically necessary.

What I saw when the whales surfaced was not absurd. It was what ought to be, what must be. Something deep in our collective psyche told us that our very essence, our very being, was trapped beneath that ice. We threw ourselves into frantic action to rescue the whales. We stripped away everything that separates us from the natural world. We disregarded all ideologies that fragment our humanity. We abandoned all self-serving enterprise and acted selflessly. We became one life form trying to save itself. We could not save all three whales, but when the two survivors swam to freedom, we had, for a brief moment, taken one step toward saving ourselves.

Because of this event I better understand the ecologists' message that we need to save the wilderness to save ourselves. I understand that it takes a life or death crisis to awaken in us an awareness of our oneness.

I wish I could have been there, cut some ice, listened to the explosion of the whales' breath, and touched them on the nose. But the truth is, I was there. I was there in spirit. If I must be counted as one of the human race that acts absurdly, then I am also one of those humans who helped save the whales. I am part Russian, part entrepreneur, part reporter, part Eskimo, and part whale. I rejoice in what I have done, even if this time I acted only in spirit. I exalt in this altruistic gesture, but I know it is an empty gesture if we do not abandon the absurd and free the rest of us who are trapped.

"Now, Mr. Melchior, what does this picture say to us?"

1

Students

Stories by My Students

Mike

THE YEAR WAS 1967, AND I WAS ONE YEAR OLD. MY family and I were visiting with relatives at my grandmother's house. The house was an old rural home in northern Iowa that had corn husks stuffed into the dead spaces in the attic to serve as insulating material, a common practice at the time.

It was an extremely hot September afternoon and almost everyone was playing and visiting out in the yard. It was time for my afternoon nap, so my mother placed me in a crib upstairs in the attic away from the commotion of the family activities. She set the crib near an open window and left to be with the others. Unknown to her and to the dozens of people in the yard, hot gasses from the husks were being released and ignited a fire through spontaneous combustion.

I watched from the crib as I became wrapped in a hot, smoky wind that seemed to pass right through me on its way to the nearby window. The heat made me delirious as sounds became muffled and there was a strange sensation of taste, smell, and consciousness all melting into one. I remember staring curiously into the gray smoke when out of nowhere there appeared a face. It belonged to my father and he rescued me from the burning house that day. My dad was always proud to say that he found me laughing when he finally reached the crib.

I sustained burns to the face, hands, and scalp. In hospital photos, I resembled a patchwork quilt. The surgeon who worked on my skin grafts recommended a hair prosthesis for proper "psychological development," so my parents bought me a hairpiece before I started kindergarten.

The hairpiece took some getting used to and I spent what seemed like hours every morning before school telling my mother, "That's too high.

That's too low," I said as she tried to get me accustomed to my new look. Eventually, she would get my hairpiece on just the way it should go and then carefully combed it into my real hair. That was my routine every morning before heading out to school.

One day in kindergarten while the class was sitting in a circle listening to the teacher tell stories, a boy named Jeff was trying to persuade a fellow kindergarten student that my hair was really a wig. In fact, he was so sure of it that he decided to prove his point in a very direct way. He sneaked up behind me and pulled the hair from my head.

From around the room I heard a collective gasp, followed by shrieking and laughter as everyone realized what had just happened. I turned around quickly to see Jeff examining the underside of my hairpiece as if there was something important in it. I asked him to give it back, but when I reached out to take the hair, he turned and passed it to someone else who threw it to someone else. Eventually, the teacher retrieved the hair and quieted the group somewhat.

My teacher led me away from the group with my arm in one hand and my hair in the other. She took me behind a bookshelf and bent down to hand me the hairpiece. Unfortunately, it had become so stuck together and so mangled that I didn't recognize it. I told her I didn't know how to put it on and would she please put it on the way my mom did. There was a strange silence. Then she said something that terrified me, "Michael, I don't really know how your mother puts this on."

She unfolded the hairpiece, trying her best to make it look as it had before. She put the hair on my head as best she could. Unfortunately, no placement of the hair could have satisfied me at that point. I took my best guess as to which way to orient it on my head. She didn't put it on like I told her, and I am sure I said something nasty to her about how poorly the hair was placed because she just handed me the comb and walked away saying, "Return to the group when you feel ready." My teacher never did have a lot of patience for the problems of young kids and I felt victimized by her as well.

I don't know how long I sat there hiding behind that bookshelf with my screwed-up hair and its tape no longer sticking to my head. I had a comb but I didn't know how to use it. I had no mirror and my belly was doing that crying thing where the more you try to stop it, the more it goes into spasm. Later I would seek out seating arrangements that backed up against walls to keep this from happening again. Unfortunately, there were never enough walls.

Finally, when I returned to the group, I found myself the recipient of playful tugs and lifting of the hair from different directions. With each lift the tacking ability of the hair tape was lessened. Soon I was holding one hand on top of my head at all times. I could never admit to the others that I was actually bald no matter how painfully obvious it had become to the class during frenzied times like these.

Later that year, while visiting with my family at my grandmother's house, now restored from the fire, I was struck by something I had never seen before: a mounted pheasant hanging on the wall. It was a rooster with its wings spread in flight. I couldn't stop looking at its feathers all laid out in a rich patchwork of colors and textures. Unlike the burn patterns on my skin, which seemed to do nothing more that to evoke a sense of horror in strangers, the patterns on this bird had just the opposite effect, making it awesome and beautiful.

I became obsessed with this thing and so I borrowed a piece of paper and a pencil from the adults' poker game. I sat on my grandmother's couch and began to sketch the pheasant. Of course, I was only five years old, but I do remember feeling as though I was drawing for the very first time. I spent the afternoon happily counting the wing feathers and memorizing the shapes and locations the feather patterns. In the end I was proud to show the finished work to the people at the poker table and they seemed to be proud of it as well.

Back at school, the beginning of each year brought with it the challenge of determining which kids would be the ones to sneak up behind me and try to take my hair. The actions of those bold little monsters encouraged the bad behavior of others. Soon it was just accepted that my hair was everyone's business. Curious interrogators would appear out of nowhere. "Are you bald? Is that real hair? Your hair doesn't look the same as mine." Even the most demure little girl in class could completely immobilize me with fear by asking me these simple questions.

Fortunately, though, I had the secret weapon that gave me power over the other kids. I could draw a flying pheasant better than anyone else in school and I was ready for battle! Some kids saw the attention my pheasant drawings were getting and they started drawing their own pheasants, but I knew how many feathers were in a real pheasant wing, and I could quickly reveal their pheasants as impostors.

My first grade teacher introduced an art project that involved the creation of a white cotton dress that she would sew together and wear in class. The pieces of material for the dress were to be covered with drawings by each of her students, and she made it clear that she wanted me to draw a pheasant in flight—very large—across the breast piece, the biggest area given to any student. When the dress was finished, I could not have been more proud to see my pheasant so big it even crept into her arms a little bit.

One day the following year, I spotted her coming down the hall towards me. She was quite a sight, wearing that same white cotton dress and walking with a man in a suit. We were just about to pass each other when she stopped me and told the man to wait for a minute. Then she called my name and made her way across the hallway. She crouched down in front of me and pointed to her chest saying, "Michael, I just wanted to tell you how proud I am to be wearing my pheasant dress today."

Fourth grade was a watershed; it marked the end of my traumatic hair-piece episodes. For some reason, my hair was no longer the focus of every-one's attention. I suppose it all ended, as so many childhood fascinations do, out of sheer boredom. Not only did the teasing come to an end, but also my fourth-grade teacher was one of the best teachers I would ever have.

She was graceful, radiant, and larger than life. She had an infectious, positive attitude and she was also Mark Hamill's (Luke Skywalker's) cousin. What kid would not have loved this woman? She said she once lived in Palm Springs next door to Bing Crosby. She was friends with Bing and even though they were friends, she said that he couldn't bear for any-one to see his bald head. At times she said hello to Bing in the backyard, surprising him without his hat, and she told me that whenever this hap-pened, he would say nothing but turn and make a mad dash for the house. She said she found the behavior very peculiar and amusing. Usually the bald guy stories didn't do much for me, but this was Bing, and this was my teacher.

One day she invited a janitor to talk for an entire hour on the topic of his life experiences. She knew all the janitors, and she knew that this guy had some real stories to tell. His name was Jim, and he had traveled the world, first in the military and then in construction. Once while clearing rain forests in the Amazon Basin, he was nearly killed by natives from a gunshot wound to the chest and was forced to settle down back in the United States. Jim had so many stories that he ran out of time telling them.

My eighth-grade teacher had as much energy as her students. She assigned a large project called "The Person I Will Become." The project explored our thoughts and plans for the future. We visualized how our lives would unfold, and as I get older, I still find myself comparing my life's path to what I wrote down on those pages. I think about whether or not I am measuring up to the person I created in that eighth-grade paper.

I took high school calculus from The Legend. He was tall and thin with a dry sense of humor. I always thought that if Abe Lincoln was ever rein-carnated, he would be something like my calculus teacher. At Christmas time he took one day and just read stories to the class by candlelight. I was chronically behind in calculus, so the fact that he constantly reminded us to focus on the big picture kept me from getting too depressed over the fact that I was underachieving amidst a group of very competitive students. While working at the blackboard, he enlisted the aid of imaginary characters such as Mr. Slope Finder and the parrot that sat on his shoulder. He knew how to bring college-level problems down to size.

My high school art teacher lived his life immersed in the arts. Opera, symphonies, plays, gourmet food, and art exhibits were constantly on his mind. He was the first teacher to become my friend and I was fortunate enough to have had the chance to spend time with him in one-on-one situations.

He took me to figure drawing classes, concerts, and plays, all during his leisure time. Once he invited me up to a Lake Superior cabin to draw and paint nature with him. We read P.G. Woodhouse stories to each other long into the night until we were so tired and silly that we couldn't read another word. He is gone now. He was the most sensitive man I have ever met.

In the same way that my fourth-grade teacher had the common sense and resourcefulness to humanize Jim, the janitor, before a class of fourth graders, my twelfth-grade English teacher used every angle imaginable to communicate his ideas. We analyzed with equal focus the classics, the lyrics of Simon and Garfunkel, the stories about Beowulf and Gilgamesh, the mythic-marketing ploys of McDonald's Corporation, the poetry of Dylan Thomas, the narrative oil paintings of the Renaissance, and excerpts from the *Upanishads*. He made it clear that no life experience was outside the realm of the arts.

While I was taking his class, I won an award for a drawing I had created in my art classes. It was an important award and one that I had worked hard to achieve. I attended a ceremony in Minneapolis for what was called the Gold Key Award, and the governor was to present it personally.

As I sat in the auditorium that night, waiting for my turn to approach the podium, I scanned the crowd and noticed that my math teacher and his wife were sitting alone in the crowd. I was shocked to realize they had made the effort spend an evening for just one of his many students.

As usual in high school, Gold Key Art Awards do not get much attention. So the next day was just another day until I walked into English class and sat down. The starting bell rang, but instead of beginning class right away as he always did, my teacher was silently at work tracing out some strange shape on the chalkboard. His movements were slow and deliberate. As he pushed the chalk heavily, the chalk dust flaked in tiny clouds to the floor. The class grew silent and all faced forward wondering what could be the matter.

He said nothing as he finished the shape he had created—a large key. He stood back and examined his work, remembering to draw the hole in the key before laying the chalk on the rail. He turned and stepped back to his usual position at the front of the class. He stood for a time, motionless, staring at a point somewhere just above the students and moving his lips slightly in thought. At this point, nobody dared move or speak. I thought, "Is this what happens when a teacher finally loses it?"

Then he turned and pointed at the board. "Does anyone know what this is?" he asked, knowing full well that only two of us knew. "Someone in this class achieved something very important last night," he said. "It won't make the front page of the school paper and it didn't happen on the athletic field, but it is important to acknowledge this achievement." He then explained that I had won the Gold Key Award and when he had finished, he just stood looking at me, beaming. The class immediately stood and applauded.

In that moment I realized a little irony. Clapping next to me was one of my old grade school interrogators. She was among the first to stand and applaud. Earlier in high school we'd become close enough for me to ask if she remembered any of the cruel things she did to me in grade school. She said she couldn't remember anything about it, but oh, how I wanted that forgotten little monster to see me on this, my best day! Instead, I had to settle for a secret moment of reconciliation with my old nemesis, who now gave me the standing ovation.

When I look back now about the Gold Key Award, I think about my art teacher who worked tirelessly to mentor me and to get my work shown. I think about a math teacher and his wife who spent an evening in a cramped auditorium to shake my hand and tell me how were proud they were of me. I also think of the day my English teacher outlined a gold key in chalk and transformed it into the golden moment of my formal education.

Scene from "The Portable Phonograph" by Mike

Carla

I first met Carla when she was a student in my eighth-grade English class. I transferred to the high school and a year later she enrolled in two of my classes. We meet every few months to reminisce and share what is happening in our lives. When I asked her what she would like to add to her story, she said, "Just say, 'Carla is a survivor.'"

I really don't know if teachers have a clue about how much impact they have on students. I've thought about their influence from third grade through high school. As cocky and difficult and dark as I became in my teenage years, the ones I trusted had an incredible impact on me even though I didn't let them know it. I had lost trust in my parents and other people around me, but I trusted a few teachers whose words and stories affected me tremendously.

In fourth grade we moved. By sixth grade I was heading downhill psychologically. I thought my parents intentionally put me in a round school to keep me confused. I had problems finding my rooms. I went around and around. I always went the wrong way. I tried to get somewhere on time, but I always chose the wrong way, and it took forever to get where I was supposed to be. I thought my parents had moved me just to be mean or make me crazy.

I had a "hippie" teacher who wore weird clothes. She played the guitar and we sang songs like "Blowin' in the Wind." She taught us environmental stuff: controlling population, taking care of the earth, and preserving limited resources. I spent hours picking up litter, one little thing I could do. It wasn't much, but it was something.

We saw a movie about hunger in school and it struck me like a ton of bricks. Suddenly I didn't see just my family and me. I saw a piece of the world. I didn't know anything about kids starving to death. I was young and idealistic. I discovered there was such a thing as starvation, and I was so naïve that I thought I could stop it. I thought, "Why hadn't my parents told me about this?" I had too much. I felt ashamed and angry. I didn't understand why people had so much of this stuff. My heart was never about stuff. I was very angry because my parents had purchased a large house for just four of us. I had all this stuff that I didn't need, and there were people who didn't have what they needed to survive.

I needed something to believe in. I needed to know there was something good out there. I saw these horrible things happening, so I searched for God, for something spiritual. I was frustrated trying to discuss things with my parents and having my mom say, "You're weird," or "You're different."

I didn't need to hear that. I wanted to be like other people. I wanted to find somebody who would say, "No, you're not strange. You're not different. You're just the way you are."

Then two things happened that changed me: an anti-drug campaign in school and drinking for the first time. Those things happened close to Christmas when I was in the sixth grade. The same hippie teacher showed us a film about illegal drugs and how bad they were. I came out of that movie feeling drugs were the only thing I wanted. Before that film I never thought about doing drugs and what they would do to me. The movie imitated an LSD trip. I got the impression that no matter what I did or what I took, I would have a high for a while, but then I'd come back to reality.

"So what's the problem here?" I thought. "I get happy for a while, and then I come back down." I didn't see any problem. The movie talked about some physical side effects, but it wasn't convincing. "Here's a way out of pain," I thought. "Here's a way to experience lack of control." I was so tired of holding things in. I wanted a sense of freedom.

At Christmas my folks had wine. I had a glass, and since it was okay with them, I had two. I went up to my bedroom and lay on the bed. A warm feeling came over me. I thought, "The pain's gone! The pain's gone!" When I felt that pain two or three weeks later, I went into the cabinet and had a drink. The pain vanished again.

I picked out every book I could find about religion and philosophy. I had a sense that there was something that nobody would tell me. The things I was learning were not touching where I was hungry. I was looking for answers: "Why am I here? Why do I hurt? Why am I so confused?"

My parents told me, "God's up there." They taught me the Ten Commandments. "Follow them and you'll be okay. Be good and good things will happen." That fell apart. I saw it wasn't true. My teacher's wife died. My teacher was a nice guy, the best teacher I'd ever had and his wife died. Things like that were not supposed to happen.

I was frustrated and disillusioned. I looked into philosophy. When I read a book or got words from a teacher that were deep, I thought, "Somebody else does know. I'm not alone. Somebody else talks about the kind of things I'm thinking about." I was unable to make contact, to really touch. I don't mean just physical touch. I mean soulful touch. Those heady things left me starving on the inside. I wasn't in contact with my parents. I wasn't in contact with kids. I was very lonely. I tried on different ideas the way people try on coats. "All right, Shinto, show me what you can do. All right, let's go, Hindu." I explored witchcraft, which appealed to me because there were exercises to make things happen because you believed them.

I read a book that said we can't trust what we see because there's more space between things than there is material. That meant if I had the right combination and knew how to manipulate molecules, I could make one thing go through another. I couldn't even trust my table. How could I trust this thing and this group of molecules no matter how it was put together since it was mostly space? I carried that to the way I saw people. I believed everybody was made up of space, so I had an automatic sense of mistrust.

On my bulletin board next to the Ten Commandments, I put up sayings like "The only real things are those that are unseen," *real* meaning permanent, things that matter, things that last. Anything I could see would turn to dust. I believed what I couldn't see. I didn't trust any one or any thing. That was scary. I can see why I went nuts. I was walking around in my private little world. Also, I didn't trust time. If I couldn't believe something is solid, how could I trust that today is today?

What guarantee did I have that the reality I was living in had a bottom-line and that my reality was in tune with that reality? How did I know that someone else was not living in a completely different reality? I couldn't trust in anything I walked on or anything I breathed.

I had a renegade spirit, so when I was in the seventh grade, I created a persona to exist "out there," so that I could live "in here" and be free of the pain. I decided how she acted, how she looked, how she talked, what hurt her, everything, so I could stay inside. I tried to put her persona "out there" and keep her skin on all the time.

I gave the other me a name. Those were big rock days and I had a picture of Stevie Nicks from Fleetwood Mac. She had long black hair, not blonde like mine. I named my new persona Child, a real hippie thing.

I admired authors who wrote about something deep. I hungered to touch minds with anyone who understood things. Through movies, books, or people I thought of myself as two people, the one "out there" and the one "in here." I could move that other one in closer and take a chance on trusting a little bit more. I developed the other persona to take care of me so I wouldn't be frightened and hurt. I drank because it soothed me for the moment. I did it to survive.

I baby-sat and drank the people's liquor. I put the kids to bed and took a couple drinks, not enough that the parents could tell. I wasn't sloshed drunk. When they came home, they paid me and hired me again.

My folks didn't drink that often. My dad put liquor on his ice cream, but he wasn't a heavy drinker. Neither was my mother, but they had a well-stocked liquor cabinet.

I walked at night and drank, even in the winter. I took their booze when they weren't home, poured it into baby food jars, and kept it in my closet. Then I waited for them to go to sleep. I took one step down the stairs and counted to thirty. I took another step and another step until I got to the back door. Sometimes I crawled out the windows.

I drank my gin or vodka straight and walked around the school and back into the woods. I hoped even in the dark of night there was someone out there who might help me. One night I got drunk and wrote "HELP!" all over our light pole with Chap Stick. I was so miserable, standing out there alone, feeling something was wrong. One time a car came up slowly behind me. Somebody ran after me. I ran to the playground and hid in one of the forts. I thought, "Why am I doing this? This is scary and stupid," but I walked at night for a long time. Sometimes I came home drunk, went to sleep, got up, and went to school in the morning.

At the same time I had allergies and coughed all the time, so I was on codeine. I took it to school, went into the bathroom, and slugged it down and then went back to class. I lived in horrendous guilt because I figured what I was doing was very much against my Christian upbringing, even though it wasn't ministering to me at that point.

I also counted to get through the pain. I've counted for as long as I can remember, but when you're young, you can't count very far. It's one, two three, or one, two, three, four, five and then start again. When I counted, I believed I could do almost anything, bear any amount of pain for a short time.

I wanted to get good grades and I enjoyed learning, but I couldn't look like I wanted good grades. I had to look a little like the other me. I tried not to look too good. I wore blue jeans. I had to look a little unkempt. I went to a few parties in the seventh grade. I was still struggling on and off with depression. Sometimes it wasn't too bad. Of course, I didn't know at that time it was depression.

You gave us an invitation to write at a level that interested me, but I wondered if you could handle what I wrote. I wondered what you were going do with it. Things got so bad that I wrote a list of reasons why I should commit suicide and reasons why I shouldn't. I wrote it very deliberately. I probably got drunk before I wrote it. I even signed it in blood.

I wrote a poem about suicide. I visualized the whole thing. I turned that poem in and we talked in the library one night after school. You asked, "Is it a boy?" You said if I needed help, we could talk. Then you directed me to a counselor at school. I tried every avenue I could. I certainly didn't trust you. I mean, to a point I did, but I thought I'd try my family's church. I took my pro and con suicide list with me. One option was to commit suicide and be done with it. The other was to run away and become a prostitute. I had no sexual experience. This wasn't about sex, but I saw that as an option because I was too young to work. Either do suicide or become a prostitute. I didn't know if getting help was an option.

I became physically ill. I drank a lot. I saw a counselor from Community Action Council, something like that. He lit up a cigarette in the school office, and I thought that was awesome. Then he offered me one. He had seen kids in trouble. He nailed me fast. He told me if I didn't knock it off, I'd never make it to eighteen, and I had to get into treatment immediately. He sent me to an AA meeting. Usually I didn't trust anyone, but when I did trust, I opened the door and walked all the way in. He could have taken me to another country and I would have gone with him.

I was twelve and in the seventh grade when I went to treatment for the first time. They said that everything we do, we do for a reason, even when we think we are doing something out of love. I had been so angry at everybody else for not caring, and then they said everything we do is self-serving. That crushed me.

In high school I toughened up. I became much more like that person I tried to create. I had a real "fuck you" attitude. I thought I was so lousy and awful that I might as well get hurt and I did get hurt. I made some very destructive choices. I tried to be a good student. I was with a group of good students, but my other friends said, "Which is it going to be? Are you going to be with them or with us?" I pulled A's and told the good students about my Fridays, going to a kegger party with older people and running from the cops. I told them I got drunk and sick and threw up. There I was sitting at their table, doing my science project. They couldn't trust me because I didn't look like the other burnouts.

A group of druggies accepted me. I went out to the parking lot and smoked pot in their car. My friends in school nailed me. "Which is it going to be?" they demanded. They wanted to know which box I was in. I was so frustrated because I wasn't in either. Finally I gave up on the kids my age.

I blame the school curriculum for some of my problems. Teachers have to teach some things, but maybe they could change how they teach and be more selective in the options they give their students. I took a class about becoming eighteen—what our rights are and what we could do as adults. It made a huge difference in my life. I was primed for that class. I was angry with my family. I had come out of treatment with all these ideas about how my family was totally screwed up.

The other choices I made were much worse than what was waiting for me at home. The class taught us how we could have power over all kinds of things we didn't know about. That's a dangerous thing to give to high school kids. The teachers taught us how to have sexual freedom, what to do about it, where to get help, things I would never have thought about. They gave out the names of clinics. I got a friend and said, "Let's get on the pill." All the girls I knew started having sex, not because they were in love, but because they had the name of a clinic handed to them.

The class also taught us about our legal system. It showed us we could be emancipated at an earlier age if we showed that we were taking care of ourselves. We learned that if we didn't like our parents and thought they were abusing us, we could get away from them. So I went to a social worker. I was very angry, very unhappy. Instead of turning my anger inward, I turned it on my parents. I wouldn't speak to my mother. I ran away and didn't tell her where I was going. Then I told the social worker, "I want to get out of my house. I can't live there anymore." I was backed by what I had learned in class. I went into the counselor feeling like I had an arsenal on me. I knew my rights and I knew what they had to do for me. Boom! I was in a foster home just like that.

I went to Abbott Hospital, too, during high school. I spent a summer and part of the fall in their psych ward, four or five months. I had already done the treatment in Chanhassen. When I got out, I did okay for a while. That's when I insisted on getting into a foster home. The first night I was there the other girl looked at me and said, "You know, she's just doing this for the money."

The foster mother took us to a bar, got drunk, and brought a guy home. She was whoping it up with him in the next room and I thought, "I've made a big mistake." The next night she gave us money and dropped us off at a rock concert. I spent my money on LSD. I took so much acid that I got extremely ill and wound up walkings the streets. I found a phone and called a sponsor for help.

I ended up back in Chanhassen detox, hallucinating from strychnine poisoning. I ran away again. I didn't want to go home, so I ran away and hitched a ride into Minneapolis. I didn't know anything about the city.

I was raped on that runaway. I had this wacko idea that the police would help me. I was too embarrassed to talk to my parents, I didn't trust social workers, I wasn't in school, and I didn't trust the treatment center, but I believed I could trust the police. I had the idea that if I got in some kind of trouble, they'd help me. That was crazy. It was nuts. That's why I wound up in the psych ward.

I walked up to this guy and said, "Do you know where I can get a cool drink?"

"Yeah, my place," he said, so I went home with him. I smoked something. I don't know what it was. It could have been hashish. I drank something, got terribly high, very sick and woozy. When I tried to leave, he laughed and locked the door. He put the chain over it. He tried to push me into the shower but then he put me into bed. I told him I would break a window and the police would come. Later when he opened the door to take me out, I still thought, "Okay, I've been through all this but at least I can call the police." I couldn't walk very well, so he dragged me down the steps and he took me behind a bar. I threw up in the gutter.

Debbie

The following story is a response to this assignment: Select a few lines from Gilgamesh and relate them to your own life.

"Some faces may be passages into a life one may imagine but has never seen."
It was a bitterly cold evening three days before Christmas when I descended upon the downtown Nicollet Mall. That particular holiday season my procrastination had reached its peak and I was futilely attempting to complete my neglected shopping. After hours of battling frantic, screaming masses of primitive humans, my mind and my pocket book were completely drained. With two dollars in quarters to my name and a pile of packages that reached to my nose, I stumbled out of the last department store.

The doors swung behind me and I was assaulted by a cutting blast of wind. The chill seeped into my bones and left me breathless. I accelerated my pace toward the bus stop. I reached the bus shelter and settled myself into a corner bench. As the walls of the shelter rocked with the wind, my thoughts strayed to the warmth of home and the food in the refrigerator. A noise to my right, barely audible, startled me from my thoughts. Expecting the bogeyman himself to jump in front of me with a knife, I turned toward the mumbling noises coming from the next bench.

I could just barely discern the figure of a man, his gray head, covered by a dirt-stained hunting cap. He bent his hands and he seemed to be communicating something important to them. I pretended not to notice, and turned my head to concentrate on a very squashed, very dead fly on the wall next to me. My curiosity got the best of me though, and I couldn't help but take quick glances at the man. He wore a torn button-up shirt, the red stripes fading and stained, and a brown cardigan missing all its buttons. The jacket he wore was too small, barely reaching to his waist, and his pants were too big, the legs scrunched up at his ankles. Boots with holes and without laces covered his feet, and I could see his sockless big toes.

He drew his attention away from his hands and looked in my direction. The moment he looked up I felt transported into another world. His eyes, covered by wrinkles and matted hair, seemed to look right through me. It was if the pain and sorrow of the world were trapped in his face, and his eyes mirrored this suffering. My cushy suburban life-style had never exposed me to the harsh realities of his world. The warmth and comfort of my home awaited me, but he had no home to return to, just a swaying bus shelter that offered little relief from the cold.

I saw the bus approaching, I felt overwhelming guilt. I knew I could not just close my eyes and walk away without helping him, yet I had only enough money to get home. My thoughts turned to the bundle of packages at my feet, and I remembered the wool sweater I had bought for my father. With only seconds to spare before the bus left without me, I ripped open the bag and tore off the tags of the sweater. Thoroughly embarrassed, I grabbed all my packages and quickly turned to the man huddled in the corner. Cringing, he looked away as I placed the sweater on his lap and muttered "Merry Christmas." I ran to the bus and climbed inside. Hesitating, but not turning around, I listened as the doors closed behind me.

Burnsville Senior High School

Nahyon

The following is a reaction paper to Albert Camus' essay on Sisyphus.

Joseph Campbell said, "Myth is that which seeks to explain the unexplainable." I believe that life is unexplainable. It is filled with happiness, sorrow, and wonder. A few of my best days were winning my first piano competition, getting my first modeling job, making the school dance line, and receiving an award for my diligence in school. Those were good days, but the day that has most influenced me to be the person I hope to be is the day that I understood and connected with my parents for the first time. It was the day we studied the "Myth of Sisyphus" by Albert Camus.

My inquiring six-year-old eyes first experienced America on July 2, 1981. As I grew up learning English and the American lifestyle, I had to put my Korean customs behind me. I remember how ashamed I was about my dark brown eyes and jet-black hair. How I wished that I could be an American.

I was ashamed of our house that smelled foreign, spicy, and different because of our Korean meals. I was ashamed to be seen with my parents because they could not speak English. My childhood relationship with my parents was filled with chagrin, hurt and a complete lack of understanding.

Sisyphus, a tragic figure, endlessly presses and shoves a boulder, attempting to get it over a cliff. The Greek gods, however, were angry with Sisyphus, and refused to let him accomplish his job. Instead, at the top the boulder rolls back down and the process of pushing the boulder is repeated once again. A Sisyphus figure in our society is a person who at the end has finally accepted a meaningless and repetitive job. Sisyphus knew the boulder would never make it to the top, but he keeps pushing the boulder in order to spite the gods.

I remember sitting in class fifth hour. My stomach was churning with hunger, as I waited impatiently for lunch. The two-day rain and the warm-smelling weather made me edgy and emotional. It was ironic that my mother and I had fought that same morning about my college plans. That day we discussed Sisyphus, and I saw my parents with respect and admiration for the first time.

They were Sisyphus figures. My dad, at the age of fifty-two, works in the scorching heat and the biting cold. My mother has cared for kids for twelve years, putting up with their crying five days a week. I saw the sacrifice that they have made, giving up their high-class life in Korea to give my sister and me a better childhood than they had.

I can see the frustration in their faces every day after work. Sometimes they contemplate why they are here. After all, they had graduated from prestigious universities in Korea and had held comfortable, high-positioned jobs. Now they have back-aching jobs in their retirement age. Now I also wonder why they sacrificed everything. However, they accept their responsibility as Sisyphus did.

Before encountering Albert Camus' essay on Sisyphus, I envied my friends. I wondered why they got to go on luxurious vacations every summer. I was jealous that other girls got new clothes, new shoes, or even a new ski set whenever they asked for it. I did not understand why we could not have a cabin up north as other families did.

Now I feel that I may have more than other families. My parents accomplished the extraordinary. I never imagined how hard living in a new country with a new language, culture, and customs could be. I never imagined how arduous giving up their old friends, traditions, and country could be, but now I can imagine how much they sacrificed out of their love for my sister and me. The sacrifice displays a greater love than a cabin or a new outfit would.

Not only have I learned the importance of family, but I also feel my relationship with my parents has grown positively from this myth. I find myself snickering less at them and making more attempts to understand and communicate with them. Our gap is slowly narrowing.

Camus said, "Myths are for imagination to breathe life into." The interpretation of this myth has begun a new relationship between my parents and me. I would not trade one award or one great day to replace the day that I learned about Sisyphus.

Marette

We had been in class for several weeks before the nurse's report arrived. I looked down the list for the names of students in my classes. Under the list of students in grade ten I found Notice from nurse. Marette Flies has lupus.

When I me her, she had battled the lupus for five years. She had entered my classroom like a silent warrior— no fanfare, no talking about past battles and old wounds. She came to fight the battle of composition just like all the rest of the students.

Marette Clare Flies

After class a few days later, I asked her how she was feeling and if she would tell me about lupus and her battle with the "wolf." She often talked about her experiences before or after school or between classes. She never talked about it in class and wanted to be "treated just like the other kids."

After class about a month later she walked up to my desk holding a stack of papers. "Here," she said, "this is my journal. Would you like to read it? I don't let just anyone read it."

I have no adjectives to describe Marette's gift. It needs one of those hyphenated, Native American words such as "this-is-my-life-of-suffering-and-rebirth" story or "this is my because-you-asked-and-now-I-trust-you" story.

Marette's story reads like the journey of the classic hero: She leaves the world of common day and enters a world of supernatural wonder where she fights her battles against her dragon.

From Marette's Journal

The Wolf

The tragedy of illness spreads through the children and weeds them out as if they were animals in Charles Darwin's natural selection. The hospital holds children prisoners as if their illness had not done that already. Soon the children learn another system to survive in. When they learn the system and finally have a way to beat it, it changes. Soon the children lose hope and accept it as a way of life and start over.

Lupus, the wolf, attacks me when I am most vulnerable. It attacks through the antibodies, which attack my organs and keep me hostage in my own body. I am a hostage confined to hospitals. These abductions separate me from a normal life.

My first weapon is prednisone, which makes me look like a balloon. It controls the lupus but makes me feel like a social outcast. When my face and body look like the Goodyear Blimp, how many guys will ask me to the prom?

My second weapon is chemotherapy, but it makes me SICK and then I miss out on what happened at school or the dance. Then I rely on my personality to regain the lost time and lost ground. I deserve some points in this war. This year I escaped my bondage. I finally put the lupus into remission. I lead a pretty normal life other than the chemotherapy every three months. I enjoy learning how to be well for a change. I am free.

When Marette confronted the dark forces, she received physical and inspirational help from others, including Penelope. Again and again she writes about how her battle awakens a new awareness.

Speech: April 27, 1987
God gave us a gift, our bodies. Our system works together to form one whole and not to think anything else is better. My gift got broken a little. I came down with a disease called lupus in which parts don't work as one and they attack each other. Your mind starts to break away from your heart and really hates God for a period of time, blaming him, saying, "Why me, Lord?" I did this for a while, still praying but not with my heart, only my mind, until I was very near death in a life-support unit.

I was scheduled for a procedure that was fairly complicated. I went and just as the end of it was coming, I started to get short of breath and tingly. I saw the face of my mom's brother who died and who I didn't remember. I saw God and myself. It stopped later and I was pushed into recovery.

Then my mind and heart did work together and I realized that God didn't give this to me. He made me discover a whole, shiny, brand-new gift, writing. I then began to write a story about my stay with I. V.s in both hands. I'm not saying I'm superior because anybody could be up here talking about their closeness to God or their gifts. Maybe your gift is music or sports. All I say is make use of it.

Dialysis
Dialysis is a four-syllable word that causes a life to change immediately. How is it possible for this one small word to carry the power of creating a whole new system? I'm finding it hard to cope with this. It feels like it takes more out of me than just excess fluids.

It's taking my spirit, my freedom to drink and eat what I want, but mainly it's taking my freedom. How do I conquer this system? Where's the flaw? Now I can't sleep and this is the dialysis' ploy to keep me sick because if I can't rest, I'll never beat the system. Help me on this one.

Penelope, March 2, 1995

Penelope is my doll. I normally don't sleep with her every night, but she's always watching over me, protecting and comforting me. She adds light to my hospital room as well as my heart. She and I went through many scary moments together. I don't think I could've made it without her.

Freshly out of the shower, I headed to my hospital bed. My hospital bed looked out onto a dingy parking lot in south Minneapolis. I plunged into my newly made bed and glanced up at the table where Penelope usually sits after my nurse makes the bed. She was gone!

At that moment I felt my heart sink to the floor. I sprang from my lounging position. I got up a little to quickly because I had to catch my breath. I rushed over to my closet, which held my belongings, dragging my I.V. pole. One by one, I flung everything out of the closet looking for any sign of hope. Taking the only course of action I felt open to me, I had a nervous breakdown. The nurse came into my room after I had given my lungs a workout. She tried to settle me down, but after I repeated my story three times, she understood my sobs.

Her jaw fell down and her eyes bugged out and then she sat me down and calmly said, "Penelope might have got sent with the laundry." A feeling of guilt washed over her face and she kept repeating, "I'm sorry."

"Is the laundry gone yet?" I said.

"No, she said, I'll round up a wheelchair and we'll look downstairs." I grew very impatient as I waited for the wheelchair. It finally arrived and I leaped into it, making sure to position my I.V. pole between my legs. My nurse took me down to the basement where the dirty laundry was held for central cleaning. When we approached the mass of laundry, my jaw fell. I saw dirty diapers, blood-stained sheets, and sheets that held the stain of someone's stomach contents. My eyes filled with tears because I couldn't dig through all that gross stuff—maybe one or two tops, but not that mountain of sickness.

We turned around and went back to the floor. The nurse suggested I describe Penelope to central cleaning and they could dig her out. I went with that idea. Depressed, with no more will to go on, I clumsily plunked back into my bed and slept.

I dreamt about how I would have to fight this disease by myself. The more I thought about who was fighting this disease, I realized it was me. Penelope was just a figure I could relate to. As far as protecting and watching over me, I had my parents and God. I was the one conquering this disease and nobody else.

The next morning my nurse came into the room with a doll similar to Penelope. The only difference was her size. She was much smaller. By the look on my nurse's face I knew it was extremely important that I accept the doll to relieve her conscience.

Two months later Penelope came back from central cleaning. I had a really different feeling about her. Now she was just an object. The two months away from her made me feel independent and confident. Penelope will always have a place in my heart, but not on my battlefront.

Marette Flies suffered a near-death attack in which she was hospitalized for thirty days in intensive care and stabilized on dialysis. Because her muscles had atrophied, she had to learn to walk again. She wrote, "I had won the race of hospital survival, but here before me awaits the real and never-ending race, the race of the real world. And as you know, the tortoise always wins."

Marette entered the University of St. Thomas. She died at age twenty-two. In the conclusion of her essay she wrote, "It doesn't have to be like this. There is one way to beat the system: the children must learn to move on to the future in the soul."

Stories About My Students

Ramon

1959, Colegio San Antonio Abad
Humacao, Puerto Rico

RAMON WAS ONE OF THE TALLEST FIVE-FOOTERS I HAVE ever met. He was an A student in my tenth-grade English class and a passionate orator on our declamation team. He won several contests pleading, "Friends, Romans, countrymen, lend me your ears." Ramon would have made both Shakespeare and Marcus Antonius proud.

We ate a variation of cafeteria style at San Antonio Abad. Students passed through the line and Chilo the cook dished out the day's specialty. Students could decline any part of the meal, but what they took they had to eat. That was the school rule.

Many of the students had never eaten spaghetti and meatballs. Chilo's spaghetti was fantastic, but the students stared wide-eyed as he plopped it on their plates. Many tried it but ate no more than a forkful.

The school rule stated that students must eat what was on their plates and they must remain in the lunchroom until they had finished. Two hours later many of the students sat before their plates of congealing spaghetti, unable to take another bite. Finally, they were dismissed.

That afternoon I met Ramon on the playground. "Ramon," I said, " some of the guys had a hard time eating today's spaghetti, but I noticed you ate it with no trouble at all."

He said, "At home we eat grass."

Barry

I coached the high school base team for ten years from 1964 to 1974. In my first year senior Barry Mott was one of the co-captains. The classes were quite small then, and since I taught only sophomores and junior high students, I didn't meet Barry until baseball practice began in the spring.

Barry Mott, senior 1964

Like many other players on the team, Barry lived in Savage. He grew up playing on a wonderful field shaded by giant cottonwoods and surrounded by a board fence—an old-time ballpark. Burnsville High School played all its home games in Barry's park.

Barry seldom spoke and he often walked under a cloud of gloom. He never talked about himself and usually sat quietly in the back of the bus or in the corner of the dugout.

I knew one thing about him, however—he loved baseball. He was a tall, handsome kid who ran with loping strides. His swing reminded me of my favorite player, Ted Williams. Barry's long arms whipped the bat through the strike zone just like Teddy Ballgame. When Barry threw, his ball tailed to the left, a trait with most lefthanded throwers. He couldn't throw the ball straight, so when he threw to any base from right field, he aimed a foot or two to the right of his target.

Barry was tormented by failure. If he struck out, dropped a fly ball, or bobbled a ground ball, he hung his head in despair. Since Barry hit less than .250, he spent more than seventy-five percent of his time flogging himself for not being perfect. I prayed that he would get a hit during his first and last at bats. The first lifted his spirits during the game and the last sparked him to look forward to the next game. A base hit in the last inning lifted him out of his despair and fended off his demons.

That spring when I was twenty-five and he was eighteen, we rode the baseball roller coaster together. He pouted and smiled. I cajoled and coaxed. He threw his bat and I tried to boost his ego. He muttered, "Damn it," and I yelled, "Good cut. Get 'em next time." He snarled, "Stupid, stupid, stupid," and I shouted, "Lookin' good! Nothin's lost. Hustle. Hustle. Hustle." He hungered for game-winning hits and I prayed he would find joy in playing the game.

Barry and I, 1964

I cannot recall one single anecdote from that season, no memorable play, no outstanding humorous or dramatic moment. Many nights I gave Barry a ride home, but we often rode in silence. He usually answered my question with as short an answer as possible. The season ended when we lost in tournament play. Barry turned in his uniform after the game and we went our separate ways.

Vietnam Memorial Web Site
"On July 27, 1966, nineteen-year-old CPL-E4 Barry Mott of the United States Marine Corps was killed by hostile, small-arms gunfire in Quang Nam Province, South Vietnam."

"Retired" is stamped on my teaching certificate, but I know I will never find peace with Barry's memory until I trace my fingers across the letters of his name on the Vietnam Memorial in Washington, D. C..

Until then I will continue to picture him standing in right field, his throwing arm hanging at his side, his right hand resting on his cocked hip. Between pitches he moves into the shade of the giant cottonwood tree that stands inside the fence near the right field foul line.

Davuth

Summer School, 1979

We were on the quarter system, so every nine weeks hundreds of students failed a class or two. We had a seven-period day, and if students passed five credits each quarter, they accumulated just enough credits to graduate. Failing one class meant taking six credits the next quarter. Failing two classes meant one very agonizing seven-hour day. Naturally students who couldn't pass five classes with two study halls sank deeper into the abyss with seven classes and no study hall. Thoughts of graduation dissolved like an early morning dream.

All was not lost, however. For those who worked late and slept through class, those who were strangers to books and could not spell "study," those who partied, those who rebelled, and those who missed earning credits for "legitimate reasons," the school board raised taxes and offered a summer session. Presto! We created academic salvation packaged haphazardly into a six-week-crash course.

All teachers taught in their major and minor fields. Classes lasted two hours, and since classes ran from 8:00 a.m. to 12:15 p.m., students could earn only two credits. The rest were doomed to "thirteenth-year-senior purgatory."

When the budget dried up, the school board reduced the number of teachers and combined courses. That summer in one two-hour block, I had three students in American literature, four in world literature, and six in American government, which I had never taught. Twenty-one years earlier I had earned a social studies teaching minor, which did not include a course in American government. I also had one student in composition. One classroom, fourteen students, and four different subjects.

My daily discussion with the two junior girls who had failed American Government went something like this:

"Mary, what's the Twenty-first Amendment about?"

"Hmmmm. I usta know but I guess I forgot. Hmmm! Bummer. Give me hint. Waida second. What's *amendment* mean again? Is this a trick question? Are you talkin' 'bout the Bill of Amendments?"

"You mean the Bill of Rights?"

"Ohhhhhh, that bill. I hearda those. Are there a hunderd of them?"

"Paula, how about you?" I asked. "What's the Twenty-first Amendment?"

"Well, jeez, ya know, I bombed this class. I don't know nothin' about this history stuff and it gives me a pain in the butt. (Gum cracking.) Ya know, well, it's like, how can I tell ya, I mean, ya know, I never got the basics. (Gum cracking.) Mr. D. hated my guts. I couldn't do a damn thing right for him. (Medium sized bubble.) He kicked me out of class every other day. (Double gum crack.) Wait. I think I know this one 'cuz we talked about it one night after school at a kegger. This one's 'bout no booze, ain't it?" (Monster bubble.)

The four male American government students sat in the back. Mary and Paula couldn't tolerate their greasy hands and motor-oil perfume, so I taught each group separately. The four guys came to class directly from work. When they could stay awake, they discussed their sexual exploits and souped-up Pontiacs. They thought the senators played hockey or football, but they were positive that Washington, D.C. was just north of Oregon. They scored about fifty percent on three-answer multiple choice questions if one of the answers was Bugs Bunny, Elvis Presley, King Kong, or the name of that month's *Playboy* centerfold.

My lone composition student sat isolated in the first seat in the right-hand corner of the room. Davuth was a twenty-one-year-old Cambodian, a stranger in a strange land, a prisoner in a summer school wasteland.

In our first meeting I asked him, "What English class do you need, Davuth?"

"Composition," he said. "I need composition."

"Do you need help with vocabulary?"

"Vocabulary poor."

"How about punctuation and grammar?" I asked.

"Not good. English hard."

We worked on sentence structure, vocabulary, and mechanics every day. "Tell me a story," I said one day as we searched for ideas. "Tell me something that happened to you today or yesterday or last week."

"Nothing happens. I get up, Come here, go to work, go home, study, go to bed, and get up. Everyday, same thing. Nothing happens."

"Could you write about Cambodia? Anything happen there?"

"I try," he said.

For the rest of the summer session, Davuth wrote about Cambodia. After I had read his first short paragraph, I asked him if he had seen *The Killing Fields*.

He hung his head and whispered, "No."

"Why not?" I asked. It's a powerful movie."

He thought for several seconds, looking down at his hands. "I was in killing fields," he said. "I saw bones. I saw rotting bodies of women and children. I don't need movie."

Day after day he wrote painful stories about his life in Cambodia after the Communists had attacked his village. His family was well educated. His father and uncles were doctors, lawyers, teachers, and professional people. His brothers, sisters, cousins and he went to the best schools. He described how he and his family hid from the Communists in the rice fields. "After curfew they shot anything that moved," he said. He described the execution of two teenage lovers who tried to sneak off.

After traveling hundreds of miles at night, Davuth's mother, father, sisters, brothers, aunts, uncles, and cousins reached the "bandits," ruthless men who charged exorbitant fees to help people escape. Sometimes the bandits simply took the money and murdered everyone.

Davuth's father and uncles paid thousands of dollars to the bandits, who loaded families into railroad cars heading for refugee camps. They crammed the women and children into the cars. "My father, uncles, male cousins, and I stood on side boards and held to boards above us. Hundreds of people rode on tops of cars."

Each day Davuth hunched over his paper and wrote his stories, so he could earn one credit in composition and graduate from a school in a country that lived by a Bill of Rights. Each day I watched him fold his hands, bend his head, and shut his eyes. I tried to imagine the movie of memories flashing in his mind's eye—a child playing with his brothers and sisters, school, rice harvests, bombs, assassinations, crowded refugee camps, landing in America, trying to learn English. He struggled to find the words that described those images.

I then realized the soundtrack of his movie was not English, but Cambodian. How frustrating it must have been to describe those traumatic events in English! How frustrating to see his life and not be able to tell his story! Every day he ground up his native Cambodian and sifted those marvelous images until they became childlike. Each day he worked passionately, oblivious to the student babble around him.

"Was it Don Quick Sot who thought the windmill was a guy on a horse? Da. Stupid. Ya'd never catch me doing something that dumb."

"So, Paula, did ya get the answer to number six? How the heck does a bill become a law anyways?"

"Who the hell cares? You think I'm gonna move to Philadelphia and be a senator in the White House? How's my blush?"

"It's all Hester's fault, man. She shoulda never gone into those woods. Who'd she think she was—Little Red Riding Hood?"

"God, I'm tired. I stayed out with Sally till five o'clock. Her old man really raised hell when I brought her home. Hey, what'd we suposta read for today?"

Davuth passed composition and graduated. On the last day of class, I put all his compositions into a folder and said, "Keep these for your children. They need to know your story. They need to know who you are."

Jenny

She walked into my ninth-grade English class about the same time the Beatles recorded *Revolution*. She always strolled into the room after the tardy bell had rung. Revolution. For nine months she wore the same torn jeans and the same red and black lumberjack's shirt. Revolution. For thirty-six weeks she wore the same scowl. Revolution. When she looked at me, she folded her arms and stared with blazing eyes. Revolution. She did her work but she never spoke.

After three or four minutes she showed her disdain for whatever we were doing by slamming shut her text and taking out her worn copy of *Bury My Heart at Wounded Knee*. While we read the latest "classic" teen novel such as *That Was Then, This Is Now* or *The Pigman*, she lost herself in the literature of rebellion and injustice. While we studied grammar, she studied the language of broken treaties and the syntax of heartache. She passed her tests, completed ninth grade, and slipped out of my life.

Beating the drum of revolution, she entered the turmoil of high school. Two years later she tried to commit suicide and was placed in a psychiatric ward in the county hospital.

I wrote to her and told her I was sad to hear that her life was filled with so much pain. I told her that I could see her waiting outside my door for the bell to ring. I told her that I could visualize the way she looked and acted every day she was in my class. I told her that despite all the scowling, glaring, and rebelling, she did one thing that gave her away—a fourteen-year-old ninth-grade girl does not read *Bury My Heart at Wounded Knee* with a heart of stone. I told her she could give the appearance that she was being treated unjustly, but she could not conceal her sense of justice.

She wrote back. Her letter was written in a nervous, sharp-angled scrawl. She told me high school was a nightmare. She said a boy she had dated since the ninth grade told her to "fuck off," so she cut her wrists in anger, but fortunately her parents found her soon after.

She ended her letter by saying, "I can't believe a teacher wrote to me, that you even remember me. That's really cool. Thanx."

For years I kept her letter in the pencil box on my desk. During those moments when I felt overwhelmed, when dark shadows clouded my passion, I re-read her letter. I thought about how close I came to not writing, about other unwritten letters. Later I didn't need to open her letter. I knew it by heart. When I questioned the sense of it all, I sat at my desk and stared at the envelope. To this day I'm not certain why I wrote, how a keener sense than I ordinarily possessed moved my hand. My official teacher duties to her were over, but for some reason that I cannot explain, she did not become one of my serious neglects.

Guy

Prelude: Turtles

I have been passionate about saving wayward turtles ever since I began biking. I have found them naively crossing county roads and busy city streets. Somehow they became disoriented and wandered from the safety of their lakes or ponds. Perhaps they think the scum is greener on the other side of the road. Perhaps they lose their sense of purpose and direction and struggle toward some turtle Garden of Eden or the Shangri-La of turtledom filled with visions of gourmet delights and sexual escapades forbidden in their home ponds.

Whenever I find a lost turtle, I stop my bike, get off, and examine what kind of fellow I'm dealing with. Snapping turtles, like some of my students, don't take kindly to someone butting into their business.

Holding the turtle with one hand and the handlebar with the other, I struggle to find my balance, so I can bike the fellow back to his home. Most of the turtles I helped thought little of my missionary zeal and tried to pee on me. I soon learned they can aim that spray at many angles, so I hold them far from my body. and tilt them just a bit.

When I reach what I think is the turtle's favorite spot, I talk to him for a few minutes. I try to comfort him and ease his fears. "Everything is going to be fine. Somehow you lost your way and ended up in the middle of the road. Didn't you notice the dangers? Some people even tried to squash you on purpose. You must have forgotten who you are and where you belong. It's dangerous wandering around out there in that turtle wasteland.

"Now I'm going to give you a ride that you can brag about to your grandturtles. Tuck in your head and legs 'cuz this'll be the trip of a lifetime."

Like a discus thrower in the Olympic Games, I fling him skyward. He spins out over the pond and plops into the water. A few seconds later he sticks out his head, blinks, and dives.

Part 1

Guy was a thirteenth-year senior in my honors English class. Usually thirteenth-year seniors return for that extra year because they have found ways to fail themselves into this embarrassing situation. This was not the case with Guy, who was a bright, talented student and a gifted musician.

He had begun his senior year at a prestigious music school to master the piano and train his voice. One day Guy was struggling with a piece by Rachmaninoff. Another student asked if he could help. He sat down and played the piece flawlessly.

That day Guy packed his bags and left the school, leaving him two credits short of the requirement needed for graduation. That's how Guy ended up in my class.

Guy sat in the middle of the room, directly in front of my desk. For a few weeks he participated in class discussions. His essay answers were written in a tiny scrawl so he could have enough space to write insightful, detailed essay answers.

Each day he said less and less in class. He wrote shorter and shorter answers and eventually he stopped answering any question. He turned in a blank page. After class, however, he hung around to discuss the day's readings. He laughed and joked when I teased him about his tests and his silence. He enjoyed playing the game.

To culminate our unit on romance and the sacred place, we gathered in the performing arts center to listen to Beethoven's Symphony No. 6 (Pastorale).

At the end of class the next day, which was Thursday, Guy said, "Beethoven's *Pastorale* is very lyrical, but I think you'll find Bruckner's Symphony No. 4 *Romantic* equally as lyrical. I'll bring the tape and the score tomorrow."

"You don't need to bring the score," I said, "because I can't read music, but I'd like to listen to the tape." He gave me the tape on Friday as he was leaving.

On Sunday night three of Guy's friends who were in the class called me and asked if they could come to my house. I gave them the directions and hung up the phone. "Something bad has happened," I said to my wife. "I know it. I could hear it in Libby's voice."

They walked into the house and Libby cried, "Guy killed himself. He bought a shotgun last night and shot himself."

On Monday when I walked into class, the room was filled with my students as well as students from neighboring high schools who had sung with Guy in summer musicals. I stood before his empty desk and looked at the faces of teenagers hungry for something to ease their pain.

That hour was the most difficult hour of my teaching career. We did not need Aristotle, Sophocles, or Shakespeare to understand tragedy. Tragedy filled the empty desk.

No college classes had prepared me for that moment. English Methods suggested ways to teach sentence structure, grammar and usage, creative writing, and literary analysis, but no professor had instructed me on how to heal a teenager's broken heart or rekindle the flame of hope and youthful joy. I did the best I could by reading them a story I had written two years earlier.

Part 2

Today I began my thirty-first year of teaching. I looked forward to work-shop, swapping stories with my colleagues and getting things ready for a new year.

In the first hour of my return, I was informed that John and Pau, two students from my spring semester literature class, had committed suicide during the summer. One born into a middle-class suburban home and another born in war-torn Cambodia were sucked into darkness. Two six-teen-year-old boys with nothing in common except their despair had taken their own lives.

The ghosts of Pau and John haunted me as I drove home that afternoon. "What a foolish thing to do!" I thought. "How could you have strayed so far from bliss and placed yourself in harm's way? How could you have lost your vision?"

The light changed. Trucks roared next to me, spilling black clouds of diesel smoke over my gloom. The light changed. The traffic inched ahead. Suddenly the traffic split apart into a V and I saw the turtle

"What the hell are you doing out there, you damn fool," I yelled. He slipped under me. I saw him again in my rearview mirror, head and legs sucked in, too terrified to move.

"Should I? Shouldn't I?" I hesitated. The traffic was terrible. It would be so inconvenient.

I whipped a right at Hennen's Station, another right on River Drive, another right back to the highway. I miscalculated. I was a block away. In the minutes it had taken me to circle back, someone had hit him and flipped him on his back near the curb.

Around the block. Down the alley. I stopped at the corner, ran out into the gap in the traffic, and picked him up. His top shell was crushed a bit and blood seeped through the cracks in his bottom shell. I set him on the floor and drove to the boat landing on the river.

"Dead! I bet you're dead. What a foolish thing to do! How could you stray so far from bliss and place yourself in harm's way? How could you lose your vision?"

He never moved.

"Dead. Dead, I bet. Killed by a Michelin. What a waste!"

I carried him down to the boat landing and set him in the muddy water. I sat on a rock and waited.

Nothing. "Dead, I bet. Betrayed by your dreams."

I nudged him until the murky water covered him.

"What a fool," I whispered, "squashed in the wasteland."

Bip. Bip. Bip. From the depths of a primeval passion to live, one tiny string of bubbles slipped out of that terrorized shell. Bip. Bip. Bip. Another string of bubbles danced to the surface.

The turtle slowly eased out its head to face a reborn world. He stretched his neck and poked his nostrils into the air. Then he flailed away with all four legs and slipped into the darkness.

Part 3

Our first task in life is to save the lost turtle within ourselves. Then we must save the lost turtles of the world.

I keep Guy's tape of Bruckner's Symphony No. 4 on my desk. Someday I will find the strength to listen to the music that "is as lyrical as Beethoven's."

Guy as St. George, The Reluctant Dragon

Photo courtesy of Guy's family

2

Teacher Training 101

Elementary School,
Junior and Senior High School

Finger Painting

FINGER-PAINTING DAY WAS THE FOURTH OF JULY, Halloween, Thanksgiving, and Christmas all rolled into one. On finger-painting day during my early grade school days, the teacher hauled out her gigantic roll of white, glossy paper and laid it on the floor. She rolled out the paper, measured carefully, laid her yardstick across the paper, and tore off a sheet for each child in the class.

We taped our sheets to the board and she coated each sheet with water from her sponge. Then she popped off the paint can lids. Bright red, blue, green, and yellow pails of paint waited for our hands. What a feast for the senses! I plunged each hand into the bucket up to my wrists. With my right hand I swirled red circles. With my left hand I swiped my fingers through the circles, creating five streaks of blue. We dabbed and dribbled, palmed and patted. Some of my classmates drew animals, houses, an oasis or two, as well as many strange-looking creatures.

I would like to claim that as a third- or fourth-grader I was an insightful prodigy who knew that nothing during the rest of my life would be so free of constraints, but I can't claim such insight. I was just a kid who loved the feel of the heavy paint, the smell of green and yellow, and the recklessness of the exploding colors flashing from my fingers. I smeared my face with the backs of my wrists as I pushed my hair from my face. Then I continued to paint memories that have remained with me all my life.

My teacher's only rule was "Don't make a mess." She laughed and painted whimsy with us. It may have been the only school activity I ever did that was completely free of fear. There was no before and no after, just now. There was no "must be," "should be," or "could have been." There were no critiques, no anxiety, no correct answers, no study guide, no homework, and no grades. We were all geniuses and our teacher pinned our songs of freedom on the bulletin board for the whole world to applaud.

My Sandbox

My dad nailed four planks square
   and wheel barrowed it heaping full of white sand
   he found on an enchanted island,
     so he said.
In that barren paradise we sculpted
   mystical castles ringed by moats
   filled by Mason jars of well water.
The knights jousted evil
   while Robin's band guarded
   an evergreen sprig Sherwood Forest
     tucked into a secluded corner.
Saturday's Movietone News transformed
   that fantasy into the North African desert,
   and five-and-dime toy tanks played at war,
   and mimicked newsreel reality.
My father's sandbox rules
   demanded that imagination play
   inside the planked world.
Fantasy confined itself within
   boarded boundaries.
Sand spilled into the real world
   was taboo.
We learned early the temptation
   to fling precious sand
   past forbidden boundaries,
   sprinkle what wasn't with
     what was, and challenge
     what should not be with
     what ought to be.
The barriers grew, and today
   imaginary sandbox walls
   tower behind me
   tormenting me with the urge
     to throw sand.

With my sister Rene

Spelling

Spelling teachers are equipped with an arsenal of spelling clichés that paralyzed me throughout my school career. Perhaps the announcement which froze my brain most often was "Now, children, there are no rules for these words. You must learn to spell each one." Following a close second was the proclamation "There are many exceptions to this rule. For example, most words form the plurals by adding *s* or *es*, but don't forget about *oxen* and *deer* and all those other exceptions."

I sat bolt upright when my teacher announced, "There are no exceptions to this rule." Three cheers for the words that allowed for no exceptions. Someone told me that Mark Twain once said, "I take no stock in a person who can spell a word only one way." Mark Twain would have loved me. I was the master of creative spelling.

During my grade school years the reading gurus announced that spelling was anathema, so I became a child of word recognition. Dick and Jane helped guide me to the hell of spelling paranoia. "Do I change the *y* to *i* and add es to make the plural of monkey or do I just add *es*?" I puzzled. "Is it Seadick run or Cee Dik run?"

Rules, rules, rules! I was cursed by rules and no rules. This is. No, that isn't. "It's not *enuff*. It's *enough*. It's *snuff*, not *snough*. I was flummoxed for life.

I studied my spelling words diligently. Every week a new spelling chapter. Every week twenty new words and their wicked stepchildren. On the day of the spelling test, I began spelling the words at breakfast and my mother corrected my mistakes. A block from the house I was still hollering them to her.

To make matters worse, spelling went hand in hand with writing and printing, and those two lived between lines. The Palmer Method died the same death that killed phonics. I adopted the Chicken Scratching Method to bring my spelling warts to life.

Unlike my finger painting, every single letter I scrawled on my paper was critiqued and graded. We never had spelling tests just for fun. We spelled, corrected each other's papers, and the teacher recorded every grade. No forgiveness lived between the red covers of her grade book.

My life as a student and teacher was filled with a great deal more spelling than finger painting.

Lines

Kindergartners
  learn quickly to respect lines—
    firm, black, wavering, wiggling lines
    that dance freely yet demand awe from
    daring Crayola yellows and greens
        and
    defiant reds and blues-
      splashes of spiritual fancy
        or
    storybook lines, Red Riding Hood, Rapunzel lines
      requiring squint-eyed, tongue-biting, knee-bending,
        crayon-squeezing homage.

Kindergartners
  learn early to caress fat pencils,
    and on brown newsprint smelling of time
    they print sound lines.
  Between parallel boundaries that rule
        yes or no
    they scrawl stately A's and B's.
  Between broken parallels
    boldly stroked t's and z's
    parade before nervous q's and
    paranoid m's and w's struggling for identity.

But kindergartners learn too
  that hands plunged knuckle deep
  into finger paints
        explode into defiant swirls and loops
        singing praise to whimsy.
  Gobs of slippery red, yellow, and green
        sprout flaming flowers hiding unicorns.
  Childish palms pat out illusions
        pranced over by flying fingers
            that defy the tyranny of lines.

The Trials

Joseph Campbell defines a hero as someone who has a mysterious birth, is orphaned, wanders far from his native land, is adopted, and receives a secluded education. The hero leaves the common-day world and enters a world of supernatural wonder. With the aid of god-teachers, he is taught how to become a hero. The would-be hero must complete the rites of passage by mastering the mental and physical skills necessary to enter the wasteland and confront the powers that seek to destroy the world of love, hope, and faith. The hero encounters fabulous forces, which seek to destroy him and turn his world into a wasteland.

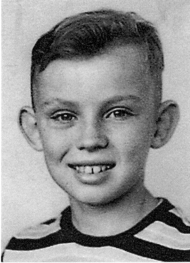

While mastering his skills, the hero must fight minor battles, play on the B team, before he takes on the dehumanizing demons. The hero will win or lose, but in winning or losing, the hero destroys the dark side and gives a boon to the world.

Campbell outlines the path each of us must take to become a hero, which also means that Joseph Campbell outlines the path each of us must take to become a teacher. Who but an idealistic adventurer would take a journey filled with fire-breathing aberrations?

Every teacher has battled Medusa, whose looks turn us to stone; the Minotaur, waiting to devour the naïve; the one-eyed Cyclops cursed by tunnel vision; and Cerberus, the three-headed, dragon-tailed dog, waiting to condemn us to darkness.

Perhaps the most important part of the hero's training is the rites of passage. Like King Arthur, we rely upon our Merlins to show us how to live outside ourselves, how to fly like a hawk and realize that boundary lines cannot be seen from above. Like Bartholomew in *The Never-Ending Story*, we become part of the this living epic. We must be willing to sacrifice bits and pieces of ourselves if we are to prevent the Nothing from destroying Fantasia and ourselves.

Like Luke Skywalker, we must listen to our personal Obi Wan Kanobies and Yodas. Before we battle the Death Stars facing us, we must master the use of our light sabers and control our minds until we can levitate our Jedi planes out of our muck. When we, like Luke, exclaim, "I do not believe it," our Yoda will say, "That is why you will fail."

Teachers training begins long before we enter the college classroom. Our teaching rites of passage begin with the trials we fought as far back as we can remember. In many ways these trials were far more challenging than the battles we would fight later in our lives. They were more challenging because our shield was innocence and our sword was naiveté. Many times our god-teachers were unavailable. Our parents were working. Merlin was doing laundry in the basement or working to make the house payment. Obie was in grade school and Yoda was just learning to untangle words and master his sentence syntax.

We rarely felt the Nothing nibbling away at our self-esteem or rosy-pink sense of morality. We still believed in adult heroes who were willing to gallop to our rescue, and so we faced our dragons. We saw them as raging, fire-breathing demons of destruction. If the adults in our world saw them at all, they saw them as tiny mice blowing smoke rings.

We seldom realized we were in the midst of anything. We accepted the trials because we were naive. We accepted the trials because we trusted our god-teachers. We accepted the trials because we had been taught to do what we were told. Sometimes we plunged into our trials because we believed that we could recognize "the right thing." Sometimes we blundered into the trials and often we were simply picked up and thrown into the mess. And many times we walked a few steps into the slough before we realized the mud was oozing between our toes.

I fought the following battles from the spring of 1948, when I entered the seventh grade, until the spring of 1954, when I completed high school. I never realized when I was fighting these dragons that I would meet their offspring during my teaching career.

Gaylord, Summer, 1949, Age 12
The Gillette Friday Night Fights

I was always broke. The world didn't pay much to a kid who whiled away his summer playing baseball. My dad seldom refused my request for a nickel or dime, but I soon blew it on an ice cream cone or comic book and was broke again.

During World War II, I collected anything that could lift me out of poverty. I scoured the town looking for tin cans and newspapers, anything that was needed for the war effort. During baseball games I asked pop drinkers if they would save their bottles for me when they had finished. When we went to my grandfather's farm, I scavenged behind the chicken house for worn-out plow shears, broken cultivator parts, and anything else made of steel. I piled the junk into our Ford.

Krebsbach's Junk Yard covered most of the southeast corner of town. I heaped my treasure into my wagon and headed for the newspaper mountain, the tower of pop bottles, and the field of rusting steel. Mr. Krebsbach weighed each piece and scratched out his calculations with a pencil he had sharpened that morning with his front teeth. I rejoiced as he handed me each quarter.

When the war ended, Mr. Krebsbach stopped collecting junk, and I went broke. But the guys and I never stopped racking our brains for money-making schemes. Schzammmmm! Bobby had an idea that would make us all rich. We would put on a night of boxing matches that would draw people from far and wide.

We called a truce with the Horned Frogs, the other "gang" in town. They thought the idea was fantastic. Although not one of us had ever boxed, this was a sport we knew well. Didn't we spent every Friday night in front of the television watching the Friday Night Fights brought to us by Gillette razors and Gillette razor blades, the cleanest shave in America" We even knew the boxing anthem—"To look sharp, every time you shave, to feel sharp and be on the ball—"

We made the plans for our fight night.

"We could build a ring in the empty lot next to the high school."

"How we gonna dig the post holes?"

"No, problem, my old man's got a posthole digger."

"Where we gonna get the stuff to build the ring?"

"Whose got any rope?"

"Aw, you guys worry too much. We'll find the stuff."

"People could bring lawn chairs, so we wouldn't need bleachers."

"My brother could referee and some of his friends could time the rounds and ring the bell."

"Where we gonna get the gloves?"

"My brother got some for Christmas a few years ago."

"Yeah, so did mine. I think they're hanging in the basement."

On and on we went, solving each problem with the snap of our fingers. Then someone asked the unthinkable question, "Hey, who's gonna fight who?" Silence, looking down, picking grass, fidgeting. More silence, a really uncomfortable silence.

"Come on. Who's gonna fight?" asked Alger, Frog's gang leader and the toughest kid in town. "It's gotta be one guy from the Alley Cats fightin' one guy from the Horned Frogs."

"Yeah, right," chimed in the Horned Frogs.

"Well, Alger is the biggest Horned Frog and Kenny is the biggest Alley Cat, so they'll be the heavy weights." One by one the gang leaders matched us up. "And, Melch, you can fight Freddy." I got sick to my stomach. Fight

Freddy? I had never hit anyone in my life. My head began to spin. I could see his fist flashing toward my nose. No way in hell was I going to fight anyone. I was chicken on a bone.

"Ya, and Bruce can fight Bobby and Hommie can fight Karl."

Finally every guy in each gang was paired with an opponent.

"O.K., next time we meet, we'll make signs to put up all over town. We're gonna make a bundle on this."

We drifted home for supper. No one ever mentioned the Gillette Fight Night again.

Winter, 1949–1950, Age 12
The Set-Up Kid

In many hero tales, the hero enters an opening in the earth and travels downward into the unknown. Leaving the light and warmth of the upper world, the hero winds his way down, down the labyrinthine maze to face evil. Psychologists interpret this as every person's journey into the sub-conscious where the nasties live.

Now that's a serious tussle. All of us need warm-up games, a year or two on the junior varsity team before we confront Big Evil. My training began the evening I opened the door to the Green Lantern Cafe and Bowling Alley. The cafe where we passed hours playing pinball and telling stories was upstairs. The steps to the bowling alley led to a grimy, stuffy world filled with polished alleys, clunking balls, and white triangles of bowling pins. Cigarette smoke hung on the ceiling and sucked into my sinus cavities. Little did I realize that this was the outer chamber of my journey into pinsetting hell.

That night I became a pinsetter. Today if I told people I was once a pin-setter most of them would look at me as if I had told them I was a cooper or smithy. "Pinsetter? Where do you set the pins? Why do you set pins? Safety pins? Stickpins? Stick-the-tail-on-the-donkey pins?"

I followed the manager. We stepped carefully on the narrow walkway between the gutter and the wall. "There," he pointed, "you work those two alleys."

This was not my first experience with setting pins. When my buddies and I bowled in the afternoons, we cut our expense by setting our own pins, but this was the real thing—setting pins for men's league bowling.

The wasteland world is filled with caves and pits. We pinsetters plunged into our pits hundreds of times each night. We sat on a board seat at the back of the pit. Under us hung a heavy rubber mat that stopped the flying pins and the sixteen-pound bowling balls.

In front of us lay the eight alleys, narrow strips of hardwood, sanded and varnished until they glistened. A few feet before the end of the alley stood ten wooden pins, placed in a perfect triangle, each pin standing proudly on its designated black spot.

Above the pins hung a huge triangular metal rack filled with ten holes that held the pins below. I sat on the board above the pit and put my feet against the rack. I crossed my arms in front my face and bent forward, touching my arms against my knees to protect myself. The egomaniacs thought that faster was always better. They thought that the harder they threw, the higher their scores. Many times pins shot out of the pit, right and left, and bounced off the back wall. The ones that hit my legs fell to the bottom of the pit.

Once the pins slid into the pit, I jumped down, grabbed the ball, rolled it back, picked up two or three pins in each hand, and threw them into the holes that matched the black dots below.

Every bowling match involved two teams, which meant they used two alleys at the same time. The partition between alleys one and two, for instance, had a two-foot by three-foot section cut out so we could jump from one alley to the other.

Each one of us set two lanes, which meant leaping from one alley to the other after each ball was thrown. Lane one knocks down five pins, jump, send back ball, set pins in rack. Lane two throws and gets a strike. Jump into pit and set all ten pins, pull down rack and set pins.

Jump back into lane one for second ball. Pick up pins and set all ten for next person. Jump into lane two, crouch; wrap arms in front of face. Speedballer knocks pin out of pit. Jump backwards, pick up pin, jump into pit, and pick up pins.

Gutter ball. Send back ball. Next lane. Pin bounces off rack and spins down alley. Slide on stomach under rack and down the alley. Slide back, set pins over and over.

I earned ten cents a line, which meant I earned forty cents for setting for the four guys on Team A and forty cents from Team B. Eighty frames, eighty cents. Most of us set two shifts, so each night I made $1.60 for six hours of work. One hundred sixty frames, one hundred sixty pennies. When I walked to the counter to collect my pay, I felt like an urchin in a Dickens' novel.

All night long many bowlers poured booze from their brown paper bags into their set-ups. They laughed or joked or razzed each other about their games. I don't remember one of those adults ever tipping me or saying, "Good job, Tommy. You really hustled tonight."

Summer, 1950, Age 13
Dad's Job

During the summer of 1950, Dad's friends in AA persuaded him to "dry out" at the state hospital in Willmar. He went to fight his lifelong dragon face-to-face and left my mother, sister, and me to fight the dry-cleaning beastie that lived in the Tip Top Cleaners.

My job was to clean the clothes. Behind the Tip Top building Dad had set up his dry-cleaning operation. He converted a shed made of red clay rectangular tiles into his cleaning plant. The building was ten-by-ten with a seven-foot ceiling. The sliding door was made of metal and filled with concrete. It weighed a ton. Inside was a metal cylindrical tub that held the dry-cleaning solvent. Inside the large metal barrel was a smaller, wooden-slatted washer.

The cleaning solvent was a mixture of two chemical solutions and a powder. I have no idea what these chemicals were, but a good whiff made my head dance like a helium balloon. I am certain the solutions were carcinogenic. Fortunately, I held my breath whenever I worked in the tiny shack and jumped out the door into the fresh air before I breathed in the toxin.

My mother checked in the clothing and separated the items into two piles, light and dark. I hauled the wicker baskets filled with suits, pants, dresses, and sport coats out to the tile shack, pulled back the concrete door, and set the baskets inside. I unlatched the top half of the metal tank and lifted the lid. The rotating wooden container reminded me of a riverboat paddle wheel. I opened the door, threw in twenty-five pounds of clothing, latched the door of the drum, pulled down the tank cover, and pressed the start button. The wooden tumbler mixed the clothing in the solvent.

When the load was finished, I drained the solvent. The tumbler whirled, spin-drying the clothing. I carried the baskets back into the shop where my mother hung each item in the deodorizing room. I picked up another basket and walked out the back door to the tile shack.

Garden City, 1951, Age 14
Chicken Killer

We moved away from town trials. Suddenly my quest became agricultural. Dad met Dean at an AA meeting in Mankato. Things were falling apart for Dad, so Dean convinced him to move. "There's a house right in town," he said. "You can get it for three thousand bucks. It's got no basement, the pipes freeze in the winter, and the grass is three feet tall. Those are just a few of the problems, but it's a good deal for the money." The place looked like Miss Havisham's house twenty-five years after her lover had abandoned her at the altar.

We had a garage, which the previous owners had turned into a chicken coop. Straw-filled coops covered one wall. The coops were reserved for hens only. They could do anything they wanted during the day as long as each laid an egg. Each morning I collected the eggs before I went to school. I wore my shirtsleeves long so the peck marks wouldn't show.

I dreaded the mornings my mother announced, "I'm going to fix chicken soup for supper tonight, Tom. Go out there and butcher three roosters before you leave for school."

"Jeez, Mom, it's almost time for school."

"Just do it. I did it all the time as a kid. Grab the rooster by the legs. Hold the tips of their wings and their feet in your hand. Lay the chicken's neck across the block and don't miss. First change your clothes so you don't get blood on them." Years later I discovered that my mother's sister Marietta had done all the chicken killing.

The roosters were maniacs. They knew a hatchet when they saw one. I grabbed one, laid its neck across the block and wham! I threw the flapping Leghorn out on the grass and watched the neck spurt blood all over the place. One down. Two to go—just like spelling tests and lesson plans.

Knee Deep

Dad's friend Dean appeared at our house when he wanted cheaper-than-cheap labor, namely me. One day he picked me up and said, "I've got a bit of a problem today." Actually his "bit of a problem" started years before and kept growing. He had had a bit of a problem for three or four years.

Three feet of chicken shit covered his chicken house floor. Now some people might criticize me for using the vulgar form of excrement, but that wasn't excrement piled on that floor. It wasn't poop. It wasn't feces. It wasn't droppings. It was putrid, festering chicken shit.

I stood on my mountain and touched the ceiling. The sun blistered down and sucked the methane gas out of the mountain below me.

I began at one end of the building and pitched fork after fork of manure out the window. Fortunately the building had several windows, so I didn't have to carry each forkful very far. By ten o'clock the thermometer hit eighty-five and the humidity closed in. By noon the temperature had risen to ninety. Each load got heavier and heavier.

For the rest of the day, I worked about five minutes and stood in the fresh air for five minutes. Every time I scooped a pitchfork full of manure, more methane seeped out. When my head began to spin, I rested under the elm trees and then charged back in. I pitched more furiously the closer I came to the end. "You bastard," I mumbled, "you and your chicken shit will never beat me."

Dean returned as I swept the last bits of straw out the door. I don't remember what he said on the way home or how much he paid me, but I owe him for showing me what it's like to be knee deep in muck. During my days as a student and teacher I often stood knee deep in "chicken shit." The deeper it got the faster I shoveled. Usually it worked.

Summer, 1951, Age 15
Weeding Them Out
Many college graduates tell of despotic instructors who began the first day of class by announcing, "This class isn't for everyone. By mid-term half of you will be gone and by the end of the term only one third of you will make it. Most of you will earn C's." Every college student understood what "weeding them out" meant.

I learned a different meaning during the summer of 1951. I lived during the pre-herbicide era. Every cornfield and soybean field blossomed with bull thistles, cockleburs, hemp, burdock, button weed, and mustard. Up and down those rows I walked, whacking every weed in sight. The "clean farmers" had few weeds. In the spring of 1950, they hoed the intruders before they went to seed.

The "dirty farmers" cursed first and hoed later, just before harvest. Many bull thistles as thick as my wrist tried to stare me down and scratch my hide. Whack! Whack! Whack! I whaled away with my hoe. "Timber!" I yelled every time one dropped.

My buddy Tony, whose dad ran 160 acres south of town, hired ten of us to pull mustard. I thought, "Great, fifty cents an hour to walk along and pull a few weeds." The green soybean field was a sea of blossoming yellow mustard. We crawled up and down each row, ten of us side-by-side on our hands and knees. From a distance we probably looked like ants inching our way forward, swallowing bits and pieces of yellow. For several weeks we crawled from seven to noon and then from one to five. My hands looked like those of a nicotine addict.

Summer, 1951, Age 15
Too Corny
"How much do you want?" asked the guy from Northrop King Seed Company. "A quarter acre? A half-acre? An acre? More than that?"

"Jeez, I don't know. How much is an acre?"

"You don't know much about this, do you?" he asked. "You ever detasseled corn before?"

"No, but I know I can do this. How much is an acre? Show me."

"Well, we're standing here at this corner of the field. See that telephone pole over there? You go that far over and all the way down the field to those trees down there."

We walked down the shoulder-high corn and he showed me where the tassels would grow. "Now the idea is to pull those tassels out before they ripen and pollinate the corn. You got to work fast once they begin to grow. If you let them pollinate the corn, well, hell, the whole operation is kaput. Can you do it?"

"I'll sign up for an acre and a half," I said.

"You sure 'bout that? Young fella like you? That corn gets pretty tall. Acre and a half's a lot."

"I can do it. I need the money."

The corn grew and I checked the field every day, pulling a tassel here and there. One day I walked into the corn and it towered more than an arm's length above my fingertips. Overnight thousands of tassels had shot out of the tops of the stalks. What had happened to the shoulder-high corn?

I jumped, grabbed the top of the stalk, and yanked out the tassel. It was 92 degrees and humid. Sweat burned my eyes. The corn leaves sliced my skin. I couldn't breath. My god, I was in the chicken house again!

I worked for hours, pulling and snapping tassels. The corn seemed to grow taller and taller as I walked down the row. The field grew larger and larger. The telephone pole moved farther and farther away. The woods slid down the hill. The cornrows marched off into the horizon. I began to shrink— 5' 8"—5' 4"—5'—4' 8."

The afternoon sun yanked the tassels right out of the stalks. The voice under the blue NK cap echoed in my ears, "If you let them fill out and pollinate the corn, well, hell, the whole operation is kaput. Can you do it?"

Each morning at six o'clock I plunged into the corn jungle. Rows I thought I had cleaned the day before again flowered with tassels. Day after day I worked from sunrise to sunset, stopping only for water and brown paper-bag snacks. The more furiously I worked, the further I fell behind. I could not fail. We needed the money so badly.

That night at supper I admitted defeat. I could not win the battle alone. I believed I could whip my dragons if I worked harder and longer, if I practiced more, if I ran faster, if I tried, tried, tried. For the first time, I admitted I was doomed if someone didn't help me.

That weekend my mother, dad, twelve-year-old sister and I pulled thousands of tassels. I could see the field shrink. I began to grow.

I had marched into battle naive and ignorant, brimming with hubris. Only the gift of family saved me.

Winter, 1951–1952, Age 14–15
Shooting Baskets

When school opened for my sophomore year, I began working for Faye Kelley, the school janitor and all-around handyman. I crawled out of bed every morning at six o'clock, ate a bowl of cereal, and walked the few blocks to school.

My job was to empty the wastebaskets and sweep the classroom floors. My last task was to sweep the gymnasium floor. Then I put on my beloved white Converse tennis shoes and shot baskets. For half an hour I filled the silence with bounce, bounce, bounce—swish, bounce, bounce, bounce—swish, bounce, bounce, bounce—clank. Morning after morning I played in front of empty bleachers.

One January morning about six-thirty I was shooting game-winning shots when I heard someone pounding on the front doors. I thought perhaps Faye had locked himself out, but the banging wasn't very loud.

I couldn't see outside in the morning darkness, so I opened the door. In walked my seven-year-old brother, jacket opened against the winter wind.

"What the heck are you doing here?" I asked.

"I came to shoot some baskets with you."

He threw his jacket into the corner and took off his sweatshirt. I passed him the ball. He dribbled a few times and pushed the ball into the air. He couldn't shoot the ball high enough to reach the rim but he never stopped trying.

I started shooting baskets when I was in the fifth grade and kept shooting for the next forty-five years through junior high, B squad, varsity, and college intramurals. Later I put up a basket on our garage and shot with my kids. I quit shooting baskets when I was fifty-five. The kids had moved away and the backboard rotted, so I took down the hoop and set the ball on the shelf in the garage.

I suppose I shot thousands of baskets in my life, but my best memory is the morning my second-grade brother said, "I came to shoot some baskets with you."

Spring, 1951, Grade Ten
Turkey Trot

One May morning after I had finished sweeping and dumping, Faye said, "Tom, how'd you like to make a few bucks this weekend? I'm going to sell my turkeys and I could really use some help."

"Sure, why not," I said. "How hard can that be? I can use the money."

"I'll pick you up at seven tomorrow morning."

An undulating sea of black gobbling spread out before me. "Don't kid yourself, rookie," they gabbled. "We know why you guys are here and we're not giving up without a fight. Think about it, buster. Some guy is waiting to change us into a meal. First they'll stuff us into a crate, drive us to the slaughterhouse, and send us to turkey heaven without blinking an eye. Then they'll pluck us, wrap us in plastic, and stamp us with some ridiculous name like Jenny-O."

Although I didn't speak turkey, I could tell they were preparing for battle, and gobbled no intention of going without a fight.

"Here, take this," said Faye. He handed me a six-foot rod with a looped hook on the end. "Try not to rile them up. Walk up behind them as casually as you can and hook one of their legs. Pull the bird toward you. Grab their legs with one hand and wrap your other arm around their wings. They can get pretty nasty, so work fast."

I walked towards them. They gobbled turkey obscenities.

"Walk casually, my eye!" I couldn't get near them.

"Retreat. Retreat," they cried. The black wave of bobbing heads and flapping wings moved toward the far corners of the pen. I spotted my first victim and hustled toward him. Just as I was ready to hook him, I slipped on the fresh turkey droppings and fell flat on my back.

"My god," I thought, "I'm back in the chicken house again, except this time I'm slip-sliding in turkey poop. When will I ever learn?"

I got up and sprinted after my turkey. I hooked him and pulled him toward me. I grabbed for a leg and missed. The bird fought for its life. It scratched my hands and arms.

I held both feet and he flew in place. I grabbed for his wings and missed. He twisted and beat the hell out of my face with his wings. He dived and pecked at my ankles. I pulled him to my chest and wrapped my arms around his wings. One down. Only nine hundred ninety-three to go.

Faye grinned. He crated four or five to my one. When we quit, I was exhausted and covered with turkey crap. My hair, my shirt, my overall, and my shoe were one slimy mess. My glasses, which had been knocked off several times, were smudged brown. The turkeys tore my shirt, raked their claws down my arms and hands, and scratched my face with their wings. I was beaten and battered, but I learned a lot about teaching junior high students that day.

Summer, 1951, Age 15
Into the Fumes
That summer my dad took a job pressing clothes at Brightway Cleaners on Selby and Dale in St. Paul. I looked forward to a summer of playing baseball, but that ended the day he announced, "They need someone to run the dry-cleaning machine. Want the job?"

I had learned that a question like "Want the job?" wasn't really a question at all when it came from my parents or teachers. "What happened to you on the test?" or "Would you like to rethink your answer?" were really commands such as "You better start studying," or "You better rethink your answer."

"I guess so," I said. "Yes, I'll take it."

We left home about five a.m. Dad pointed the '51 Studebaker's silver-bullet nose toward St. Paul and once again I became a stranger in a strange land. Although we lived in the big city, my world was quite small. We lived with my mother's uncle and his wife on Stanford Avenue. After work I took the streetcar from the corner of Selby and Dale to Snelling Avenue. For the first month I paid each time I got on the car. When someone told me about transfer tickets, I cut my fare in half. I walked the few blocks down Stanford.

I worked in the back of the building. Mountains of clothing were stacked on the workbench in front of me. Many of the buttons dissolved in the cleaning solvent, so I cut them off and put them in bags, making certain I identified them properly. Many times I thought the buttons were the kind that would not dissolve. I pulled many buttonless items out of that machine.

The dry-cleaning machine was the large, improved model, unlike Dad's old rig at the Tip Top Cleaners. The fumes, however, were just as noxious and I couldn't run outside into the fresh air.

Dad and I left for work about 7:30 A.M. and I worked until 5:00 p.m. The clothes heap grew from early morning until about two o'clock. After that the race was on. The machine ran continuously, so I ate my lunch at the worktable as the machine roared behind me.

Someone might say, "What a wonderful opportunity for a father and son to bond! All that time riding to and from work and all those hours working together." We usually ate breakfast in silence and seldom spoke as we rode to work. I went to my fume-filled purgatory and Dad went to his inferno.

Since I couldn't see him from my workbench, each day I walked a few feet, leaned against the sidewall, and watched him. He worked in northeast corner of the building. I never saw my dad's face. He never saw anything but the steam press in front of him and the landscape of the gray concrete block wall. The clothes I had cleaned were thrown into carts, which surrounded his press.

We had no air conditioning. While the summer heat blistered the building, Dad slammed the cover down and steam poured from the press. He lifted the top of the press, flipped the garment, and pulled down the press. Again the steam enveloped him in a white cloud. He was drenched in sweat and the muscles in his shoulders tightened every time he pulled down the press.

I knew he was in hell every minute he stood in that corner. I felt nauseated, but I wasn't smart enough to understand why seeing him like that depressed me so. I wasn't yet wise enough to ask him, "How do you survive back there? What do you think about all day? Do you dream of better days? A better job? Are you in pain? Do you think about your wife and children who are struggling to survive back home?"

The worst part of my job was cleaning the dry cleaning machine. Every few days I had to shovel the powdery residue from the machine. There were about three feet between the machine and the wall. I crawled into that space and removed a panel from the back of the machine. I scooped out the powder and dumped it into a pail.

The fumes gushed out of the opening. I held my nose with one hand and scooped with the other. Just before I ran out of breath, I grabbed the pail and crawled backwards. There were no vents or windows. I ran outside to dump the pail and breath some back-alley air. I sucked my lungs full and went back for another load. Soon my head reeled and I thought I would pass out before I got outside. My head ached and felt as if it were cracking open.

I said good-bye to my dad at five o'clock. My great aunt and uncle had little to say to a fifteen-year-old. I had no buddies to play catch with, no television, no radio, no nothin'. I hated work and I hated the loneliness. One night I discovered a cache of their son's hot novels by Mickey Spillaine. I became a very avid reader. I became a very fast reader.

I was asleep by the time Dad came home, and the next morning we enacted the same routine. At five o'clock on Friday afternoon, we aimed the Studie south for home. I slept most of the way and Dad stared straight ahead. We spent the entire summer together. My dad learned little about me and I learned even less about him.

I learned one thing about summer jobs—the more horrible they were, the more I yearned for school to start.

Summer, 1953, Age 16
Block Heads
In the fall of 1952, we moved to Belle Plaine. Dad got a job at the Model Clothing Store, where he had worked as a student. For the first few months he and I lived with his parents, Grandpa Pete and Grandma Clara. I went to school and played football. Dad worked during the day and built our house on the weekends and after work. When it was framed in, my mother, sister, and three brothers joined us.

EASY WASH, INC.
ST. PAUL, MINN.

PERIOD ENDING JUN 14 1952 195

EMP. NAME *Tom Melchow*

REGULAR HOURS @		
OVERTIME HOURS @	*R.W.*	
TOTAL EARNINGS ☞	*45⁰⁰*	
OLD AGE BENEFIT	*67*	
WITHHOLDING U. S. INCOME TAX	*90*	
TOTAL DEDUCTIONS ☞	*957*	
NET PAY	*25⁴³*	

We made 9970 blocks at six-tenths of a cent and 560 blocks at nine-tenths.

The next summer my friends John, Pat, and I got a job at the Belle Plaine Block and Tile Factory. We made eight- and sixteen-pound concrete blocks. Our work was appropriately named "piecework." We began by shoveling sand into a huge bucket that sat in a pit ten feet below floor level. Next we tore open bags of cement and dumped it into the bucket. We added the water and switched on the automatic mixer.

Many times we shoveled the gravel and cement into the pit when the bucket was still at the top of the hoist. We took turns shoveling our mistake out of the pit. Our piecework was first shoveled into the pit, then thrown out of the pit, and then thrown back into the bucket.

When the sand, cement, and water were properly mixed, we pressed the button, which set the cables moving. Slowly they pulled the bucket high above the hopper and dumped the concrete mix into the hopper. We were now ready to make blocks. We set metal pallets in the steel molds, which would shape the blocks.

When we pressed the button, the machine vibrated in agony. The molds gave birth to twin concrete blocks. We lifted the pallets with two short pieces of angle iron. Next we carefully lifted the freshly packed blocks and set them on the drying rack. Press the button. Buurrrrrr! Another block. For eight hours. It was money out of our pocket if we bumped the block on the rack or nicked it in any way. Once we had filled the rack, the forklift driver picked up our rack of fragile blocks and drove them into the kiln. We held our breath because one day he bumped a rack of tile and leveled every one. Green concrete mix lay in little piles under the rack. No pay for that!

At that point we still had no money in our pockets. Piecework meant we would not be paid until the job was complete. When the blocks were dry, they were hauled into the yard. Naturally the metal pallets were still stuck to the bottoms of the blocks, so we knocked the pallets off with a hammer. Once they were stacked, they were money in the pocket.

My job at the block and tile factory made me very cynical about merit pay for teachers.

Human Relations

In 1973 the state of Minnesota passed a law requiring all teachers, except those with life certificates, to take courses in human relations in order to renew their teaching certificates.

MINNESOTA STATE DEPARTMENT OF EDUCATION

The Minnesota Human Relations Program is a state requirement for all applicants for licensure in education to be issued on/after July 1, 1973. This course deals with the following components: a) understanding the contributions and life styles of various racial, cultural and economic groups in our society; b) recognizing and dealing with humanizing biases, discrimination and prejudices; c) creating learning environments which contribute to the self-esteem of all persons and to positive interpersonal relations; and d) respecting human diversity and personal rights.

Why were we "lifers" excused from this mandate? Perhaps the legislators assumed that those of us who began teaching in the '50s had honed our skills in cultural awareness. Perhaps they assumed that our years in the classroom had instilled within us enough cultural sensitivity that we didn't need the course.

Perhaps they assumed that we were children of the Greatest Generation, nurtured on a diet of ethical and moral absolutism. After all, we had been raised in a mythology of Super Man and "God Bless America."

Perhaps they assumed anyone trained before God died in the '60s was free of bias. The youth of the nation cried, "Trust no one over thirty!" Many who made the laws thought young people were anarchical, long-haired hippies, mired in a slough of rattle-brained ethics and morality. The logical conclusion was that we old timers were as unchallengeable as Newton's laws of physics.

Naturally we lifers congratulated ourselves for our cultural sensitivity. Not only were we finely tuned to the nuances of our culture, but also we were practical. Who wanted to shell out cash for another education course?

Perhaps we were excluded because legislators believed time and money spent on us would be wasted. Perhaps they looked at the longevity statistics and decided not to waste money on teachers who could do little damage before they retired. Perhaps they thought we were so deeply entrenched in our tunnel vision and prejudices that we were beyond reclamation.

I was delighted to be a lifer. I certainly would have benefited from the class during the remaining twenty years of my career. What scared me about the class were all the "deal withs" in the course description. "This class deals with …understanding the contributions and life styles of various racial, cultural, and economic groups; [This class] "deals with dehumanizing biases, discrimination, and prejudices." "Deals with" sounded a lot like taking a bloody beating from Tuffy Anderson in the alley.

Cynics may argue that our trauma from being ignored by the state lawmakers is no more than infantile whining, much ado about nothing. I disagree. A lifetime certificate does not insulate one from the slings and arrows of administrative shunning. We, too, feel pain. Believing that the decision to pardon us from our obligation was made by disinterested lobbyists and legislators had not soothed our feelings of rejection.

After giving years of thought to my shunning, I have arrived at the following conclusion: The legislature must have decided that we lifers were without harmful bias, prejudice, or tunnel vision. Perhaps they thought that we harbored few flaws in sensibility and compassion and that we had been nurtured during the decades of authentic character building. Perhaps they decided that family nurturing, religion, and public education had given birth to a generation of teachers of sound intellect and character—lifers. Perhaps they concluded a sound foundation of ethics and logic had freed us from the present and future generations' predisposition toward self-righteousness, egoism, and demagoguery. Perhaps they believed that the folks down on Main Street had pointed us straight down the narrow path of righteousness.

Perhaps these were the reasons I was excused, or perhaps they looked at my youthful experiences and decided I had already taken the class.

The following excerpts are from the *Human Relations Education of Thomas Melchior* (Complete work yet to be written.)

Gaylord Elementary and Junior High Schools, 1946-1950
The Protestant churches towered over the other buildings in town. St. Michael the Archangel Catholic Church was one the smallest buildings in town. It towered over nothing. The tiny house of God was tucked neatly between two homes, both bigger than the church. St. Michael's architectural significance matched the lack of interest and respect it held in the hearts of local Protestants. A statue of St. Michael waving a sword over the dragon-snake of evil guarded the church and all who worshiped within.

The Lutherans received a daily dose of religion at their school. We warriors of St. Michael descended to Mamie Deis's basement each Wednesday afternoon. She guided us gently through our *Baltimore Catechisms*. We recited terse-memorized responses to questions such as, "Who made me?" or "Why did God make me?" or "Where is God?"

We tried to catch up with the Protestants each summer by attending religion classes for a week or two. I wasn't the holiest or most astute student, but I won my share of holy cards.

My buddies and I seldom discussed religion. We knew, however, who believed what and who was going where. We battled often but neither side had much ammunition. Occasionally we public school kids (Papists included) played the kids from the Lutheran school to settle any unresolved disputes about the Reformation. Instead of swords and spears we used a softball and bat to prove who was holier. I didn't care about winning any holy war. I just wanted to beat Allen Zachow, probably the best player in town.

The highlight of this crusade came the day I slammed a long drive across the field. The ball ricocheted off a light pole and I waltzed home with the Holy Grail. I guess that settled who was saved. No problem dealing with religious differences that day!

Gang Problems
This class deals with understanding the lifestyle of another cultural group, recognizing and dealing with dehumanizing biases, and respecting human rights.   Minnesota Public Relations Program

When the Alley Cats got their dander up, we were forced to deal with some serious problems. Again and again in our secret meetings we resolved that nobody was going to push us Horned Frogs around. As usual we settled our disputes with a game of whatever sport was in season. By the time we went home and gathered our equipment, the issue was forgotten, but we played for a while anyway and quit when we got bored. I discovered early that boredom deals with adversity very effectively.

Our problems with the Alley Cats never ended. They smoked, drank, swore, and talked as if they knew everything there was to know about sex. Rumors spread that one of the Horned Toads had brushed against the breast of an Alley Cats' girlfriend. Someone also said a Horned Frog had paraphrased the lyric "I'm lookin' over a four leaf clover" on the walls of the girls' toilet in the park and substituted obscenities. The same rumor claimed the villain had also written a fearsome obscenity next to the girl's name. We Horned Frogs weren't that stupid. No Frog had the guts. Someone had set us up.

The Alley Cats intimidated us, but we Frogs knew how to "deal with"these cultural clashes. We sacrificed our self-esteem. First we groveled and then we hid.

Garden City High School, 1950-1952

Our move to Garden City made us outsiders. We looked like the Joad family, leaving our roots and heading to the Promised Land. The white Congregationalist church was the tallest building in town. I didn't need to deal with religious bias because we were the only Catholics in town. The nearest church was fourteen miles away. We were a religious nonentity.

The red barns dotting the countryside made a clear statement about the people and their values. I was a town kid in the midst of farm kids. Although I had spent months on my grandparents' farm, I knew nothing about the lifestyle of my farm buddies.

That summer I worked in the fields pulling weeds and hoeing thistles. Whenever I defended my position as an overworked peon, my farm buddies exclaimed, "Ha! You think that's work? You should have done what I did today. I got up at 4:30 a.m., milked the cows, and cleaned the barn before breakfast. Then I—"

How did I deal with this plunge into an agrarian culture? Did I stand my ground? Did I create an environment of respectful diversity? No. Usually I agreed that that nothing in my life compared to milking forty cows before dawn, scooping manure from barn-length gutters, picking forty acres of corn after school, milking the cows again, and making the honor roll every quarter. Acquiescing requires nothing more than sacrificing self-esteem.

Veryl
There were twenty-four students in my class. A few of them came from Vernon Center, six miles south of town, but the majority of the students were farm kids. There were only five guys in town who went to Garden City High, two seniors, one-eighth grader, and two of us freshmen.

On the first day I walked the two blocks to school and picked up my schedule. I recognized all the course titles except one—Ag. 1 "What the heck was Ag.," I wondered, "and who signed me up to take the class?" I went to English, history, physical education, and algebra.

Finally it was time for Ag. Every guy in my class walked into Ag, which I discovered was Agriculture 1. What did I need to know about crop rotation, animal medicine, and pig breeding? I was a town kid. What the heck was I doing in Agriculture 1?

I tried to get out of the class, but there were no options. Since most of the guys in the school were farmers, all of us were required to take the class. I didn't realize it at the time but the dictate to take Ag. was my first encounter with administrative expediency. It was cheaper and easier to force us to become pseudo-farmers than to offer other electives. Every administrator, parent, teacher and student knew there was no chance that Fred, Gene, Burt, Frank and I would ever become farmers.

The class was taught by Veryl Rollings, one of the most lovable, dedicated teaching tyrants who ever lived. Veryl was a young man when I met him, but a small spare tire was already ballooning just above his belt. His face glowed with excitement while he talked about farming. He loved to laugh. He was the only teacher I ever had who could smile the same smile whether he was enjoying a joke or ripping the hide off us for fooling around.

The first six weeks my grade was C+.

Veryl was the favorite teacher of many of the school's students. He was perennial Teacher of the Year for all the farm parents and their sons. He was their counselor, teacher, and friend. After school and

Veryl Rollings, Mr. Agriculture

on Saturdays, he traveled from one farm to another, helping the parents of his students. In time, these parents would retire and turn the farms over to his students. He taught what he lived and lived what he taught.

The second six weeks my grade was C+.

Ag was the first of many required classes which would torment me during my career in education. I was bored much of the time during Veryl's lectures about cultivating corn, farrowing pigs, injecting antibiotics, and curing worms, but when he told stories, I came alive. A lecture on bovine tuberculosis became "A few years ago I went out to a farm and every one of those damn cows—." Just the mention foot and mouth disease, scrapie, or trichinella sent Veryl into storytelling ecstasy.

Veryl was an expert on manure management. I had to listen carefully to determine whether he was informing us on the value of spreading natural fertilizer on the fields or just spreading a little of his own around the classroom. He taught me that the innocent and the unthinking accept manure as willingly as Mother Earth. He taught me it is as easy to spoil the mind as it is to desecrate earth, water, and air. Spreading manure must never be done perniciously.

I loved Veryl despite my frustration with his grading system. Each day we stampeded into his classroom, and in a few seconds he rounded us up and began the day's instruction on chicken lice or intestinal fungus.

The third six weeks my grade was C+.

Enrollment in Ag. made us automatic candidates for FFA, Future Farmers of America. I suspected that most members of FFA nationwide joined of their own free will, but I ended up with a membership card and I don't remember volunteering.

Veryl taught me that two things are really one thing. I may have thought that Ag class and Future Farmers of America were separate, which they were, but all of us knew Veryl believed two were married. Belonging to FFA. meant we could join one of the activity groups, so I joined the Wildlife Identification Club. For weeks before the big meet, I studied dozens of stuffed birds and four-legged creatures. Most of the specimens had been stuffed before I was born. The red fox looked more like a well-fed fox squirrel and the fox squirrel looked like something long extinct.

I accompanied the team to Mankato State Teachers College for the district FFA contest. I was the only freshman on our team, and naturally, I took home the most pathetic score.

I studied so hard to earn a good grade in Ag. I did extra credit. No matter how hard I studied, however, no matter how high my test scores were, it seemed I was doomed to C+. Joining the FFA judging team didn't help. The fourth six-week grading period I again received a C+.

I delivered the Minneapolis Sunday *Tribune* to the folks in Garden City. Veryl lived about two miles outside of town on the Highway 169 curve that bent into town. Every Sunday despite hail, heat, and blizzard, I biked those two miles, fighting traffic, weather, and nipping dogs to deliver one lousy paper. Shouldn't that count for at least a B?

Four grading periods had passed and four C+'s marched across my report card. I had to make the B honor roll. One day before class I asked Veryl what I had to do to earn a higher grade.

He looked at me for a few seconds and smiled. "Mr. Melchior," Veryl announced, "you can't learn how to castrate a pig by reading a book."

When I considered my options, I decided C+ was good enough.

Fall, 1953-1954
Belle Plaine High School
Most of the Catholics attended the Catholic grade school. Most of the Lutherans attended the Lutheran grade school. The others attended Belle Plaine public school. Ninth grade mixed everyone together in Belle Plaine High School. My parents pitched me into this melting pot when we moved to town in 1953.

The German Catholics attended Sts. Peter and Paul, where the gothic spires reached higher to heaven than anything or anyone else in town. The Irish Catholics worshiped comfortably in a much less ostentatious church. The Protestant faithful, including a multitude of German Lutherans, worshiped in several other churches.

The town was founded and named Belle Plaine by a traveling Frenchman. After years of genealogical sifting, the Irish and the Germans fell through the smallest holes. Dealing with the problems created by all this mixing resulted in the Belle Plaine Holy War.

Years later the Catholic archbishop dealt with the problem by tearing down Sacred Heart and re-naming Sts. Peter and Paul. Reluctantly the German and Irish Catholics and all the other "foreigners" gathered to worship at Our Lady of the Prairie, but that all happened after I had left town.

Each spring an annual battle of this war was fought in the high school gymnasium. How and when these battles began remains a mystery. Someone years earlier had decided these disputes about nationality and religion would be settled every St. Patrick's Day on the basketball court.

Ancient cultures offered human and animal sacrifices to appease the gods in their spring rituals. We played the Irish-All-Nations Game instead.

Perhaps the challenge originated late in the evening after hours of cele-brating St. Patrick's victory over the snakes. More than likely a few Irishmen boasted that they could defeat the whole world and the world accepted the challenge. Perhaps there were too few non-Irishmen to quiet the blarney and the game was on. The battle lines were clearly drawn. Anyone with a drop of Irish blood (Northern Irish blood excluded) battled the world.

Not just anyone could play, however. Teams were chosen from members of the varsity and B squad teams. The ritual was held during the last hour of school. The Irish followers dressed in green sat on one side of the gym, and the All-Nation fans sat on the other. They dressed in the colors their great grandparents honored in the old world. The All-Nations were lead by their polka band and one cheerleader with German ancestry. Minton, Moriarty, Murphy, Mahoney, and Doheny cheered for the Irish.

Belle Plaine *Herald* March 12, 1953
Irish vs. All-Nations Tuesday
The annual inter-squad St. Patrick's Day basketball game between the Irish and All-Nations will be held at 3 o'clock Tuesday afternoon.

The traditional post-season game is gaining a lot of enthusiasm this year with the sons of Erin confident they can regain cage supremacy over all comers on this magic day of days, March 17. On the other hand, the All-Nations is sure they can out-do the Irish as they have for the last few years.

At any rate this will probably be one of the closest St. Patrick's Day games in many years with almost an even split on the high school's first ten men on each team.

Belle Plaine *Herald*, March 19, 1953
Irish Win
It was a great day for the Irish Tuesday when the sons of Erin trimmed the All-Nations team 33-18 in the annual intersquad St. Patrick's Day game. At halftime the green led 26-13.

The following March the question of religious and cultural superiority erupted again. The administration, caught in the storm of historic ritual, deferred again to battle as the method of settling this steamy problem.

Belle Plaine *Herald*, March 1954
They Got Their Irish Up
The school was alive with the usual St. Patrick's Day spirit. All the Irish were a wearing their green and humming their Irish tunes. Of course, the Germans were trying to get back at the Irish. They were wearing red and whistling their German tunes.

Front Row: Martin, (Irish), Mc Raith, (Irish), Lynch, (Irish), Grosser, (All-Nations), Melchior, (Irish), Back Row:Olson, (All-Nations). Hottinger, (All-Nations), Moody, (All-Nations). Larson, (All-Nations), Engfer, (Irish)

At two-thirty everyone was dismissed to go to the basketball game. When we arrived in the gym, the Irish theme song, "McNamara's Band" was playing. But soon the German band started to play and drowned out the Irish music. There were cheerleaders for both sides. The Irish had a mascot, Timmy Melchior. The Irish team was decked out in green suits. They even had green and white basketballs. The Germans wore red suits.

The game was very close with little lead for either side. Both teams were trying very hard and they kept the score quite close. The final score was 54-51 with the Irish winning. This victory made St. Patrick's Day perfect for the Belle Plaine Irish.

These are some of the cultural conflicts I experienced in my youth. Did they qualify me for exclusion from the human relations requirement? Certainly not. The reason we lifers were excluded from taking the class was a simple matter of the law. Once the law had been passed making us "lifers," we could not be "unlifed."

Plunging

I was born a plunger. Let's get to it. Time to act.

Fortunately, many of my teaching colleagues thought first and then cautiously stepped into the darkness. They did not follow me as I leaped into the unknown or paddled toward the sirens' songs.

They reasoned things as they relaxed in rocking recliners. They used logic and sipped elixirs of insight while stretched on padded chaise longues. They sat patiently like Rodin's *Thinker* and weighed the consequences of impulsive, untested academic gymnastics.

Meanwhile, I walked the teaching tightrope or flung myself from one pedagogical guru to another. I followed my instincts, believing I was doing the right thing, and leapt.

If I thought about reasoning in a recliner or stretching out on a chaise longue to apply logic, the gods of education whisked me away before I could relax and meditate. "Hey, Melchior," they yelled, "what the heck are you doing? Get with it. We need some reckless abandon over here. Jump right in."

I would like to blame those gods for my tendency to leap without looking, but in truth, I think they gave me many opportunities to correct my leap-first, think-later compulsion, but gradually plunging became part of my Melchiorness. People would look at me and say, "Oh, that's just the way he is. He'll outgrow it."

Like everyone else, I leapt into the world and was greeted by a firm slap on the butt. "There you go, laddie," said the doctor. "Take a deep breath and howl your head off. This is just a sign of things to come."

Later I jumped, leapt, and plunged while the gods frowned and said, "Someday he'll catch on. Someday he'll think before he jumps. He's a good candidate to teach the youth of the nation, but he's a bit reckless." Meanwhile, I perfected my dives.

When I was ten, my mother said, "Don't go swimming in the lake." The murky lake was coated with ripples of green algae. I closed my eyes and jumped off the dock into Lake Titloe, the laughing stock of lakes, partly because of its name, but mainly because it is a mud lake that tries to pass itself off as one of Minnesota's 10,000 crystal clear waters.

I took a few steps and cut my heel on a broken pop bottle. In twenty seconds several leeches selected me for lunch. I crawled onto the dock. Blood seeped from the cut on my heel and a bit more oozed out every time I pulled off a bloodsucker.

The next summer I spent a few weeks at my cousins' farm. I jumped from the top of the storage bin. Before I sank into the wheat, my cousins Pat and Mike pulled me out. The Gods of Teaching just shook their heads.

When I was in the seventh grade, I went to visit my grandparents in Belle Plaine. I met some guys who took me swimming in a backwater lake off the Minnesota River. I waded in and stepped into a drop-off. This time the Madden twins pulled me out. The Gods began to mumble.

In high school my friend said, "Hey, Melch, I met this girl from (a neighboring town). She wants me to take her to their prom. Her best friend is looking for a date. How about you taking her and we'll double. I'll drive. Come on, pardner. I need some help here."

We walked into the gym and every head turned to stare. I knew immediately I had dated Hester Prynne. Her classmates' stares lit up the scarlet letter on her prom dress like a neon sign. I danced through the night as happily as if I were having a colonoscopy.

After my second year of teaching in Puerto Rico, I agreed to act as tour leader for twenty-five recently graduated college students. Eighteen of the twenty young women on the tour had graduated from prestigious eastern schools.

The day we toured the Swiss Alps, the temperature rose to ninety-four degrees. We were roasting in the bus. We stopped for lunch near a mountain lake fed by melting snow. "Hey, let's take a swim," I said. "I know I'll never come back here again and I want to say I swam in the Alps."

I sprinted into the lake and dived. My stomach and chest froze before my back felt the water. One of the Swiss tourists laughed and checked the water. The mercury pushed up to thirty-five degrees and stopped.

When I was thirty-one, we moved into our new house. In November I hid the boys' Christmas presents. One of our bedroom doors opens to the rafters to which the sheet-rocked ceiling of the family room is nailed. I tip-toed across the rafters and hid the kids' presents behind the chimney.

On December 23 we packed the car to head to my father-in-law's house for our Christmas ritual. I had only one task left before we headed for Faribault—retrieve the presents. My wife and children watched me walk down the basement steps. "Daddy has a few things to do in the basement before we leave," said my wife. "We'll wait up here."

I walked out the basement door, sneaked in the front door and walked up the stairs. I opened the bedroom door and retraced my steps, making certain I placed each foot securely on the ceiling rafters. I reached around the chimney for the presents and slipped.

My right foot crashed through the ceiling and tore out a huge triangular piece of sheetrock. The boys were standing directly under the falling plaster. When my leg shot through the hole and dangled above them they screamed, "Mommy, there's a robber up there, a robber."

I swore like a maniac, my crotch impaled on the rafter, my other leg bent like a pretzel. Presents flew as I grabbed the rafters to keep from smashing my other foot through the ceiling.

The story of daddy's plaster plunge sent my in-laws into holiday hysterics. For years I could see nothing funny about the story, but now it has become a family favorite, just another of Tom's leaps into the unknown.

I have a doctorate degree in plunging. I would like to say I am the only person who has earned this accolade for stepping blindly into the darkness, but that would be naive. Therefore, I have used discretion to select the following stories, which appear in Melchior's *Dissertation on Plunging*.

1960, El Yunke National Rain Forest, Puerto Rico
The Great White Whale

Seve, Teresa, Pat and his fiancé Naomi and I climbed hundreds of steps to reach the pool at the top of El Yunke. During the 1930s the Civil Conservation Corps carved the Bano Grande Pool out of the mountain. Every year 240 inches of rain fall on the mountain, 100 billion gallons of water. The Commonwealth of Puerto built a diving board and each year would-be divers swan-dived, cannonballed, flipped, and belly-flopped into the dark abyss. Although the water was crystal clear, the black rock made it impossible to see a foot below the surface. Divers hit the black water and disappeared.

When we reached the pool, the drama had just begun. A Puerto Rican grandmother stood off to the side with her son and daughter. Dressed in their swimsuits, two young Puerto Rican women sat on their towels, admiring the antics of their dates, two American sailors from nearby Roosevelt Roads Navy Base.

One paced back and forth along the side of the pool.

The main character pranced back and forth on the high board, flexing his muscles. "Take a look at this," he yelled. "Is this the body of Mr. America or what?" He struck three of four poses, popping muscles like bubble gum.

"Big deal!" laughed his buddy. "Who do you think you are, Tarzan of the Jungle?"

"Ugh, me Tarzan. You Jane," he grunted, pointing at his date.

"Come on, Tarzan. Show us how you dive," she giggled.

Grandma shook her head.

"Watch this," said Tarzan. He strutted to the back of the board, sprinted a few steps, bounced, and arched into a spectacular swan dive. He slipped into the pool, no splash, a perfect 10.

His head popped out of the water and he screamed, "Oh, my God! I lost my suit. It ripped off when I hit the water."

We all moved closer to the pool.

"I can't see it." He dived into the darkness and two white cheeks broke water like the Great White Whale.

"Ave Marie, que Gringo!" moaned Grandma. "Que pasa aqui?"

The girls shrieked. Grandma covered her eyes but spread her fingers for a good look.

Again and again he dove. We hooted and hollered every time his butt broke water.

"Hey, Moby, you look like the Great White Butt of the Ocean," yelled his buddy.

"Goddamn it!" Moby screamed. "Don't just stand there. Get me a towel."

White Cheeks dived again.

"Que barbaridad! Que desgracia!" scolded Grandma. "Que bruto, Gringo!" Grandma whipped her shawl over her shoulder. "Jose, Anita, vamanos. Que sin verguenza!" She led the way down the stairs but the kids kept watching until their heads dropped out of sight.

Gringo number two threw his buddy a towel. He wrapped it around himself under water and walked up the ladder.

"Bravo! Bravo!" we cheered. "Great show! What a performance!"

"Thank you. Thank you," he grinned. "It was nothing."

I knew just how he felt.

In 1958 I plunged into teaching. For years I climbed the ladder and dived again and again. Occasionally I scored a nine or a ten. What a grand feeling! Many times I nearly lost my suit and once or twice I did lose it. I'm proud to be a plunger. Sitting around the house swimming in memories of teaching is nice, but it's the diving I miss the most.

It Ain't Just a Game

I have seen guys fooled so badly by a slow-breaking curveball that every joint in their bodies struggled to keep from popping a socket. In a lunging, sweeping whirl, they waved their Louisville Sluggers at strike three. After unscrewing themselves from the ground, they laughed at their Charlie Chaplin routine and headed to the dugout.

I have seen guys measure their lead off first base, sprint for second, execute a perfect head-first slide, and plow to a dusty stop three feet short of the bag. Pounding their fists in feigned anger, they laughed as the shortstop knighted the fallen heroes, tagging them gently on the helmet.

I have always envied people who could see the humor in moments like these. How much of my obsession to take life seriously is genetic, I can't say. I do know that my youthful mastery of two sets of commandments won for me a life-long hair shirt and a cat-o'-nine tails for psyche flogging.

The Commandments

I learned the commandments of the Church and the commandments of sport about the same time. I traveled through my childhood and adolescence learning to be a "good" Catholic. This happened in the late 1940s and 1950s before Pope John XXIII spun the altar around and changed the liturgy from Latin to English. Religion was no laughing matter. I memorized the commandments, but I understood only a few.

I placed no false gods before me, at least not until I was about twelve. I never took the Lord's name in vain. My vocabulary was filled with one-syllable words. No problem honoring my father and my mother. They took care of that commandment. They took me to Mass every Sunday. I fought with my sister but murder was never an option. I had no idea how to commit adultery, nor did I have a clue what coveting meant.

Religion was a serious mixture of humility and razzmatazz. I could recite every prayer but didn't understand what most of the words meant. I did, however, understand the necessity of praying to win. Losing to the opposition would result in more than a mere tongue-lashing. Losing meant burning in the fires of hell. The Act of Contrition helped me form my blossoming scrupulous conscience. "O, my God, I am heartily sorry for having offended Thee," I proclaimed, "and I detest all my sins not because I dread the loss of heaven and the pains of hell, but most of all because I have offended thee, my God." I claimed I was contrite not because I feared the fire of hell, but my whole being said, "Are you crazy? You're terrified you'll burn and sizzle and explode like popcorn for all eternity." Well, of course I was cooked anyway because I uttered a solemn prayer that I didn't really mean.

Word Magic

No one tells little kids about Word Magic. Adults don't explain that words are just words because that would sap grownups of their power. Some adults even believe the word is the thing.

About the time I started pitching peewee baseball, Word Magic was smokin' major league fastballs by me. Not much of a match. "Thy will be done on earth as it is in heaven" kept me wide-eyed under my covers for many nights. I wasn't certain what Thy's will was. I didn't even know who Thy was. Having Thy watch me day and night was a heavy burden.

"Forgive us our trespasses" didn't bother me much. The only time I trespassed was when Jimmy Breagle and I crawled into the game preserve, trying to pick off a couple of mallards with our 410s. We never associated the "No Trespassing" sign with the "trespassing" in the "Thou shalt nots." I mucked up my shirt and jeans, which put more fear in me than sullying my conscience.

One day our motherly religion teacher was sick. Well, that's what we were told. Word Magic took her place. He looked at us wrinkle-browed and sour-faced above a black suit and white collar. When he dismissed the girls, I knew we were in trouble. Then he announced that it was a big-time sin, maybe even a mortal sin, to have impure thoughts and I froze to the chair.

The old fast baller fired "immoral," "shameful," and "obscene" past me before I could blink. "You're out!" my conscious screamed! Before I had time to walk to the dugout, I was back in the batter's box. "Wicked," "unclean," and "despicable" struck me out again. Then Word Magic cut loose with the fastest blazer I had ever seen: "No impure touching!" he growled. I squirmed to escape the flames.

"Shame, shame," he snarled. "Repent or else." We knew what that meant—confession every Saturday.

There wasn't anything to laugh about here. If I was going to grow up to be "a good person," a person "with character," I had better learn to walk the straight and narrow path. There was no room on that path for humor or fun, especially delicious impure thoughts.

Only a few Catholic guys lived in town and we were too embarrassed to talk to each other about the Enchanted Kingdom of Impure Thoughts, where we frolicked in rapturous fantasy. How we envied those lucky Protestant guys who could enjoy impure thoughts whenever they floated into their imaginations! No Saturday confession for them!

The white collar whistled a few fastballs under my chin and screamed, "Shame on you for wallowing in hedonism." I had no idea what wallowing and hedonism meant, but I knew from those snarling lips and pinched eyes that I was destined for trouble.

Confiteor Deo: Mea Culpa, Mea Culpa, Mea Maxima Culpa

Shame and Guilt soon had me begging for repentance. Off to confession I went every Saturday afternoon. "Bless me, Father, for I have sinned. I trespassed once in the slough, I called my sister "Fatso" five times, I got really mad at my mom three times, and I had seven thousand impure thoughts, every day, during math class, except for the day we had religion." I wondered if he would be able to tell I was fibbing at that small number.

Bit-by-bit I honed my scruples. By the time I was pitching for the midgets, I experienced enough to know "I was a sinner in the hands of an angry God." The priest said, "Now I absolve thee of thy sins. Say ninety-eight rosaries and tell me you will sin no more."

"I will sin no more," I echoed.

"Go in peace," he said. "I'll see you next week" and I left the church cleansed of my transgressions.

Unfortunately sports had no absolution for strikeouts, missed shots, or or bobbled ground balls. I could only mumble, "My fault. I should have (fill in the blank)." My teammates offered offered absolution and hollered, "Forget about it," but I never forgot.

The Chosen

About that time I was given the privilege of becoming an altar boy. I memorized the Latin words and walked to the priest's house at 5 a.m. in -20 degree weather to serve Mass. I never ate breakfast, so I was starving by communion time. By second-hour geography I folded my growling stomach behind my belly button to stifle the angry lions looking for a feeble zebra.

The worst thing about serving Mass was that I became an automaton, mouthing words I didn't understand at a babbling pace to compete with my serving partner. We slurred Latin words with lightning speed.

My dad had been an altar boy, so I followed his lead. I did what was expected of me and carried out my role in the ritual. This conditioned me for an adult life in which I would obediently act out incomprehensible rituals or dance unquestioningly through situations from which I thought there was no escape.

Serving as an altar boy was advertised as a unique privilege offered to the most deserving. I had memorized my Baltimore Catechism and could answer simple questions such as "Who is God? Where is God? Why did God make us?" I had accumulated my share of holy cards and other sundry awards for both my knowledge and obedience. Therefore, I was chosen.

I realized years later, however, that being selected to kneel beside the priest and rattle off words I didn't understand was based on expedience, not holiness. Few Catholic boys my age lived in town, so the selection committee dipped deeply into the well no matter how bitter the dregs.

Being an altar boy taught me to revere God's sacred place. The tiny church demanded total reverence. I entered a sacred, humorless world when I crossed the threshold. At Christmas I stood next to the organ where we kids gathered to sing hymns. Since nothing could silence me from singing, this seemed to be an ecclesiastical faux pas. I belted out those Christmas hymns with unrestrained good humor and joy.

The solemnity demanded by this emaciated building, however, quieted even the most rambunctious spirit. If I forgot where I was, either the priest or my dad silenced me with the same stern glare as the plaster martyrs staring down from their pedestals. Years later when I visited the Vatican, Chartres, and Notre Dame de Paris, people wandered around during Mass, extolling the beauty of the great works of art and chattering as if they were at their high school reunion. I saw the statues still staring.

Thou Shalt Not!
The moment I walked into the sanctuary behind the altar to pull on my server's gown, I was immersed in a world of black and white. Most of the time we dressed in silence, the priest a few feet away from my partner and me. This entire ritual helped me understand the power of the other sacred places I would encounter during my life. It certainly helped me move smoothly from the altar of God to the altar of sports.

St. Michael's Catholic Church

The tiny church breathed, "Thou shalt not." The priest scolded, "This is the house of God, not a place for horseplay, giggling, or passing gas." The crucifix hung as a reminder that I was a sinner. Bobbling spiritual ground balls demanded hundreds of spiritual pushups.

The message was clear—"Thou shalt not talk, daydream, and fail to genuflect and bow at designated times and places. Thou shalt not screw up." Failure to place wine and water cruets in the proper place or handing them to the priest in reverse order earned me a well-practiced seminary scowl. Cutting across the altar, burying the candlewick in hot wax, and genuflecting half-heartedly earned me post-Mass lectures.

"Thou shalt not touch" could have been brought down from the mountain by Moses with the other "Thou shalt nots." I was convinced that I was condemned to Purgatory whether I brushed against Rose Ann's angora bosom in school or touched the chalice on the altar. The lines were clearly drawn as to what a Catholic adolescent could and could not touch. Flickering flames of fire and brimstone awaited wandering fingers.

The philosophy of religious and athletic rituals was exactly the same. Winning was everything. "Thou shalt not" allowed no exceptions. "Thou shalt hustle on the playing fields of religion and sports. Sitting on the bench terrified me as much as sitting in the purgatory of the soul. I quivered at the thought of either one. It wasn't long before my mind was doing spiritual pushups for morally striking out. Soon anxiety ticks danced in my eyes. Migraine fireworks exploded in my head. There were no humor pills to ease the pain. I persecuted myself for fumbling a "thou shalt not" or muffing a fly ball. The lessons were always painful.

Serious Stuff

I cannot remember a priest laughing. Each catechism class, confession, and Mass was the seventh game of the World Series. There was no margin for error. The game must be played by aspiring saints who boot no rubric or swing wildly at temptation. "Step out of the batter's box and you're out! Fumble the communion platter and you're dancin' in the flames."

Tragedy and comedy, however, are the same muscles pulled by different gods. Yin pulls them one way, and Yang tugs them the other. One person's yin is another person's yang. I'm not certain why I couldn't laugh at myself when my body betrayed my mind, when I fired a fastball that sailed two feet over the catcher and bounced off the backstop screen or punted the football thirty yards straight up for a next gain of three yards.

"Get serious out there. Bear down! You're letting the whole team down!" yelled Yin. "Did you see that?" howled Yang. "That's the most hilarious thing I have ever seen!" People who weren't yanging at the same vibration that I was were greatly amused. There was always someone who could laugh at me as I acted out life's absurdities and the more sacred the event, the more yanging I heard.

Going, going, gone!

"Thou shalt fast before communion." Every Christmas eve my family ate oyster stew for supper. Then we opened our presents and waited four or five hours for midnight Mass. Throughout those years migraine headaches plagued me. When I was tired or nervous, a vise gripped my head and screwed the pain through my eyeballs.

When I was thirteen, I served midnight Mass for the robot priest. Just before communion the seeds of a blistering migraine sprouted and blossomed. Stars sparkled and burst before my eyes. My head throbbed. As I waited to ring the bells at the consecration of the bread and wine, the large red flowers in the carpet revolved in slow motion. Picking up speed, they spiraled into a whirling vortex and sucked me down. I dropped the bell and fainted. I struck out in the last of the ninth with the bases loaded. I struck out before a packed church! Sit down! No confession for that blunder!

I found nothing humorous about my dive at the holiest moment of the Mass. Not so with my serving buddies and classmates. With roaring bursts of laughter, they described to each other again and again my swan-divine into oblivion. Only the passing of time and their embellishment of the tale enabled me to laugh with them.

My education by the good father was not finished. Winthrop, seven miles away, was the priest's mission church. They did not have an altar boy and I was "volunteered" to serve. It was another of those late night services, and after Mass the priest talked and talked and talked with one of the parishioners.

I sat in the pew and waited. Like a kid waiting for his dad to come out of a 3.2 beer joint, I got bored. I closed my eyes. I stretched out on the pew and fell asleep. "What do you think you're doing?" thundered over me. "Don't you know this is the House of God?" The scolding lasted long enough to carve "Thou shalt not" a bit deeper in my conscience. Strike three again! Zip! Zip! Zip! Three fastballs and "You're out of here." I never got the bat off my shoulder!

I moved rapidly from innocence into the impending doom of those who cannot score a perfect ten in spiritual gymnastics. St. Augustine sent me to the plate to face Original Sin. I never saw the three strikes, but I heard them whiz by. I walked back to the dugout, knowing I would face a life of broken psychic bones. I treated my conscience for some ache or sprain every Saturday.

When I worshiped by numbers, I did quite well. I knew every page of the spiritual rule book for rote religion written in Baltimore. I didn't know why and I didn't ask questions. I just kept genuflecting, making the sign of the cross, and following the numbers.

Almost magically the philosophy of sport blended into my religious truths. Both high priests stood on their respective altars and proclaimed the same dogma: "Fire up. Say your prayers. This is more than just a game. A mortal sin is a bad as taking a third strike with the bases loaded. When you are on this field, you must give 110% or turn in your uniform. Sit up straight. Don't slump when you're kneeling. Hellfire and damnation to the guy who quits! Venial sins can lead you to hellfire. Screw up and you sit on the end of the bench!"

The angel choirs and my coaches chanted, "Buckle down. Bear down. Dig deeper. Don't make any foolish decisions. Stay away from girls. You can't concentrate if you're thinking about them. You've gone too far to qualify for Limbo. Can you pray ten seconds and not think of sports or girls? Purgatory has a long bench.

"Winning is everything," they cried. You're here to serve God and hit homers. Winners never quit and quitters never win! Who remembers who finished in second place? This isn't sport; it's religion! This isn't religion, it's sport and there ain't no difference! Hustle! Hustle! Hustle! Only the true believers get to play in the big game."

My luck got worse. Teenage girls started firing more fastballs than usual, and the day they threw curves, they had me swinging like a baseball clown. "Bear down out there. Keep your head in there! You're stepping in the bucket! Concentrate. You're pulling your head out. You're stepping in the bucket again. Swing that bat. Clean up your act. Wipe the slate clean. Don't just stand there gawking. Screw up and you gotta pay. Misplay that commandment and you're history, baby."

Love of the Game

I cannot remember when I wasn't kicking, throwing, shooting, or dribbling a ball. My dad ran the Tip Top Cleaners. Next to our building was Lee Warnke's Hardware Store, which was forty or fifty feet longer than our building. Mr. Warnke's shop faced our yard. An enormous window stretched the length of his workbench.

After I had hauled a load of clothes out to the red-tiled block building that housed the dry-cleaning machine, I stopped for my daily ritual, pitching practice. I fired butternuts against the wall beneath Mr. Warnke's window. Suddenly I was in Fenway Park pitching for the Red Sox against the hated Yankees. I cut loose a high, hard butternut to back Joe DiMaggio away from the plate. He leaned back and the butternut shot through Mr. Warnke's window. But no shattering glass! Just a butternut-sized hole in that gigantic window!

I waited for hell fire and damnation to sizzle me from above. My dad would lock me in the house until Mr. Warnke sent me to Alcatraz. When Mr. Warnke and my dad looked at the hole, Lee Warnke laughed and said, "Someday that kid's gonna be a pitcher. I never saw anything like this in my life." I don't remember what my punishment was, but it wasn't much. Like most of my blunders, I couldn't see the humor in the butternut fiasco until years later.

In the winter I nailed a Hunt's tomato soup can to the wall. Hour after hour I dribbled and shot my tennis ball. When the Minneapolis Lakers played, I became Slater Martin, Jim Pollard, and George Mikan. I announced the game as I played: "Martin brings the ball up the court against the Zoller Pistons, cuts left, and fires a pass to Jim Pollard. The Kangaroo Kid scores." The closer the score, the louder I called each play. By half time my voice was hoarse and I was soaked in sweat. When I went upstairs to get a drink, my mom doubled over in spasms, trying not to laugh. Nothing funny here. This was basketball, serious business.

I was short. I wanted to be 6' 7" like Jim Pollard and have a nickname like the Kangaroo Kid. Every time I walked through a door, I jumped up, grabbed the top of the doorjamb, and hung like a chimpanzee. I prayed to the god of basketball: "Get tall. Stretch. Get tall." My mother stuffed her apron in her mouth to stifle her laughter.

During the summer of 1954, I went one-on-one against the Kangaroo Kid. This time, however, it was in baseball. Pollard was pitching for our archrival, the Jordan Brewers. I was a seventeen-year-old high school grad- uate, playing for my beloved Belle Plaine Tigers. That night I hit one ball off the end of the bat and blooped a single over second. The next time I hit a ball six inches above my fists and sent a hand-tingling blooper over short. The last time up I hit a feeble ground ball up the middle. Three for four against one of the greatest basketball players in the NBA! "There is a God and He is good!"

Imaging

Sports psychologists make millions of dollars helping slumping prima don- nas master the art of positive imaging. By the time I was in the sixth grade, I had imaging down to an art. I dribbled an imaginary ball to school, mas- tering my head fakes and footwork. Dribble slowly, fake left, burn to the right, and lay the ball softly against the backboard. Practice. Get serious. Beat the other guy to the bucket.

My imaging took me three times as long to get from point A to point B as it should have. One day I went to Jim Breagle's house two blocks away. The Lakers were having a tough time against the Rochester Royals, and Slater Martin was working his butt off bringing the ball up the court against the press. I cut left, dribbled low to the ground, and leaped above those giants to get my shot off. Again and again I sailed skyward, shooting spec- tacular jump shots. I hung in the air and watched the ball rotate and then rip through the net.

When I finally got to Breagle's house, Mrs. Breagle was hysterical. She had watched the whole game. She was a loud, boisterous woman with a voice and laugh that could huff down the proverbial brick house. "Have you lost your mind, Melchior?" she shrieked. "Who won?" I got out of there as fast as I could.

My passion for basketball survived that humiliation. I certainly didn't see much humor in my behavior then, but now if I saw a kid walking down the street, playing imaginary basketball, I know I would grin and rifle him a behind-the-back pass.

Shootin' Hoops

We had a broken-down garage next to the alley. My parents gave me a basketball for Christmas, but they forgot about a hoop so I built one. Making a round hoop out of two-by-fours, however, is a difficult task. I tried cutting a hexagon using a handsaw, but I couldn't cut the angles properly. In  frustration I nailed four boards together and nailed my square basket to the garage. Foolishly, I made the inside of the square the same size as the ball. Later someone gave me a homemade hoop and I made a backboard.

On Saturday mornings from late fall to early spring, the janitors opened the high school gym. Every guy who loved hoops gathered for two or three hours of horse, around the world, and half-court games. If we were really lucky and only ten or twelve guys showed up, we used the whole court.

It was pure bliss, but as I learned in catechism, bliss isn't free. The two janitors were gods in overalls. They had the keys to the Promised Land and they weren't about to let us enter without a sacrifice. "You got to pay the price. You got to offer it up. You got to bow down and obey our commandments." If it snowed on Friday night, each of us was given a shovel and a designated number of sidewalk sections to shovel. The more guys, the fewer sections. Obviously, the less passionate guys stayed home on those snowy days, so the rest of us paid a heavy price.

Any concert or gathering meant we had to fold, stack, and wheel the metal chairs to their resting place. If the basketball team played the night before, we had to restore the gym to a pristine state. The Oshkosh gods hooked their thumbs into their pants and watched. We humbled ourselves while they puffed their pipes. If it snowed on a game night, we worked more than we played. "As flies to wanton gods [were] we. They kill[ed] us for their sport." Shakespeare never had to shovel snow or stack chairs to shoot hoops, but he knew his gods.

High Hopes

I entered the eighth grade in 1949. I was one of two or three eighth graders to make the B squad. We practiced every night and no shoveling! That year Gaylord had a terrific team that eventually won the town's first district championship since 1926. I dressed for all the B squad games and rode the bus with my heroes and the cheerleading goddesses decked out in their fancy purple and gold outfits.

Gaylord's court was approximately ten feet below the bleachers. It was surrounded by a concrete wall except on the stage side, which was about four feet above the floor. Fans sat above the floor and looked down on the court. That gym was the only basketball court I had ever played on until my B squad days.

Morton High School's court was elevated, a stage court with walls on three sides. Spectators sat at floor level and in the balcony. My routine for most B squad games was to dress as quickly as possible and to get out on the floor first, shoot as many times as I could, sit down when the game began, watch the action from the end of the bench, and dress after the game. The night we played Morton, however, I played in my first game. We were so far ahead there was no way we could lose, so the coach put us tail-enders into the game. My heart raced and the saliva in my mouth dried up as I reported to the score's table to give my name and number. There was little more than two minutes remaining when I entered the game.

Naturally we all wanted to make a basket. Five hearts pounded like sledgehammers. Five benchwarmers stumbled over each other. "I'm a guard. No, you're a forward! You guard number four. No, he's my man. You've got number three." If someone got close enough to shoot, he shot.

Suddenly I found myself unguarded. I was about fifteen feet from the basket so I let it go. The ball sailed over the top of the backboard and crashed against the iron-mesh screen, guarding the window ten feet above the basket. The ball clanged against the screen. A cloud of dust jumped into the air and drifted down to the court. It had waited all those years for me to set it free. The referees stopped the game and the janitors mopped the floor before we could continue playing.

There was no place to hide. Coaches and guys on the bench went crazy. "Geez, Melch, what was that? You really cut that one loose!" There was no escape. My buddies tormented me throughout the varsity game and all the way home. Every time someone described my missile launching, the bus rocked with laughter. Purgatory isn't very entertaining to the sinner.

More Lessons

We played a peewee baseball game against Glencoe. I can't even remember how old I was, but I know I was still pitching from the front of the pitcher's mound. Our game lasted only two innings because I walked twenty-two batters. I bounced them in the dirt, and threw them inside, outside, and over the Empire State Building. It was a Charlie Brown fiasco.

I have no idea why the coach kept me in there. Maybe he enjoyed humiliating little kids. Perhaps he thought making me do it until I got it right would make me a better pitcher and a better person, but, of course, I was well indoctrinated. I knew all the right responses to the baseball commandments—"I'll bear down. I can do it. The obstacles are never too great. I'll try harder." 'Tom, Tom, he's our man. If he can't do it, nobody can.'

"I had read the *Little Engine That Could*. All I had to do was try harder, throw faster. If I can't do it, I'll flog myself because 'It's all my fault.'" I was well conditioned— pray harder, try harder, fret and flog but never, never flee.

Baseball wasn't my only catechism. I remember only one thing about junior high football. One night we were practicing hand-offs. Time after time the ball was fumbled. Every time I blamed someone else.

Coach Gislason, our eighth-grade math teacher, looked me squarely in the eyes and said, "Melchior, accept the blame for your own mistakes. Your hand-offs are lousy." Of course, he was right. I had been taught not to blame the gods or anyone else for my screw-ups. I have never forgotten Coach Gislason's words. Of course, I haven't always accepted responsibility for my behavior, but the commandment whispers in my ear and I pay. Teachers can be powerful gods.

At All Costs
Fear of losing and fear of humiliation kill our spirit of adventure, our desire to "let it rip" even if we lose. Ridicule shrivels the spirit, and every adolescent understands that even though his buddies know this truth, they will be the first to mock and razz the one who gambles with his ego. I discovered I would do just about anything to win rather than subject myself to ridicule.

Our junior high physical education teacher decided we were going to have a unit on wrestling. He taught us a few holds and then he matched us up with an opponent. While the two know-nothings flailed around on the mat, I agonized.

I was skinny and weak as a noodle. The thought of having to wrestle someone made me nauseated, but I knew my catechism. "Stand in there. Be a man. Thou shalt not vomit from nervousness or show sign of sissiness."

My opponent was a wiry, country kid. We pawed around a bit. Then somehow I grabbed him around the neck with one hand and under the leg with the other. I clenched my hands together and held on. I'm certain he hated the whole business as much as I did. Nothing really happened. I held on and he tried to wriggle free. I played it safe. No adventurous moves for me. No experimenting with this new sport.

We stayed like that through our entire match. No way was I going to take a chance and lose. My classmates were hootin' and laughin'. They thought it was a riot. Not me. When the time ran out, I was declared the winner. What had I won? Nothing. "Don't take any silly chances out there. Keep the pressure on. Don't worry how you win, just win." Perhaps that day was the first time I realized that sometimes winning is losing.

World Series Debacle

That summer we challenged the guys from Arlington to a World Series. Not one adult was involved. We hung our gloves on our handlebars, taped on some bats, and biked the ten miles to Arlington for game one.

Our balloon tires crunched the gravel and twisted up trails of dust. We used their catcher's equipment. We were on our honor calling balls and strikes. We never argued, swore at each other, or huffed and puffed. We played baseball—free of all the "Thou shalts" and "You gottas." Sometimes the guys from Arlington made great plays and we hollered, "Way to go, Jack! Nice play. Way to hit that old apple!"

Sometimes we chased third strikes that bounced three feet in front of the plate, dropped easy pop flies, or threw the ball like madmen. And we laughed. We made fun of each other. We called each other "Klutz," "Iron Hands," and "Whiffer." The names flew but shattered no fragile egos. We just played some ball. We lost ourselves in the pure joy of throwing, running, and hitting.

We had planned to play a World Series. The winner had to win four games out of seven. All games were to be played during the two weeks before school began. But something happened that July afternoon when I was thirteen that was incomprehensible at the time but became crystal clear in later years.

By the fourth inning the game began to deteriorate. When we played by ourselves, we filled up the day. We resolved every dispute and continued to play for hours. No one organized us or coached us. We quit because we had to go home for dinner, or because we were tired.

That day in the middle of our World Series game we became bored. The game became a "game." We started fooling around until the game became a shambles and we quit a few innings later. We weren't having fun, and there was no joy in going through motions that were not governed by the nature of the game, by competition and rules and by someone to enforce these rules.

We couldn't articulate what was happening. We couldn't recognize that some guys were satisfied to fool around with the game while others knew it was not the real thing. The game was meant to be played inside both literal and metaphorical lines. There was little joy in playing outside those lines. Playing without those prescribed rules stole the game's poetry and reason for being. We were unable to discipline ourselves.

Unceremoniously, we picked up our gloves, re-taped our bats to our bikes, and headed home. We biked in silence, no bragging, no remorse, no excuses, just balloon tires crunching gravel. We had violated the sacred rituals. I yearned to confess to the gods of baseball. I had defiled the purity of the game I loved. The sun burned down from above and the gravel dust choked us.

I have never forgotten that fiasco. I scourged myself as I peddled home. "That wasn't funny," I said to myself. "Whatever gave you the idea that you could make a mockery of something so important to you?"

I replayed that game each September before the first day of school and told myself again and again, "This is not a game! This is serious stuff."

Attacked by ninth-grade girls, 1971, a not-so serious day: "I'm really sorry about that kiss," said Sue, "but I just couldn't help myself."

Deus Ex Machina

Deus ex machina from Greek *theos apo mekhanes* to Latin *deus ex machina*: *deus*, god, + *ex*, from, + *machina*, machine.
Definition 1: *Deus ex machina* in Greek and Roman drama a god lowered by stage machinery to resolve a plot or extricate the protagonist from a difficult situation.

I'm trying to imagine what kind of contraption was used to lower the actor-god from the clouds to pluck his favorite human from death. What was the "god" doing up there while his protégé was upsetting the balance between god, humans, and nature—puffing on a cigar and watching the soaps? Did the poor fella down below use his will to get himself into such a pickle or were the gods playing puppet-in-the-park with his life?

Homer said the gods on Mt. Olympus manipulated us for their amusement. They liked nothing better than whipping up a good brouhaha down on earth and messing around in our affairs, as if we couldn't do the job ourselves.

The gods on Olympus threw a wedding banquet and neglected to invite Eris, the Goddess of Discord, the only deity snubbed. She engraved "For the Fairest" on a golden apple and rolled it between Hera, Athene, and Aphrodite. They fussed over the ball and decided that Zeus should choose. Zeus was no one's fool, so he panned the job off on Paris, the King of Troy's naïve, bad-news son. Paris was lying in a field, tending his flock, and daydreaming of Oenone, his live-in nymph.

"If you choose me, I'll make you Lord of Europe and Asia," claimed Hera.

"Say I'm the fairest and I'll make certain Troy whips the Greeks!" exclaimed Athene.

Aphrodite bent over and brushed her breast against his shoulder. "I'll give you Helen, the most beautiful girl in the world," she whispered into his ear.

Paris handed the golden to Aphrodite and she spirited him to the home of Tyndareus, Helen's father, who had just pledged Helen to the warrior-king Menelaus. The newlyweds welcomed Paris into their home, and Menelaus took off for Crete. Paris kidnapped Helen and the war was on.

The gods chose sides and stuck their noses into the fray whenever their favorite Greek or Trojan was in trouble. Sometimes they lifted the guy up by the helmet or hid him is a whirlpool of sand. They would *deus ex machina* here and *deus ex machina* there, but they couldn't *deus ex machina* forever. Eventually, nearly every guy who was saved ended up as ashes.

Definition 2: *Deus ex machina* came to mean unexpected, artificial, or improbable character, device, or event introduced in a work of fiction or drama to resolve or untangle a plot.

Things usually look grim until Beowulf, Superman, Mighty Mouse and Obie Wan Kanobi, and the rest of the *deus ex machina* crew arrive. The more god-like the heroes are, the better chance they have of saving the day. Beowulf slays Mama Grendel and Grendel, Arthur saves the folks around Camelot, Perseus slays Medusa, and Obie Wan slices off the villain's arm and saves Luke Skywalker.

Sooner or later, however, they all discover the clock is ticking. Whether the hero is a 9.9 or a 1.0, the arrow will still hit Achilles' heal. Superman, perhaps the least vulnerable, succumbs to kryptonite and his writers' whims.

Chances are those .3 heroes who would like to provide the unexpected solution and save us from distress need just as much help as we do. Dragons seldom choke on their own fire and the beasties seldom retreat to the closet. Whether heroes leap buildings with a single bound or step over tinker-toy castles, they are still coming down, and so, eventually, will the victims they saved. *Deus ex machina* is not one of life's guarantees.

Definition 3: *Deus ex machina* is now a metaphor, which refers to any person or event that provides a sudden or unexpected solution to difficulty. *Deus ex machina* is the pabulum of our mythology. Feed on it and magical metamorphoses occur. Rely on it and become disillusioned. The results are tragic.

Boaters floating around in toilet tanks and little guys in dirty ovens make our lives clean and stain free. Football heroes sipping beer by cool mountain streams and gigantic human Kool-Aid pitchers crashing through walls offer us magic elixirs. Spray-ons, roll-ons, and rub-ons restore youth. *Deus ex machina* becomes expected and less surprising. A solution is at our beck and call.

What does our *deus ex machina*, our magical metamorphosis imply? At times it becomes nothing more than fermenting bushwa; at times it's a glorious salvation. The person saved is in distress, often through his or her appetite for the excitement or passion and not through some accidental quirk. The person plucked from the jaws of accidental distress may walk away rejoicing with no psychic pangs.

The person plucked from the jaws of passion or hubris, however, walks away with psychic baggage. It happens to King Arthur and Oedipus, and to all the rest of us. It's part of our mythology. I learned this from the student side of the desk.

A *Deus Ex Machina* Parable

The day he turned seventeen, December 19, 1953, the temperature dropped to ten degrees below zero. His parents gave him a pair of shoes and an orange plaid shirt. That night his sister and Merlyn, her husband-to-be boyfriend, and his date, Murph, and he celebrated his big day by going to a movie in Le Sueur. Merlyn drove his '36 Chevy six or seven miles south of town to Murph's farm. Her parents, Emmett and Florence, gave the obligatory parental advice—"Drive carefully. Be home early." They offered no admonitions to their daughter, for she had dated many suitors and was as pure as the winter snow that would fall later that evening.

As they drove back toward the farm, it began to snow. Wishing to discuss some ethical and philosophical issues, they pulled off the county road and parked in a nearby field road. Soon they were lost in a winter wonderland. He and his date sat in the back seat, discussing the nuances of Lady Macbeth's erratic behavior. As they sat in the darkness, inches of snow covered the ground. Although the car was running and the defrosters blowing, the windows fogged up from the heat of their passion. It has been said that they gave lip service to each issue.

When they had resolved the debate, they decided it was well beyond Cinderella's bewitching hour, and they had better drive that last mile home. Merlyn shifted into reverse. The tires spun and whined, but the car didn't move. Six inches of snow covered the ground. The car was parked on an incline. "How are we going to get out of here?" groaned Murph.

"You guys push," said Merlyn. They pushed and pushed but could not move the Chevy.

The four of them, dressed in light jackets, bucked the snow and wind and headed for Murph's farm.

"What do you mean, 'You're stuck'?" Emmett grumbled from his bedroom.

"I'm sorry, Daddy, but we can't get the car out."

Emmett walked down the steps bucking his overall. His wife Florence followed in her nightgown. "I'll make some hot chocolate," said Florence.

Emmett put on his coveralls, cap, and gloves and walked out of the house. The guys followed him to the shed. He motioned for them to stand on the hitch and hold on to the seat. *Deus ex machina* sliced through the winter night. He whipped the tractor around, backed up, unwrapped the log chain and hooked it to the car. "You guys sure picked a helluva spot to park," he snarled, his only words of the night.

They drove back to the house and picked up his sister. "Murph went to bed, so I was left there alone with Florence," she said.

They headed back to town, embarrassed survivors, rescued from the slippery slope by a knight on a shining red Farmal.

Note: I grew up watching western heroes throttle cattle rustlers and save damsels in distress. The Saturday serials featured Mighty Mouse, and each week Pauline was plucked from her perils. I followed the comic book heroics of Superman, Batman, and the rest of the super-hero gang. Deus ex machina poured from radio with the exploits of Jack Armstrong, the All-American Boy, and the adventures of Sky King.

I didn't find much *deus ex machina* in the real world, however. Dad dolled out ice cream and popsicle money, and my teachers and coaches helped me master my skills. But when I sat over my arithmetic tests or faced an ominous fastball, I was on my own.

In the first Star Wars movie Luke Skywalker wants to be a Jedi knight and play the role of the hero, but he's disillusioned about his powers. If Obie Wan Knobie and Yoda had not helped him, he would have been no more than fodder for evil. Aspiring humans who believes *deus ex machina* hovers about waiting to bail them out of the clutches of dragons, essay tests, and blazing fastballs have purchased a pile of fermenting bushwa.

Learning to travel alone is a necessary rite of passage. We may get help from Mom and Dad, Coach, and Teacher, but the pencil and Louisville Slugger are not in their hands when the history test or fastball comes zipping past.

Many books have been written about the art of teaching as well as the science of teaching. Each one of us who has been a student knows that "good teachers" have inspired us with their gifts. Luke's god-teachers help him find the "force" within, and our job as teachers is no different. If we teach our students to rely on some form of *deus ex machina*, they are doomed. Perhaps we cannot agree on what makes "good" teachers, but we can agree that they make a difference. We are barraged by a culture that sets a pantheon of *deus ex machina* figures before us and promises magical metamorphses with little or no effort. Occasionally we make the mistake of believing we are *deus ex machina* figures ourselves. Our task is to give our gifts and help our students find the hero within. Who knows? There may not be a *deus ex machina* with a red Farmal tractor in sight.

Jim

The story of Gilgamesh and his friend Enkidu was carved into stone tablets two or three thousand years before the birth of Christ. It's a story about the death of a friend and the quest to find out what happens after death.

Jim Ciminiski

Jim was dying from Bright's disease because his kidneys didn't work. The first time I met him I tagged along with my buddies who had know him all their lives. We wore our letter jackets, solid black with a black and white tiger sown above out hearts. "This is Tom," said Lee. "He just moved to town."

"Hey, how ya doing?" said Jim as he reached for my hand. He had baseball hands with fingers that loved a long floppy mitt. He stretched out on his bed, elbows and knees wrapped in a crumpled sheet. The year before the *Herald* had written, "Sophomore Jim Ciminski is the likely candidate for first base." Then he became ill and the doctors said, "Forget about baseball. You're too sick."

I listened as my friends talked about things past: Catholic school, ballgames, teachers, and girls. In the fall we replayed each football game for Jim. Winter came and we talked basketball. I visited him a few times by myself. I saw the ravages of his pain, but I couldn't talk about it. I didn't know how. The best I could do was to ask, "Hey, Jim, how ya doin'?"

"Pretty good," he answered, always "pretty good." I could never ask honest questions and he could not give honest answers.

Gilgamesh has never seen death. While Enkidu lies dying, he is unable to tell Gilgamesh what he is learning about dying.

Jim and I had no past, so we talked about what we loved the most, baseball. Baseball's past became our past. Neither of us had ever seen a major league game, but we read everything we could find about baseball. Players jumped from the pages of *Sport Magazine* into our conversations. Baseball's memorable moments made us soul mates, Cobb sliding into second, spikes high, Babe belting one to right, Feller blazing a fastball, and Joltin' Joe DiMaggio leading the Yankees. We traced our genealogy to the Thumper, the Mick, Stan the Man, Sal the Barber, Jackie, and Spahnie. We searched the radio dial for the voices of Red Barber, Curt Gowdy, and Mel

Allen to spirit us away and set us in the first row behind home plate. We played a board-game version of baseball by rolling dice. We picked our favorite major league teams and filled out the lineups. Base hits, strikeouts, groundouts, and fly balls played out before us with a flick of the wrist and a roll of the dice. Roll the dice. Call the play. "Musial rips a line drive to right. Furillo can't handle the carom. Slaughter heads for home and Musial glides into second. Cardinals lead the Dodgers one-zip."

Jim changed positions every few minutes to find the most comfortable position. We played the full nine innings when he was able. We played our games in Ebbetts's Field and Yankee Stadium, far from his bedroom.

We knew this wasn't baseball. Chance controlled everything. We could do no more than roll the dice. Real baseball is filled with magical moments as dramatic as a home run in the bottom of the ninth or as subtle as a sacrifice bunt. In real baseball, players throw and hit and run, and everyone who plays the game knows he will fail. Baseball games are filled with imperfections, so players have created a language of clichés to salve wounds from striking out and fumbling balls: "Forget about it! Shake it off! Nobody's hurt!" echo throughout the park. But anyone who has played the game knows these incantations are wasted energy. Mouths say what hearts cannot do. The game is unforgiving and so was Jim's disease.

Telling Jim to forget about baseball was like telling him to forget about dying. We talked about baseball but we never talked about dying. We didn't know how. He wasted away before our eyes, but I never believed he would die. I would like to say I was more sensitive than my friends, more in tune with the drama being enacted in that bedroom. I would like to say I was mature beyond my years, but I can't. I knew nothing about dying.

Sometimes he was too ill to talk, too ill to throw the dice. His muscles wasted away. He stretched out on his back, a skeleton covered with skin. I sat, made small talk, and looked at him when I had the courage.

Enkidu tells his friend Gilgamesh that he will have to journey alone, unable to understand death. Gilgamesh's innocence about death will change. Nothing will be as he thought it was.

We knelt before the casket at the wake, trying to figure out what kind of God we believed in or if a God really existed. We walked through the line, fumbling for words to tell his parents how we felt. We stood in the back of the room, stuffed our hands into our pockets, and watched our classmates and others who loved Jim file past his casket.

Enkidu tells Gilgamesh that he will see that things die, but his only choice will be to recover. What is will never be again.

We carried our friend to his grave. We knew how to punt footballs, shoot jump shots, and throw curve balls, but we knew nothing about grieving. We had nothing to say.

Enkidu tells Gilgamesh he will learn how painful it is to lose a friend.
When I began teaching, it never occurred to me that some of my students would die. I should have known this, but I didn't. And when they died, I didn't realize I was meeting Jim again and again. The names were different but it took me years to make the connection. Some had taunted Death with their hubris and lost. They didn't know that the domain of the gods belongs to the gods. Others waged had war against Death and asked, "Why?" And some had been consumed by Darkness.

The words *teacher* and *friend* seldom mean the same thing. Most of our students will remember us as teachers, which creates the image of a dispenser of facts and skills. "You taught me how to read, how to add and subtract. You taught me how to write, read music, and play the clarinet. You taught me how to analyze literature, solve calculus problems, and appreciate the arts. I would like to believe many students would also call us friend, but more likely they will call us teacher. In my heart they were all so much more than students. They were part of me. They were the fire that made my spirit blaze. John and Brian and Marette and Steve, and all the others, were so much more than passing students, occupying a desk, taking notes, daydreaming, fooling around, and plunging into life. They were more than student, more than friend. When I want to say, "Marette was—" there is no word in my language that names her, so I use *student.*

I dreaded attending Jim's wake and funeral because I did not know what to expect. After all, I didn't know who I was. I dreaded attending the wakes and funerals of my students because I knew what to expect. I wanted to be that which has no name, but I was *teacher* to my grieving *students.* We usually shook hands and mumbled something inadequate. Sometimes we held one another and cried to ease our pain. I was again a seventeen-year-old kid, living in a thirty-, forty-, or fifty-year-old body and spirit. Sometimes they asked me, "Why," and I remembered Jim.

When Enkidu dies, Gilgamesh feels the heaviness of death. He tries to speak but he cannot find the words. When he does speak, the words have little meaning. He turns to silence. When his friend dies, Gilgamesh, like me, like my buddies, like my students, wanders through the desert, no longer a king, just a man, seeking someone who can explain why his friend has died, seeking someone who can tell him what happens after death.

Like Gilgamesh, my students and I journey through life trying to find this "someone." Our quest is the story. The journey is not to possess the Rhinegold or the magic ring. Our journey is not physical, social, or psychological; it is spiritual.

Gilgamesh searched out the wisest of men, seeking the answer to his question: "Can I bring my friend back from Death?" The wise man told him about a plant in the river that would prick his fingers but would give him new life. Gilgamesh tied rocks to his feet and plunged into the river. He grabbed the plant, which cut his hands. He cut the rocks loose and swam to the surface, rejoicing in his victory.

The wise man left Gilgamesh on the shore. What rejoicing! He now possesses the mystical plant, the answer to life after death. He is more than a king. He dwells in the realm of the gods. Gilgamesh set the plant next to the pool and slipped into the water to bathe and rejoice. When he came out of the pool, he discovered a sloughed snakeskin where he had left the plant.

"What's that ending mean?" my students asked. "Is the snake the devil? Mr. Melchior, what do you think that ending means? You must know the answer. You're always talking about metaphors and symbols."

What could I say? No one has given a definitive answer since the tablets were unearthed in Mesopotamia thousands of years ago. "I think we are all Gilgamesh," I said. "We want to know all the answers. Perhaps the story asks us if we are meant to possess the plant of immortality. Why can't Gilgamesh keep the plant? In the Christian religion the snake symbolizes evil, but this story comes from the East. Would that change the story? How? Why is Gilgamesh unable to possess the plant? Why does he shed blood? What's all that mean? What are we to make of the snake sloughing its skin?

"Great literature asks the questions," I said. "Each of us must make the journey to answer them."

Belle Plaine High School, 1954, from The Tigerian, our yearbook

Teacher Training c. 1942: Gone Fishing

The King of Cold and Don't Worry

I began my course in teacher training the year I turned six. That fall my

Dad

mother spiffed me up and escorted me to Mrs. Oranger's first-grade room. A few months later when the lakes froze, my dad stuffed me into never-enough winter clothing and lured me out on the frozen tundra to pass on to his firstborn his wintry passion, ice-fishing. On some forgotten, frozen wasteland with the arctic wind whistling through my shorts, my dad introduced me to Professor Fishing. Not until years later did I realize how similar my dad's passion for fishing and my passion for teaching really were. Dad thrived in weather that hovered around freezing and then dived below zero. Perhaps he mastered the elements when he was a Boy Scout. By the time he was sixteen, he was an Eagle Scout, sporting a sash decorated with thousands of merit badges.

How many sons have yearned to have their fathers teach them the art of fishing? To share precious moments while their fathers passed on honored fishing rituals? To stand out in the middle of nowhere, side-by-side with the man who gave them life? To turn their backs to the wind and squirt steaming arcs of urine into the pure white snow? How fortunate I was to be among the chosen!

On our ice-fishing excursions Dad drove our 1941 Ford onto the lake, following the ice road toward the spot where were going to catch our limit. I was cursed to be born before fish houses were really popular. Back then real men fished right out there in the middle of the lake.

We parked at least a half mile from the shoreline. Boom! Boom! The rumbling sounded as if bombs were being dropped next to us.

"What's that sound, Dad?" I asked.

"Aw, pay no attention to that, Tommy. That's just the ice cracking because it's so cold. It happens all the time. You'll get used to it. It sounds worse than it really is. Don't worry about it."

Those hours on the ice introduced me to an educational litany that I would hear as a student and as a teacher: Fill in the blank with the correct answers: "Don't worry about that, it's only—(a) the bogeyman (b) the ghost of bad boys (c) a case of the sniffles (d) one little zit (e) a little quiz (f) your college entrance exam (g) a blue book essay final (h) a new approach to teaching grammar (i) a new method of discipline (j) a good salary increase (k) all of these (l) none of these.

What anxiety I developed at the Church of Don't Worry! What a lucky boy I was to receive such wonderful lessons that I could pass along to my students years later!

The Sculptor

Dad always parked the Ford so it would block the wind. I sat on the running board. Then he wrapped the leather strap of his ice chisel around his hand and began chopping my fishing hole. Ice chips shot through the air. Whether my dad was laying maple strips for our hardwood floors, altering the cuffs on a new pair of pants, wallpapering the kitchen, or fitting limestone slabs into freshly mixed concrete to build his fireplace, he accepted only one result—artistic symmetry.

Dad was the Michelangelo of the ice chisel. Down, down the chisel went. Dad left a thin layer of ice on the bottom of the hole while he chipped away each side until he had shaped a perfect circle. Then he drove the chisel through the thin glassy layer and the blue-black water gushed into my fishing hole.

"Here, you try it," he said, handing me the chisel.

It was tall and unwieldy. I could barely lift I. The chisel had a mind of its own. It controlled me. I raised it to strike, and off it went. It refused to strike where I had aimed. I seldom hit the same spot twice as I staggered back and forth. Finally Dad would take pity on me, grab the chisel, and chip, chip, chip—another perfect hole.

I had no idea at the time that I would spend much of my life hollowing out space, chipping away the debris, trying to create perfect teaching moments. My dad made the task look so easy, but I didn't realize at the time that he had chopped hundreds of holes before he chopped mine. I chipped lots of unteachable debris before I ever saw my students' passion gush from the deep.

Dad always made certain that my ice hole was within sitting distance of the running board of the Ford. He measured the depth of the lake, set my cork, and baited my first minnow. Then he packed his gear, walked forty or fifty feet away and began the chopping ritual again. When the Ford pulled away at the end of each fishing outing, he had chopped ten to twenty holes trying to discover where the fish were vacationing. I often felt the same way driving home after a day of teaching.

Numbed to the Bone

Again and again I find myself wanting to say, "Now if there was one thing which prepared me for teaching, it was—" and off I go recalling those memories, only to find myself saying again later, "If there was one thing that prepared me for teaching, it was—." Fishing was not the "one thing" that prepared me for teaching, but it taught me more than I learned in my first methods class.

Once Dad had chiseled my hole, I settled down to some serious fishing. I sat on the running board and stared at my red and white bobber. Nothing. The cold began to seep up out of the lake into my overshoes. I stood up and stomped my feet, waved my arms, and sat down again to participate in the joy of fishing. Soon a thin film of ice had formed on the hole and even if my minnow tried to entice some voracious walleye, its seductive wriggling couldn't move the bobber. I hesitated. "Should I do the right fishing thing," I asked myself, "or should I just sit here and let the cold have its way with me?"

On my first ice-fishing excursion I learned that that it's nearly impossible to fish with double-jointed fingers. My fingers looked and worked like those of any other kid when they were snuggled safely within my woolen mittens, but when that hook came out of the hole minnowless, I was doomed.

I took off my mittens. Then I had to capture a minnow from the freezing water in the minnow bucket. Usually the minnow slipped out of my hand and wriggled around on the ice for a few seconds before I could pick it up. Next I held the minnow in my left hand and the hook in my right hand. I hooked him easily because he, too, was nearly frozen.

By the time I had finished the impaling, my fishing hole had frozen over, so I had to scoop away the glassy film. By this time my minnow was stiff, but I dropped it into the hole anyway.

Only the joints that connected my thumbs to my hands could move. I could not move my finger joints no matter how hard I tried. From that time on I sat on the running board and watched my body turn into the abominable snowman.

I dreaded seeing my bobber dive into the lake. It usually meant I had caught another stunted perch, which meant I had to again take off my mittens, unhook a perch, usually taking a dorsal fin in the palm, and repeat the baiting ritual.

What great teachers training that was! Little did I know then that as a teacher I would sit on the running board of my desk, bait my hook before frozen eyes, and cast my offerings into the darkness, hoping for a catch.

Pillow Talk
For years I refused my dad's invitations to go ice-fishing. I did not go with him again until 1954 when I was a freshman in college. By that time he had abandoned the Ford and settled for a second-hand Chrysler.

At that time my dad had become the envy of every ice fisherman who rented a cheap one-man, five-by-five clapboard fish house from the resort owner on the east side of Mille Lacs Lake. Dad's fish house was the Taj Mahal, the Windsor Castle, the Hotel Royale of icehouses.

The insulated walls were paneled with birch. The house slept five—two beds over the wheel wells and two fold-down beds above them. The fifth bed was a large fold-down near the door. Every time Mother Nature called during the middle of the night I had to maneuver around the bed where the boss slept.

We could sit on our bunks and fish through the holes, which were strategically placed below the bunks. The ice palace was heated by a propane stove, which also lit the gas burners on the cooking stove.

Ice-fishing for Dad was not a raucous, card-playing, male-bonding, chug-a-lug, backslapping, tall tale-telling escape-from-the-Mrs. social event. He was a man of few words, and when he stepped into that fish house on Mille Lacs, he slipped into monk-like silence. Once the ice auger had set the tinnitus humming in our ears, we settled down to fishing, sleeping, and eating, almost always in silence.

Dad had to solve the paradox of his ice-fishing credo: How could he fish and sleep at the same time? Fishing is fishing and sleeping is sleeping, but to Dad ice fishing was fishing-sleeping or sleeping-fishing. It was all the same. He solved that problem with his usual ingenuity.

When I was a boy, every man wore a hat to church. How was he to keep that hat neatly blocked while his children squirmed up and down the pews? Some clever entrepreneur invented a hat clip that was screwed into the back of the pew. Push on the top of the device and the jaw of the clip opened and clamped the brim of the hat securely in place.

Somehow Dad secured four of those clamps. He attached them to each bunk and wired them to a car battery and an electric buzzer. Once he had determined the proper fishing depth, he cut a piece of electricians tape and taped it to the fishing line, making certain he had a tab of tape attached to the line, which he then inserted into the clasp, breaking the circuit. When a fish took the bait and pulled the tape out of the clamp, the buzzer awakened Dad. He pulled in his walleye, changed bait, and easily slipped back into his dreams.

I was not fisherman-sleeper. I was a teenager caged in semi-darkness. Paneled walls, bunks, and a stove entombed me. The escape door opened to a barren, frozen wasteland. I was a hyperactive seventeen-year-old trapped in darkness, caged by a lethargic, hibernating parent. I spent a lot of time walking outside in the cold just to keep from going stir-crazy.

When Dad's growling stomach woke him, he fixed supper. He was not a gourmet cook. He carried only one cooking utensil with him wherever he went—an eight-inch, crusty, black, cast-iron frying pan. Whether he was fixing his supper after working the night shift or preparing our meal on the tundra, Dad's main course was always a fried hamburger—a huge patty of fatty ground beef an inch thick. He heated the frying pan, threw in the meat and fried it just long enough to brown the outside and congeal the bloody juice inside. He wrapped two slices of Wonder Bread around the meat to sop up the juice and bit into cholesterol ecstasy. For dessert on these outings, we had one or two of Mom's chocolate cakes, covered with a half inch of Hershey's richest chocolate frosting.

Stuffed and ready for the long winter night, Dad checked his minnow, made a few comments like "It's pretty slow," or "It's gonna be a cold one tonight," and then he settled into his bunk for the night.

In a few minutes a hoarse, chainsaw roar filled the fish house. Measure after measure of basso profondo snorted from his nostrils in stereophonic aggravation. After fighting this battle for an hour, I knew I was whipped unless I took drastic action. I shoved him in the back.

"Huh, what?" he grunted.

"You're snoring. I can't sleep. Turn on your side," I ordered.

"Oh, O.K.," he mumbled and caught the second half of the snore I had so rudely interrupted.

I pulled my belt out of my pants and slipped the belt through the buckle to make a loop. I placed a pillow against each ear and lassoed them to my head. I sat down and rolled onto the bunk, holding the belt with one hand and pulling up the covers with the other. Then I tightened the lasso until silence smothered the snoring.

Although my dad spent many more days and nights in that fishing house, I never again baited a minnow in cold weather. I moved on to larger fish houses—college classrooms, lecture halls, auditoriums, and outdoor arenas where pontificating educational snorers, far less humble than my dad, filled the air with the fortissimo of "truth."

When the snoring became too pompous and I thought the "truth sayers" were too self-righteous, too dogmatic, too tyrannical, or too illogical, I pulled the belt on my pillow just a little bit tighter.

The Marvelous Martin

My dad was as passionate about summer fishing as he was about ice fishing. In the middle of winter he began to fine-tune his outboard motor, a behemoth black Martin that tormented my dad for years.

The Martin weighed a ton. Slaves building Egyptian pyramids had an easier time moving their burdens than we did carrying that lazy Martin. I had to grab it with both hands, rest it on my thighs, and stagger from the car to the dock, setting it down and picking it up seven or eight times.

But worst of all, the Martin had the disposition of an uncivilized, schizophrenic mechanical wolf-child. At some time during its engine infancy, the black beast must have been abandoned by its parental engines and brought up by two corroded hippie spark plugs in the backroom darkness of an outboard motor repair shop.

There it was taught to defy proper two-cycle rhythmic purring. "You are your own engine," preached the former Champion spark plugs, "the offspring of our refusal to conform to factory specifications. Don't let anyone think he can run your engine by simply pulling your starter rope. Purr when you want to, but never hesitate to cough, sputter, and choke if you are not in the mood to serve your master."

And so my dad bought the Martin, a ten-horse dynamo, to replace his anemic, but trusty, one-horse Johnson. Little did he know that beneath that shiny

Dad's nemesis, the Martin 60

black cover lived a dysfunctional engine determined to test the nerves of one of the most patient men who ever lived.

As he carried the motor to his car, he imagined the front of the boat spearing the sky as the propeller dug into the lake and whisked him to his happy fishing grounds. Little did he know that he had purchased the most manic-depressive outboard motor ever manufactured.

Like most people who work diligently during their probationary period, the Martin worked perfectly while it was on warranty. When the warranty expired, the Martin willed its first schizophrenic attack. It couldn't decide whether it wanted to be a precision instrument or a motley collection of scrap metal. My dad spent half his precious fishing season pulling hoses, adjusting the carburetor, changing spark plugs, and performing other futile operations on his nemesis.

As soon as the season was over, Dad took the Martin to the repair shop. The owner dissected malfunctioning organs and transplanted defective parts. Then he attached the engine to a huge, wooden barrel filled with water and started up the Martin. It purred for an hour. He started it over and over. It never missed a beat. The black beast traveled forty days and forty nights in that fifty-gallon lake and never conked out once.

Convinced that his Martin was tuned up and ready for the fishing season in the spring, Dad set the engine on the workbench in the basement where it plunged into depression and paranoia during the winter darkness. By spring it was manic enough to make Dad ecstatic for the first two or three hours of trolling before it quit again

By the time Dad traded the Martin for a new Johnson, I was teaching, where I battled the Martin's brothers, sisters, and cousins: film-eating movie projectors, temperamental video players, and the most Martin-like demon of all, the personal computer. There is no escape from the Martins of the world.

The Phoenix

In 1967 my wife and I built our house. That same year Tom Swope and Jim Keelin, two of my teaching colleagues, set out in search of public land on Minnesota's lakes where they could lease the property and build cabins.

They headed for Akeley to find Bass Lake. The Department of Natural Resources' description stated that a lake of approximately 130 acres, reaching great depths, was located a stone's throw from Eleventh Crow Wing Lake north of Akeley in Hubbard County.

Tom and Jim searched the area and explored every lake, but they found nothing fitting that description named Bass Lake. So they went into town and asked one of the old-timers if he knew of a lake about 130 acres located north of town. He said, "The only lake I know of around here that matches your description is Big Bass. Take the first right, turn past the entrance to Crow Wing Resort."

Tom and Jim went back to the lake and found the survey stakes which had been set in the 1930s. No one had ever claimed the lots because the state had the right description but the wrong name. Other people searching for the lake became frustrated and quit looking.

Jim took the lot on the north end and Tom took the lot on the south end. Word of the newfound Eden spread like wildfire throughout the school. For just twenty-five dollars a year we, too, could lease a lot on this idyllic lake. Jerry McCoy, the principal of our junior high, took the lot next to Tom's, we took the next lot, and two other administrators took the next two lots.

Paradise was ours. The only problem was that our cabin had to be built within two years, and so with no money in our pockets, we built a house and a cabin at the same time.

The other guys bought their white pine lumber from the Nevis Lumber Yard. Not us. Grandpa Pete, my dad's father, took the design and figured out the exact number of boards needed to build the cabin and took his calculations to the lumberyard in Belle Plaine. Wally said, "Ya, I'll make a bid on that cabin and the lumber will be fir. And if you buy from me, I'll haul the lumber all the way up there."

That weekend we went to visit my father-in-law. We sat on the porch talking about the cabin, and he said, "We're going to bulldoze a house in Northfield on Monday. It's got a big eight-foot thermopane window in it that you might be able to use."

I called my brother-in-law. We chopped a hole in the side of the house and I cut out the window with my chain saw. Then we cut out a few more windows and operated on the kitchen cabinets.

Wally, Grandpa, and I hauled the lumber, windows, and cabinets from Belle Plaine to Big Bass, more than two hundred miles. That summer Dad, Grandpa Pete, and I built our cabin.

We had a cabin on a lake, but we owned no boat, motor, or fishing gear. The next summer we bought a canoe, but my dad, the walleye and northern fisherman, couldn't troll from a canoe.

I never knew where or how my dad acquired the Queen Mary. One weekend he and two of his fishing buddies hauled the boat to Big Bass and launched it from the public access. Sporting a glossy white coat of paint, Dad's prize slipped smoothly into the lake.

During her glory days from the 1920s to the 1950s, before aluminum and fiber glass, she and thousands of wooden boats like her ruled 10,000 lakes. Our Queen was almost as heavy as her namesake.

When we were at the lake, she stayed tied to the dock. When we left, the entire family and a few of the neighbors slid her up the bank and rolled her over.

During the week my dad worked nights, keeping an eye on the boiler gauges in the Plymouth Building in Minneapolis. His weekends were Mondays and Tuesdays. As soon as he could get home and pack their gear, he and my mother wound up the old blue Chrysler and headed for Big Bass. His ritual seldom varied. First he hauled in the weekend supply of groceries and then he cleaned the refrigerator. My dad fussed about a lot of things, and cleaning our messy refrigerator was right up there on the top of his list.

The first time he came to stay with us at the cabin, he greeted us, chatted a few minutes, and then attacked my wife's refrigerator. She was stunned. Who was this person who had the audacity to clean her refrigerator? Once she realized that he meant no harm and was simply following his compulsion to order the universe, she welcomed him with open arms, a bucket of warm water, and a few sponges.

Often my mom and dad were the only people on the lake. My dad was more at home alone than anyone except Henry David Thoreau. Two chairs, one for himself and one for Mom, were Eden for Henry and Dad.

Once he had cleaned and stocked the refrigerator, he walked down to the Queen Mary, rolled her over, and slid her down the bank into the lake. Then

Paul, Marty, and Meg

he fastened his beloved ten-horse Johnson to the boat and trolled alone for hours.

The boat was also the heart of our family's summer rituals. Because I taught summer school, we usually arrived during the first week in August. By then the lake was warm enough for us to begin our cleanup campaign. I paid Paul and Marty five cents for each piece of debris and trash they could retrieve from the lake. I manned the oars and rowed around the lake. They sat on the side of the boat taking turns playing Jacques Cousteau.

Each time we spotted something alien floating in the weeds or resting on the sandy bottom, one of the boys jumped in and grabbed it. They filled the boats with aluminum cans, pop bottles, Styrofoam cups, and candy wrappers, as well as unique throwaways such as Barbie dolls and GI Joes.

Paul, Marty, and I spent hours fishing. When the three of us tried to fish from the canoe, each outing became a disaster. During these fishing fiascoes, I discovered a truth about teaching: I could not do and teach at the same time.

I could not concentrate on my own fishing if I were teaching my kids how to grip the pole, throw the lure, and release the line. I could play or I could teach. I couldn't do both at the same time. If I were just interested in playing at whatever I was doing, I could do both and no one need pay a price. I knew, however, I could not play at teaching. If I did someone had to pay.

Time after time I climbed into the canoe with my sons to cast for largemouth bass. When I took them out to teach them how to fish, I had every intention of fishing just as passionately as I did when I set out alone in the early morning mist.

We knew the bass were lazing about near the shoreline, so we tried to lay the surface plugs between the fallen trees. Marty sat in front and Paul sat in the back. I maneuvered the canoe into position.

Hula poppers danced on the ends of our lines. Marty snapped his rod back and hit the release. The popper dropped into the lake behind him. He whipped a limp line toward the shore.

Paul fired his plug into a birch tree ten feet above the shoreline. When he yanked the line trying to free his popper, the two treble hooks dug into the bark. I paddled toward the shore and grabbed branches as I stood on the front of the canoe trying to free the bait. I wriggled the front hook free. When I twisted the back hook free, the front hook dug into my thumb. I crawled back to my seat and twisted the barbed hook out of my thumb. It hurt like hell, but nothing was going to stop me from fishing and teaching my kids how to cast.

I pushed the canoe away from the shore. The wind came up and blew us backwards towards jack pine branches sticking out of the water. Marty's line tangled. I untangled his line. Paul wrapped his plug around a branch from a fallen tree. Marty snagged my shirtsleeve with his rubber frog. I tore my shirt and freed the frog. I unwrapped Paul's lure. We drifted. I paddled. Marty sent a rocket into a white pine.

I snarled. I grumbled. Marty cried. Paul sulked. We quit.

Then we started fishing from the Queen Mary. No rods touched and no lines tangled. No wispy breezes blew us across the lake or into the beaver's underwater aspen forest.

Paul sat in front and Marty sat in the back. I operated the oars. "Try holding your thumb like this. Don't whip your rod so hard. Great cast, Mart. You dropped it right between those two logs. Way to go, Paul. Now you're fishing like a pro." I became a better teacher when I left my snarling and grumbling in the cabin with my rod and reel.

We had little space for playing near our cabin. It was claustrophobic in the wild. The brush, trees, and mosquitoes owned the acre behind the cabin. Five feet in front of the cabin the bank dropped thirty feet into the lake. Three feet from the shoreline the lake was four or five feet deep. The McCoys had about ten feet of beach so the kids played there.

When the boys yearned for freedom and a sacred place, they found it in the Queen Mary. Paul pulled the right oar and Marty struggled gallantly with the left. The oars won every battle. Paul was bigger and stronger so they usually toured in a circle.

As the years passed, they mastered the oars and passed their solo exams. Marty usually rowed Mary Beth and Paul McCoy a few yards down the shoreline where they fished for stunted sunnies with canned corn. Some days they parked the boat over the sunnies' spawning beds and watched the fish swirl the sand into nests.

Paul soon tired of rowing back and forth in front of our cabins. A slight adjustment to the choke, a yank on the starter rope, a slight nudge of the shift lever, and a twist of the wrist freed him from childhood. As he cruised back and forth past our cabins, I thought of those high school Friday afternoons when my friends and I drove around town looking for the girls who broke our hearts.

Paul cruised from grade school into his early teens, sitting in front of my dad's ten-horse Johnson. He eased down the lake past Keelins, turned and headed back, stealing a glance to see if Peggy McCoy was watching, and then moved down the shoreline past Swopes.

Another twist of the wrist and the boat shot out of sight and into the bay where he could buzz around unseen. Then he cut the motor and the Queen Mary bobbed for a few seconds in her white, glassy shadow. There in that tiny bay guarded by giant pines, he sat in silence, flicking bass plugs between flowering lily pads.

My dad never stopped believing that giant northerns lurked in the depths of Big Bass. He was convinced he knew how to catch them but only the boat would go fishing with him because his "can't fail" method drove my sons and me stir-crazy.

Dad's Pflueger reel

He bought half a dozen huge sucker minnows and set out for his favorite spot. He tied on a number six hook and impaled the minnow behind the dorsal fin. He slid his red and white bobber to "just the right depth" and set the minnow into the lake. It dived into the depths to escape Dad, who hoped the minnow would be devoured by a voracious northern.

Then he poured himself a cup of coffee and sat and sat and sat for hours watching his berserk minnow drag that bobber around. When one minnow gave up the ghost, he hooked on another, poured more coffee and sat and sat and sat. I am certain my dad may have been as close to heaven as he ever got on earth sitting out there alone in his boat.

As the years passed, our boat began to show its age. But my dad replaced every piece of rotting wood, repaired broken seats, replaced the oarlocks, and recaulked when the water seeped through the cracks. He scraped off the flaking paint and brushed on a coat of improved spar enamel. She was his child and he cared for her with the same quiet tenderness he had cared for us when we were children.

When my dad died, so did our boat. Without his loving care or perhaps because her spirit left with his, the paint peeled and the boards began to rot. One late fall day Paul, Marty, and I pulled the boat up on shore and I cut her up with a chain saw. That night we built a fire with the wood from our Queen.

We sat silently in the darkness. The rotting wood smoked, but the dry pieces snapped and cracked and shot sparks up to the guy fishing for lunkers in the stars.

Paul now teaches biology and ecology to college students. Marty builds and restores trout streams. Both dream of water free from pollution—water like the Big Bass Lake of their youths.

Marty's fishing dream

3

Teacher Training 102

Fireflies

EVERY JULY NIGHT THE FIREFLIES PERFORM IN OUR flower garden. I know they are driven by firefly nature, doing something very practical like dining out. But I like to think they are just out of firefly school for the summer, ecstatic, showing off, cruising around on hot summer nights.

I stare at the blackness, letting my eyes take in the entire canvas. Dots of blinking lights—blink, blink. If I stare and try not to focus on any single point, they sprinkle the night with tiny stars. Sometimes I try to pick out one and follow its flight. There, a flash. There, another, moving across the garden. But how do I know it's not the same one? How do I know its not two or three out for the night just fooling around? Lights flash and fade. It's impossible to predict where and when the neon bulbs will glow.

When they fly close to the flowers, I can pick up splashes of poppy orange, rose yellow, and iris purple. The magic really begins when I take off my glasses. What a blessing to be nearsighted when the fireflies feel like playing! The darkness lights up with blurry sparklers, a firefly Fourth of July. I'm convinced the first impressionist painters were nearsighted. They painted the world the way I see it when I take off my glasses, colors washing together, dreamlike, fireflies dancing on black velvet. I know what's happening out there is chemistry at work, but where in the world would we find poetry if we saw the world as only a science textbook?

If I listen carefully, I can hear them chatting. "Hey, guys, it's dark out. Time to shine. I think I'll flit around a bit before I get serious about supper. Now's a good time to try out my new bulb. Wow! Cool! Think I'll try that again in a few seconds. Hey, there's Tom. Hey, Tom, watch this." Bzzzzt! Bzzzzt! "Whadaya think? Am I hot tonight or what?"

I have always been a daydreamer, drifting off into fantasy worlds. When I was a kid, I read all the classics. No, not *Treasure Island*, *The Three Musketeers*, *Great Expectations*, or *Tom Sawye*r. The only way I would have read Stevenson, Dumas, Dickens, and Twain was if they had been listed in the Boston Red Sox lineup.

I read the classics—every baseball novel written by John R. Tunis. I became the kid from Tomkinsville, signing a big bonus after my last high school game, a no hitter. I played my way through the minor leagues until I was called up to the big leagues. I was the rookie sensation who lifted my floundering teammates to a World Series victory. But those fantasies were never fireflies lighting up my mind. They were other people's stories. I just borrowed them for a few moments and added a few variations. Although I loved school and eventually plunged into the ideas of the world's great writers, I could not see the fireflies of literature.

In high school I read Milton, Keats and Shelley and all their literary companions in Harcourt Brace's *English Literature 12*. I studied the poets, playwrights, and novelists to which the literary world tipped their hats and lit votive candles. But no words from the masters lit up my page. The assignments short-circuited any fireflies that tried to shine for me. "Read. Memorize. Cram. Read. Regurgitate. Fill in the blanks. Read. Choose the correct multiple-choice answer. Read. Circle T for true and F for false."

For years the words danced across the pages, but I saw no fireflies. Even the words of the great William, who left his wife and family in Stratford-on-Avon to give us Hamlet, Macbeth, and Caliban, were presented as mere exercises in identifying which character said what.

Although the fireflies never danced for me in high school, I had starred in my English classes. On Mr. A.'s *Macbeth* final I had correctly identified obscure passages by such minor characters as Angus, Young Siward, the Scottish Doctor, and Banquo's son Fleance.

I can still recite with passion Macbeth's immortal "Tomorrow and tomorrow and tomorrow" speech, but at seventeen the words "Life's but a walking shadow, a poor player that struts and frets his hour upon the stage/ And then is heard no more" didn't even stir up a twenty-five-watt bulb firefly to light up my awareness of how the lines applied to my life.

I spit out the words and got an A for total recall, but the words leapt from my mind and flew out my mouth, never stopping to visit my heart. I woke each morning and sprinted headlong into hope and light.

Even the renegades in my class who coifed their Brylcreamed hair into ducktails, drove souped-up Fords, dated fast girls, and chug-a-lugged Hamms knew that life was good.

Few of us were aware that we were living in a world where idiots were telling tales filled with sound and fury signifying nothing. Even if someone had stood on an academic pulpit and pointed out the idiots for me, my fireflies would have yawned. I could resurrect the facts and fill in the blanks with Lady Macbeth, the porter, and good old Macduff, but my naive, youthful ears had no ears for meaningless words mumbled by idiots. After all, wasn't I pitching that afternoon against New Prague?

Shakespeare's witches whipped up a nasty concotion, tossing in "fillet of a fenny snake ... eye of newt, and toe of frog." They could chant, "Double, double, toil and trouble" 'til that cauldron bubbled, but it meant little to me. I was so busy worrying whether I could snap off a few sharp curve balls against those Trojan hitters that I never smelled their polluted brew. Armed with my high school storehouse of nearly useless information and my honor roll accolades, I charged into my college freshmen English class.

Professor L. was a brilliant young scholar from St. Louis who lived on an ethereal planet peopled by the spirits of Rousseau, Thomas Mann, Katherine Mansfield, Albert Camus and other players who had never once appeared in my starting lineup. Each day he assigned us stories and poems that I read several times. Each day he walked into class, sat in his chair and took roll, "Mr. Melchior?"

"Here."

Mr. Archbold?"

"Here."

When he had finished roll, he began the daily ritual of examining the molding around the ceiling. "Mr. Melchior, what do you think about the main character?"

"Mr. D., do you think the protagonist was immoral? Why?"

"Now, Mr. N., how does William Carlos Williams use the red wagon as a symbol in the poem?"

"Mmmmmmmmmmmm. Interesting," was Mr. L.'s usual response. No-fill-in-the-blank or multiple-choice, just, "How? Why? and When?" The questions struggled to escape and once they did, they headed for the ceiling where other monastic abstractions had gathered for one hundred years.

For fifty minutes he grilled us, never once looking directly at us. There must have been something captivating about that molding, something that escaped the rest of us. He started in the far left corner in the back of the room. He moved his head slowly inching his way across to the right corner, then along the side wall. He had to pivot in his chair to run his eyes along the piece behind him and then shift again to follow the journey back to the right corner. For one semester, three times a week, Professor L. discussed the works of literary greats selected by the editors of *The Omnibus of English*, works chosen to ignite literary fireflies in the minds of seventeen- and eighteen-year-old college freshmen. If they ever charged up their batteries and lit up the darkness, I never saw them.

I remember only one incident from that entire semester, and it had nothing to do with literature. It happened during a Saturday morning class. We were discussing a review of *Victory at Sea* and Professor L. asked for the definition of one of the words in the assignment.

Silence. More silence. Painful silence. Perhaps some of us had drifted into never-never land. Perhaps some of us knew but were intimidated. Of course the obvious reason was that we didn't know the answer and that we had no idea what the word meant.

Bernie Archbold raised his hand.

"Yes, Mr. Archbold."

Bernie defined the word.

"And how is it that you know the meaning, Mr. Archbold."

"I looked it up."

"And did you look up the meanings of all the words you didn't know, Mr. Archbold?"

"Yes," said Bernie.

Mr. L. opened his grade book and wrote one letter. Then in his what's-happening-on-the-ceiling-today voice, he said, "Mr. Archbold, you have an A for the semester. "Bernie was a quarterback on the Johnnie football team. When the mid-semester marks came out, that A in Freshman English saved his eligibility. Of course I could have looked those words up, too, but I didn't. I could have received an A, too, but I didn't. If I had looked the words up and received an A, I still wouldn't have seen the fireflies. To see them, I had to find my own way in the dark.

St. John's Gymnasium and Field House, 1958: I spent several nights a week here during my junior and senior years working off my grant at less than one dollar an hour. The white birch in the left-front foreground was planted in honor of our classmate Bill Foreman whose plane was shot down in the Vietnam War.

The School of One-Two, One-Two

At the end of my eighth grade, my geography teacher joined the line of the hundreds of country schoolteachers and gave us the hated State Board Examination even though she was not required to do so because we were a town school. I never questioned why she didn't make up her own final exam the way the other teachers did. I never asked her why she wanted to add such misery to our lives by making us study for hours and hours. I had been well conditioned during those eight years. I knew that "Mine was not to reason why; mine was but to do or die."

A great liner-upper, hands folded in prayer, posing obediently with his sister Rene.

I was one of the best liner-uppers in my class. All the teacher had to do was whisper or blow her whistle and I charged to that imaginary line wherever it might be. From first grade on, the teachers blew their whistles just as the first bell rang in the morning rang. If I were playing ball in the far corner of the play-ground, I was standing in line before her final toot.

I may have been a finger-counter in arithmetic, but I was a champion at lining up. I lined up for restroom breaks, fire drills, fingernail inspection, the morning milk break, and recess. In the primary grades we practiced marching in the gymnasium. I high-stepped on those out-of-bounds lines and never missed a beat. At the corners, I pivoted ninety-degree turns like a well-trained soldier. Some kids were good at spilling food, teasing girls, and erasing holes through their newsprint. I was good at lining up.

In fifth, sixth, seventh, and eighth grades, we played games that required us to stay inside the lines. Of course, first we had to line up for roll call, but then we were turned loose to play within the lines. I was as good at staying inside those lines as I had been at staying inside my coloring-book lines.

Throughout those years, the teachers taught us many games in physical education, but they all had one favorite for us boys, dodge ball. We stood in line and counted off one-two, one-two, one-two until we had two teams. One team formed a circle while the other team milled around inside the circle. We started the game with one or two volleyballs.

The task for the guys lined up in the circle was to hit the guys inside the circle with the ball. Actually, our objective was to fire the ball as fast as possible and stagger the "dodgers." The harder we could nail them, the better. It was a modern day version of the Romans throwing the Christians to the lions. Those of us "who could fire that old tomato" tried hard to bounce the ball off the back of an unsuspecting skull, thereby "knocking" the person out of the game. If someone were agile enough to escape the single ball, the teacher simply threw us two or three more volleyballs until the poor guy in the center thought he was in a hailstorm. When we began our insane chicken acts inside the circle, the guys now armed with the balls got their revenge.

Years later when I was teaching several incorrigible students, I realized why all the teachers loved subjecting us to dodge ball. Perhaps they saw it as an appropriate metaphor for life. Perhaps we begged to be blasted for an hour. Perhaps we weren't "lining up" as obediently as we had in the primary grades. Perhaps some class rebel defied the Pavlovian one-two, one-two conditioning and asked "why?" when he should have been hopping in line. Perhaps watching the gladiators cringe under the tyranny of the lions made a frustrating day tolerable.

Whatever the reason, I maintained my position at the head of the class as the champion liner-upper. I never defied authority's whistles or commands. I lined up or jumped the required distance. Even when I was angry or felt Nero was unjustly signaling thumbs down, I obediently obeyed "the rule of the line." I was too naive and well-conditioned to pound my fist in righteous indignation and say, "I'm not lining up unless you can give me a good reason why I should." Little did I realize that the Gods of Teaching were already considering me as one of their leading future teacher candidates.

I wasn't perfect, however, and during those years my reputation suffered two staggering blows. In the fourth grade I discovered swearing. Two concrete bastions guarded the steps leading into the school. One day I decided to combine my printing skills with my profanities which consisted of hell, dam (spelling was a definite weakness), and a long list of nouns and verbs labeling bodily functions. I borrowed a piece of chalk from the room and wrote the words on the walls, steps, and sidewalk.

The teachers were flabbergasted that their blond, curly-haired angel had strayed so far from the line of saintliness and desecrated their hallowed concrete. They didn't wash my mouth out with Ivory soap to make it 99 and 44/100 percent pure, but they did provide me with a bucket of sudsy water and a brush. Who knows what path my career might have taken that day if my teacher had not grabbed my unleashed id and set it firmly back on the straight and narrow. Left to wander aimlessly, I might have made millions writing and misspelling my way through seventeenth-rate pornographic literature including such classics as *The Nakit and the Dammed* and *She Was Hellfire and Damnation.*

By the time I finished my scrubbing, my mother had been informed of my moral meandering and she exacted the expected revenge on my tongue, which didn't find those words quite so delicious after the scrubbing.

That day I discovered the difference between willingly walking the line and being forced to walk the line. I also noticed the line became much narrower after my transgression. The Gods of Teaching had mixed reactions. Several were so disappointed with my behavior that they voted to cancel my 1954 scholarship to the One-Two, One-Two Teachers College. Others felt my walk on the wild side would help me know when my own students stepped off the sacred line.

The wisest and most powerful gods were quite sure they were creating an educational servant who would suffer a nervous breakdown before clamoring for justice. Most believed I would line up nicely with thousands of other teachers and make an ideal employee. They decided to give me an out-of-school exam, however, to determine whether my instruction in toeing the line would last a lifetime or whether I would become a rebellious, revolutionary. They certainly didn't intend to hire any teachers who walked a line that was a half-mile wide.

Flattened: A Tragedy in Five Acts
There were only two "gangs" in town. The guys in my gang had no money, but we were easily entertained. We loved to play the pinball machines, but those beasts gobbled our precious nickels and seldom spit out free games. Therefore, we used cunning to defeat the Miser at the Green Lantern Cafe.

Act I: We flattened a penny with a hammer and shaped it so it would slide smoothly into the nickel slot. The machine was near the door where the morning sunshine lit up the crime scene. Most of the bar was poorly lit on Saturday mornings and few people came in for an early beer. The bar was at the other end of the room, and only one person worked those odd hours, Harold, the owner. He was one of my heroes on the town baseball team. My job was to divert his attention by asking him questions about how to improve my pitching. That was really a labor of love and he gladly abandoned his clean up chores to talk baseball.

Act II: While Harold showed me how to grip my fastball, my buddies lined up on each side of the pinball machine and lifted up the front end. The first player, who usually wore his brother's shoes so his toes wouldn't get smashed, slid his toes under the legs. Then very nonchalantly the others set the machine on the toeless toes. The shooter then carefully placed the flattened penny in the coin slot and slid it into the machine. The penny passed for the real thing, dropped into the coin box, and the lights glowed. The game was on.

Act III: Next came the real test for the shooter. If his toes even thought about wriggling, the machine tilted and the day was ruined. He pulled back the springed knob, dropped the first ball into place, and shot it onto the playing field. Since the table was level, the ball rolled at turtle speed. Even the worst shooter could rack up twenty free games with the first ball. By the time the fourth ball dropped through the slot at the bottom of the table, he had usually accumulated seventy or eighty free games. When we set the legs on the floor, the tilt light flashed.

Act I. V.: For the next four or five hours we took turns playing the machine, trying to win legitimately. We took turns going home for lunch. Guys who had paper routes or jobs finished them as quickly as possible and came back to play. If we ran our free game number down to ten, we repeated Act I. By one or two o'clock everyone was bored, so we quit until the following Saturday. In my moral thermometer, this chicanery wasn't hot enough to qualify it as a venial sin. I certainly didn't consider lining up along that pinball machine to be stepping out of line.

Act V: That summer I did most of the dry cleaning at my parents' business, the Tip Top Cleaners. One day while I waited for the load to clean, someone tapped me on the shoulder. I had never seen the man before, but I could tell he hadn't come to congratulate me for my diligent work.

"You've been playing the pinball machine at the Green Lantern," he said. Not "Have you been playing the pinball machine?" but "You've been playing."

"And you've been flattening pennies, too," he snarled, jabbing his finger into my chest. "Do you know that's a federal offense, defacing government coins?"

I was too terrified to answer.

"You could go to prison for that crime."

He didn't wait for me to speak. He turned and walked away.

How effective was his threat of turning me in and sending me off to prison? My gang and I never played the pinball machine at the Green

Lantern again, and since that July day over forty-seven years ago, I have never put a coin into any kind of pinball or slot machine. I have never pulled the handle on a one-armed bandit.

This story would have more punch if I said that I was so traumatized that day that I could never walk within thirty yards of any money-eating machines. The truth is that for years the trauma of that day did keep me from slipping a coin in any kind of machine that wouldn't drop a bag of peanuts or candy bar immediately. After a while I realized I was probably one of few members of Pinball Anonymous, so now I abstain from dropping coins because I'm still a champion liner-upper.

IT

In high school and college the game was still line up and play one-two, one-two. The instructor asked the questions, and I tried to fill in the correct answers. Playing the one-two, one-two game of education is built on the premise that there is a sacred IT and only the teacher or professor knows for certain what IT is. Tyrannical teachers keep students lined up and cowering, begging for enough IT to pass the class. "Test tomorrow, class. Study hard and line up to play one-two, one-two. As usual the test will be true-false, fill in the blanks, multiple choice, and word-for-word short answers."

During my four years of high school, the only time I was allowed to step off the line was in speech where I was required to select topics in which I was allowed to dance 1-4-3-2 or 1-3-6-9 to fill Miss Lang's dance card.

High school passed quickly, and except for never really discovering the IT of physics, I did quite well. The closest I came to screaming in righteous indignation about my cold-blooded physics teacher was to reel off a string of obscenities on my way to football practice. I tap danced madly and survived. I was an experienced twelve-year-line-walker by that time.

IT became more sacred in college and its guardians more impersonal. For the first time on my quest to become a teacher/guardian of IT myself, I had to pay to dance one-two, one-two. I had to pay tuition to line up. I also learned that although I paid to pursue the sacred IT, the giant egos of the guardians seldom tolerated outbursts of righteous indignation.

Although I was an English major, I wrote only for exams and research. The dreaded "blue books" demanded that my pen dance one-two, one-two across the pages. Quietly I lined up just I as I had in grade school but with less confidence and enthusiasm.

Throughout those years of academic dancing, one great love affair fired my passion to tolerate inflated egos and impersonal instructors—baseball. How I yearned for spring and the poetry of baseball.

Truth

In college the professors asked, "What is truth?"
I read Aristotle, Jesus and St. Paul.
I reasoned inductively and deductively.
I wrestled with philosophy, theology, and logic.
I couldn't find the answers; the words were too heavy to move.
Sitting in the library struggling with Plato,
I daydreamed about a day when I was twelve.
We were playing a pickup game on a hot July afternoon.
Jackie led off second, stomping hieroglyphics in the dirt
    with his new Fred Taylor Converse. "Win it! Win it!" he yelled.
I cradled my treasured cracked DiMaggio slugger,
    nailed together and wrapped with sticky black electrician's tape.
In one flashing moment,
I smashed a fastball perfectly, right on the *o* in DiMaggio,
    and ripped a game winning white streak over short.
I realized I had learned the answer
    to the professors' question at that moment.
Truth is a baseball smashed sweetly on a wooden bat.

Give It Up

During one of my conferences with my advisor, he encouraged me to abandon my physical education minor and change to drama. "No one will ever hire someone to teach English, teach physical education, and coach," he decreed. "English majors direct plays, not pitchers and catchers." My combination certainly did not fit education's cry for one-two, one-two teachers.

Surrounded by the writings of the world's greatest thinkers, I tried to explain that whatever baseball was, it was part of who I was. I could live happily without teaching drama, but I could not be happy not coaching and playing baseball.

He listened to me talk about the poetry of baseball, and how it was tragedy, comedy, and romance played between two chalk lines. Baseball had shown me villains and heroes, compassion and treachery. By striking out with the bases loaded or driving in the winning run, I had felt the same sorrow and joy he was trying to teach in Tom Joad or Huckleberry Finn.

He smiled when I told him that at that point in my life I could no more give up my dream of coaching than he could stop reading the literature that fired his soul. He had been my teacher and advisor and he had watched me play for three years, but he really didn't know me. He didn't know me, but I loved him because he cared. I had few teachers like him.

Righteous Indignation

Many of us slammed our fists in the privacy of our dorm rooms and damned the weaknesses of our professors, but only once did I see someone express indignation where it really mattered—face-to-face with injustice and irresponsibility. Our professor had scheduled a major exam in World Literature, which required us to identify the play and speakers' lines from several plays by Euripides, Aeschylus and Sophocles. My friend Bob, one of the brightest students in our class and a dedicated line walker, had capped several days of studying by staying up most of the night mastering the material. He probably knew every line from *Iphigenia at Aulis.* How he suffered the foolishness of one-two tests! When the professor entered the room and said he decided not to have the test, six feet, three inches of blazing anger stood up and slammed the huge lit book on the floor. "Damn it!" Bob yelled. The professor was old and a bit deaf. Bob's angry words fell where we had learned they would usually fall. The professor looked up, startled not by the angry words, but by what sounded like a deer rifle exploding as the book slammed against the wood floor.

Those of us who had been trained to dance one-two, one-two followed the line through college. The cost of not lining up became more and more expensive each year. We had not been trained "to give the world the finger" and confront injustice, especially when it was something personal. We were better at condemning events in Europe or Washington than we were at challenging our own tyrants.

Butch

Although I played football and basketball against Robert (Butch) Ilg in 1952, I have no distinct memory of him until the spring of 1953. I was a junior at Belle Plaine and Butch was a sophomore at Montgomery. We played the same positions in three sports: in basketball we brought the ball up the court and often guarded each other; we both played quarterback; and we pitched against each other often.

Butch was a fifteen-year-old going on twenty-five. He had a face full of black whiskers and he walked with legs like parentheses. He loved to chatter, heckle, and laugh. When Butch was a first or second grader, I have an image of his mother saying, "Robert, we are going to start calling you Butch because that sounds much more intimidating. Now you go out in the backyard and ride that old rain barrel until you look as if you were born on a horse. People will never be able to predict which way you are going, and you'll never be a great liner-upper.

"Mind me now, Butch, you taunt those older boys until they try to beat you up. Then you insult them in your best Bohemian. Be clever, but snarl a little when you insult them,

Butch, bottom row, left, is the only player wearing a block M on his cap.

so they don't really understand you but they're afraid to mess with you. And Butch, you practice pitching rocks at the telephone pole until you can hit any spot you aim at. Mind you, Butch, you throw sidearm. If I ever catch you throwing overhand, I'll clip you a good one. Then you come in and rub some of that whisker-growing snake oil I bought from that flim-flam salesman. It will make your whiskers grow and the other kids will think you are as tough as you look."

In the spring of 1953, Butch and I were pitching against each other and the game was close. His team was ahead by one run in the bottom of the seventh inning. We had the tying run on base and Pete Johnson, one of the best high school players in Minnesota, was our next batter.

Butch's coach wanted him to walk Pete, but Butch remembered what his mother had taught him. He loved a challenge and he believed he could win. Butch insisted he could "get him out" and the coach let him pitch to Pete. On the first or second pitch, Pete ripped a screamer over the right field fence and we won 8 to 7. A few weeks later Pete signed a professional baseball contract with the St. Louis Cardinals.

That summer Butch and I faced each other again in an American Legion game. We were leading but the game was close. I reached third base. The next batter hit a little dribbler between the mound and the third base line. I thought, "I'm heading for home because Butch will field the ball and throw to first." Instead of throwing to first, he faked the throw and trapped me in a rundown. I dived into third and the umpire called me safe. Butch stomped exclaiming, "I nicked him on the jersey. He's out!" When it was evident that the umpire was not going to change his mind, Butch pleaded, "Ask him. He's a good Catholic. He'll tell you."

"Play ball!" growled the umpire. I was so happy to hear those words. What would the champion liner-upper like me have said? Butch and I both knew I was out. He pitched the final innings, frustrated and angry. He fired one sidearm curve ball after another. We stepped in the bucket, thankful to get back to the bench safely. There were no batting helmets in 1953.

Butch stormed off the field at the end of the game. As he walked to his bus, he turned and said, "You just wait. We're gonna kick your ass in football this fall." Then the two parentheses marched to the bus.

Butch could have been a prophet. That fall the Redbirds with Butch Ilg at quarterback beat us 49 to 16. Our coach was so disgusted he wrote the summary of the game for the local paper himself. His article began, "The Tigers were mere kittens last Friday night."

Teammates

In the fall of 1954 I went to college and in the spring while I was going 0 for 14 for the St. John's baseball team, Robert (Butch) Ilg was named Minnesota Athlete of the Year. He certainly would have received my vote. That fall Butch received an appointment to the U.S. Naval Academy in Annapolis. One year later Butch enrolled as a freshman at St. John's. Ironically, the two of us were now playing on the same team. We played together for the next three years. I played the outfield and Butch saw limited pitching action. During my four years at St. John's we won two conference titles and tied for another.

In my senior year I was elected co-captain. In one of our final games, Goliath came to play David in Rox Park in St. Cloud. The University of Minnesota under legendary coach Dick Siebert was one of the best college baseball teams in the United States. My mother and dad drove up from Belle Plaine for the game. They had never seen me play a college game. In the seventh inning we were leading the University by two runs. Pat Dolan was pitching a fantastic game. With two out in the seventh inning, Minnesota put two guys on base with two outs. It was now twilight, and I had a difficult time seeing the ball if it went higher than the seats in the stadium.

A loyal Johnnie outfielder, 1958

The next batter hit a lazy fly ball to center field. The runners took off for the plate. I never saw the ball until it bounced about ten feet from me. The runners scored easily, tying the score. The next batter hit another fly ball into the gray sky, and I lost it the second it rose above the grandstand. Another runner scored.

I watched one of our players grab his glove, climb the dugout steps, and run out to take my place. I ran toward the grandstand filled with my college friends. Now that I have children of my own, I know that my parents were in as much pain as I was. I knew my professor was sitting somewhere in the crowd.

In the infield the lights were brilliant. I could feel my feet leave the dew-covered outfield grass, crunch on the infield dirt, more grass, more dirt, and finally the concrete steps. I slipped through a dark film of silence. My head started to spin. I sat down and bent over, driving my head between my knees to keep from vomiting. I cannot remember the rest of the game. I remember riding back to school with my parents. I couldn't speak. They dropped me off in front of the gymnasium door. I grabbed my clothes from my locker and headed for my room before the team bus arrived.

I played hundreds of baseball games before that game and hundreds after. I played baseball because it was as much a part of me as my heart, my hands, my spirit. I played for the same reason I ate. I would have starved without it. But when we sit around and tell stories about the games we played, the first thing I recall is the anger and humiliation I felt running into that dugout. I did not know that while my teammate was picking up his glove and running out to replace me, Butch was storming in the dugout, hollering at the coach, "You can't do that. You can't take him out in the middle of an inning." I don't know what else he said, but knowing Butch, I'm certain he put on quite a show. I had seen his routine many times.

The season ended a few days later. I graduated and my teammates and I went about the task of discovering what life was like beyond the college world of one-two, one-two. I have not seen Butch since we said good-bye after our final game. I never thanked him for his passion and righteous indignation. Beneath those whiskers and bravado lived a spirit that was not afraid to tell the world it was out of kilter and there was a better way than standing on the line and dancing the one-two step. I wasn't surprised that he did what he did. I had played against Butch long enough to know that he would confront any dragon.

When my teammates told me what Butch had done, I thought at first he did it because we had competed so passionately against each other, that there was a bond between us going back to our battles in high school. But I think I was wrong. I think Butch would have raged against authority because he couldn't line up and live his life one-two, one-two.

1953 Belle Plaine American Legion Team. We lost to South St. Paul 2-1 in the regional finals. Mascot, John Spellacy. Front Row left: Bill Buesgens, Ewald Gruetzmacher, Jerry McRaith, Roger Martin, Keiran O'Brien, Roger Hoelz; Second Row: Manager BobSmith, Bob Dahlke, Lee Engfer, Lee Lynch, Earl Olson, Tom Melchior, Erwin Heitkamp, Herb Kosmen, and Edward Duffy, commander of American Legion Post No. 144.

The Three Professors

During freshmen orientation I met with my advisor to schedule my classes.

"What will be your major?" he asked.

"English," I replied.

"And your minor?"

"Physical education and education. I want to teach and coach," I said.

"To earn a Bachelor of Arts degree," he said, "you are required to take two years of a foreign language. Which language would you like to study?"

"French," I replied.

Professor Paranoia (No record of his name in my yearbook.)

Our French I professor shuffled into the room. He bent forward as if he carried the burden of the world on his shoulders. He looked at the floor when he spoke. He felt more at home with his back to us as he scratched out his lessons on the blackboard. Every few seconds he turned around and looked at us as if someone had called his name.

He mumbled when he spoke and became more unintelligible if we asked him to repeat himself. He filled his message to us with a litany of "well, ah, uh, oh, ah, what I mean to say, ah—" He rarely called on us to recite or read. When he did, he cringed in regret. He moved like a wind-up toy, darting one way, then another.

One day I watched him walk from the refectory to his room. He slouched forward, head bent. Suddenly he stopped. He stood still for a few moments. Then he looked back, first left, then right. He charged ahead ten or twelve yards, stopped again, and spun around. He snapped his head to the right and left. He searched for someone, something, his eyes darting wildly. He charged ahead a few paces, stopped, and whirled around. Again and again his demon called. He escaped into the dormitory.

The second semester I changed my major to social studies and dropped French. No foreign language was required! A few weeks into the semester the dean of the university summoned me to his office. "Tom," said Father Arno, "I'd like to ask you why you dropped French."

"Oh, my god," I thought, "I'm doomed."

"Many of the students in your class have dropped out of the program. I'm wondering why you dropped French." My left eye-lid twitched the way it did before the first pitch of every ballgame. I swung at the first half-truth I could think of. "I decided I would rather major in social studies than English," I half-lied. The twitching stopped. Base hit!

Father Arno threw me a few more curves, but I didn't swing. I knew if I told him the other half of the truth, I was doomed.

Father Clarus

The second semester of my sophomore year I changed my major back to English. With a year having passed between French 1A and French 1B, I

Father Clarus Graves, O.S.B.

walked into Father Clarus's classroom. He was noted for his kindness and willingness to tolerate shaky syntax, limited vocabularies, and fractured fricatives. Several other refugees from Professor Paranoia's class were seated in the room.

Father Clarus had long abandoned the textbook used by other professors. His philosophy of teaching required his own text, which focused on vocabulary development. We spent little time conjugating verbs or delving into the passé indéfini. Since we lived in the world of here and now, Father Clarus must have thought the present tense was perfect for us.

When we read aloud and butchered his language, his response was, "That's not too bad" or "Improvement comes with time" or "Keep trying." We learned little, but we received high grades. And we felt good.

I switched back to social studies the first semester of my junior year. No more French. I switched back to English the second semester, too late to begin French IIA, which was offered only the first semester.

Father Roland

In my senior year I joined the sophomores in French II, which meant I would meet Zee Monk, Father Roland Behrendt, O.S.B. Roland Behrendt was born in Danzig, Prussia, on March 27, 1901. He studied law at universities in Frankfurt, Berlin, and Leipzig, where in 1930 he was awarded a doctorate *cum laude* in both civil and canon law. He served as legal advisor in a private banking house in Berlin until 1938 when he was forced to leave Germany as a Jewish refugee during the Nazi regime. He became a Benedictine monk and was ordained a Catholic priest in 1951. We met six years later. What a comedown it must have been to teach French to the likes of me!

Father Roland terrified me. When he walked into the classroom, I wilted. My eye twitched uncontrollably. My stomach boiled. Garbed in his Benedictine habit, he looked down on us from on high. (My fellow classmate said, "Father Roland was not born. He was created somewhere in Transylvania.") His white crew cut bristled. Behind his horn-rimmed glasses his blue eyes measured me. "Melchior: completely illiterate, infantile vocabulary, sloppy syntax, grade school grammar, thinks conjugation is a sexual act."

At the beginning of every class, he folded his hands and prayed the Sign of the Cross and the Lord's Prayer. "Unt so, jettlemen, ser is your first assignment. Learn soze prayers by Vensday."

Father Roland Behrendt, O.S.B.

Father Roland's teaching philosophy was simple: "Memorize, memorize, memorize. Recite, recite, recite. Test, test, test. He barked and we jumped. We stood to answer questions. No one dozed, doodled, or day dreamed. No one chewed gum, diddled with a pencil, or cracked knuckles. No one passed supercilious glances, crib notes, or gas. He clasped his hands, furrowed his brow, and shrank us where we sat.

When he said, "Melk-eeeee-your, rrrrrrrrrrrrread, he trilled that r so long it froze my vocal chords. A pre-adolescent voice squeaked, "Bonjour, Monsieur. Comment allez-vous?"

I did everything possible to make myself small. I sat behind one of the biggest guys in class and tucked myself into the back corner seat. I never entered class first or last. As we left class, I melted into the group. I never raised my hand or volunteered for anything. I struggled to become forgettable.

The hot fall sun baked our room and Father Roland scorched us three times a week. He made me more nervous than confession during Lent. The minute I walked into class, sweat welled up in my armpits, drenching my shirt. At first I thought it was the fall sun, but during the January blizzards I realized it was the sweat of fear.

After class I returned to my dorm room and enacted the après-French ritual. First I changed my shirt. Then I wound up and fired my book against the concrete wall. When Zee Monk had made me that day's sacrificial victim, I pitched several innings.

Mr. Holmes

No one skipped French II, and skipping class to play basketball or baseball was anathema. Dave played basketball and the team often left Friday afternoons to play Saturday away games. One Monday Fr. Roland asked, "Mister Holmes, vere vas you last Frrrrrrrrrriday?"

"Basketball, Father," Dave mumbled.

"Baskeetball, baskeetball," Roland groaned. "If I hear baskeetball one more time, I vill lie on the floor and retch."

A few weeks later Dave's chair was again empty on Friday. On Monday Zee Monk snarled, "Mister Holmes, vere vas you last Frrrrrrrrrrday."

We cringed, waiting the explosion.

"I got married, Father," whispered Dave.

"Evreevon, stand up. Let's hafe a big hand ver Holmes." We hooted and hollered for Holmes. He never heard another word about "baskeetball."

Zee Monk and Pat

Spring and baseball season finally arrived. While our teammates were knocking the ball around, Pat and I were trapped from 2:00 until 3:00 every Monday, Wednesday, and Friday. When we opened our schedule, we both expected the Mr. Holmes treatment.

By that time, however, I had become a nonentity to Father Roland. He expected mediocrity from me and I seldom disappointed him. If I missed class for a ballgame, it was neither here nor there. I had disappeared. This was not the case with my teammate Pat Dolan, who had doomed himself at the beginning of the semester.

The Gospel According to Pat

"One day early in the year, before Roland found out what a perfect dunce I was, I actually started a conversation with him. I had been to Germany as an American Field Service student before coming to St. John's. I lived with Frederic Ruge, who was a retired vice-admiral in the German navy. I loved the Germans who despised and ridiculed the French for their laziness.

"So that day before Father Roland found out what a dunce I was, I told him that I had lived with these wonderful Germans, who thought the French were slightly above slime. Unfortunately, I didn't know he was a German Jew who had escaped Germany and was hidden and saved by the French, whom he respected and loved.

"Then in the spring I missed French in the afternoon because of our baseball games, and the next class Father Roland questioned me. 'Unt, Mr. Dolan, vere ver you yesterday?'

"We had a baseball game, Father," I replied. His face flushed. Then the red pooled into purple and I thought one of us was about to die.

"Mistair Dolan, Mistair Dolan," he groaned, "if you menshun beisbol von more time, I vill rrrrrretch on zee floor!"

Shortly after the retching scene, we were scheduled to play Gustavus. We would be leaving in the late morning, before French. To make matters worse, there was a very important test scheduled for that day. At the time I was Father Dunstan Tucker's assistant prefect. I worshiped Father Dunstan. I told Father Dunstan I was afraid to miss class. Lo and behold, Dunstan said he was scheduled to monitor Father Roland's classes that day, so I suggested I come to the 8:00 a.m. class rather than my 2:00 p.m. class to take the test and Father Roland need never know. Unfortunately, Father Roland gave two different tests, which Father Dunstan didn't realize. When the tests were corrected, there was my exam in with the 8:00 batch.

I really didn't get kicked around that much, but I assume Father Dunstan had to submit to tongue-lashing for his part in the deception. Father Dunstan and Steve Humphrey saved me. I was allowed to take the correct test. By the time that was scheduled, my class had gotten its tests back, and I got some Christian soul's copy and memorized the correct answers. I also memorized the wrong answers because I didn't know enough to fake a wrong answer.

I'm certain Rather Roland felt something was wrong when he stood near me as we recited the Our Father in French, and he heard, "In noming the Father et Sunny et Holly Ghostee."

Pat and I both passed French II. He went home for the summer and began his senior year that fall. I graduated and began my career teaching English.

"Au nom du Pere, et du Fils, et du Saint Esprit."

I passed French. Graduation Day, May, 1954, with Dad and Mom.

The Can-Do Kid

During my junior and senior years at St. John's University, the education department tried to prepare me for my teaching career. I took Ph 25, General Psychology; Ed. 31, Educational Psychology; Ed. 44, Guidance in Secondary Schools; Ed. 48, Principles of Education; PE. 41, Directed Teaching; Ed. 41, Special Methods; Ed 42E, Observation and Student Teaching, Ed. 32, Secondary School Methods, PE. 44, Directed Coaching; and PE. 42, Directed Teaching.

Leo and I, spring 1958

I have written about some of my experiences in other stories, but most of what I learned in those classes disappeared like foam and fog. I vaguely recall lectures about talent, skills, dedication, creativity, and ingenuity. Most of the lectures were general textbook exhortations. Many of the lectures helped fill my storehouse of useless information. Not one of my professors had taught in a junior or senior high school. They told no anecdotes to whet my appetite for teaching.

At the same time I was taking Leo 101. Actually I started taking Leo 101 early in my freshman year. Leo had been all-everything in Cando, North Dakota. We both played all sports in high school and hoped to play college basketball and baseball. We tried out for basketball and soon realized we were two 5' 8" castoffs laboring under the armpits of giants.

Leo was talented, creative, ingenious, skillful, and dedicated (if the cause interested him). He sailed through his math classes with little effort. While he may not have studied for hours on end, he spent hours perfecting his basketball skills. He soon earned the title Chief of the Gym Rats.

Somehow we ended up on the same intramural basketball team and played together for four years. Leo handled the ball like a magician and seemed to score at will. When he started wheeling and dealing, we moved out of the way. The only thing that frustrated him was his inability to dunk the ball.

We also played intramural flag football, a freewheeling game in which any player on the team could be a pass receiver. When Leo started making his moves, we moved out of the way. In the huddle he looked like a kid diagramming plays for street football. "Archie, you take ten strides and hook. Bill, flare to the right. I'll fake to Len and hit one of you guys." I learned more about creative thinking from Leo than I learned in my ed. psych. class.

One afternoon during our sophomore year, Leo and I were watching the varsity basketball team practice. The team was short a few players and the coach, who was also our baseball coach, asked us if we would like to help out and scrimmage the varsity. At long last we would be vindicated!

Our job was to play defense while the varsity practiced their half-court offense. Leo guarded a 6' 3" cocky, slick, ball-handling guard who had just returned from the Army. The vet loved fancy behind-the-back passes and nifty dribbling. Leo drove him crazy, stealing the ball again and again. Once he drove the baseline and went up for a jump shot. Leo blocked the shot, "stuffed" him clean with a great leap. The guy got so frustrated he threw a punch at Leo, who was also too quick for the punch. The coach thanked us for our help and sent us on our way. There was no question in my mind who should have been playing for the varsity.

In my education classes the professors often raised the question of whether teaching was an art or a science. Why wasn't every teacher a master teacher? What was the art of teaching? Could one identify the qualities? What was the science of teaching? We raised questions we seldom answered.

Leo "did" the answers. He was the Nike logo, "just do it," before Nike existed. He didn't discuss the "art" of accounting or the "art" of mathematics. When the problem arose, he solved it.

In the spring of our senior year, we were scheduled to play Gustavus at St. Peter, but the game was cancelled and we stayed on campus. The Minnesota Intercollegiate Athletic Conference held its meet that day at St. John's. One of Leo's track friends told him St. John's was short a broad jumper, so Leo asked Coach Gagliardi if he could jump. "How far can you jump, son?" asked Gagliardi?"

I don't know," Leo said. "I haven't jumped for four years and that was in high school. I didn't jump often because I played baseball, but I think I can jump somewhere between 16 to 20 feet."

"Go get a uniform and shoes," said Gagliardi.

Leo jumped close to 21 feet and took fifth place, good for one point. St. John's won the meet by two points. The problem was simple: conquer gravity. The school required the trackmen to earn a certain number of points during the season or to score at least one point in the conference meet to earn a varsity letter. Many guys on the track team practiced all year, but never scored enough points or scored a point in the conference meet.

The track team had made no provisions for a "Leo." The team met and awarded Leo a trophy and a letter. So much for protocol! So much for the science of broad jumping!

Cabin fever finally caught up to Leo after spending almost four years in the woods at St. John's. He rebelled and set a record for consecutive nights going to St. Cloud. Leaving campus in 1958 was not easy. Only a few guys owned cars. Somehow Leo blazed the trail to town each night. He abandoned his role as the ideal college student and athlete. I was learning another lesson about human nature from Leo 101.

Leo and I had one major thing in common, severe myopia. We were the proverbial blind bats without our glasses. Before one of our final baseball games, Leo walked up to me while we were taking batting practice. He was dressed in his street clothes. He couldn't tell who I was because he wasn't wearing his glasses. He knew I played left field, and since someone was standing in left field, it must be Melchior.

"What the heck's wrong with you?" I asked. "Aren't you playing today?"

"Mel-kee-or," he squinted, "do you have another pair of glasses?"

"Just my good pair," I said. "What happened to yours?"

"I lost them," he said.

"How'd that happen?" I asked.

"I was necking with some girl in the quarry," he grinned, "and I lost them. Can I use yours?"

"I guess so," I said, "but they probable won't help much."

Twenty minutes later he showed up wearing his uniform and my horn-rimmed glasses. "How'd they work?" I asked.

"Jeez, pretty good," he said. "I only fell down twice."

Somehow Coach Osborne found out that Leo was wearing my glasses and sent him to the outfield to prove that he could see well enough to catch fly balls. Coach hit them as high and as far as he could. Leo caught each one with ease. For his *coup de grâce*, Leo caught the last few behind his back. Leo played, got two hits, and we won.

My classes in Leo 101 ended a few weeks later at graduation. Many people may argue that a kid from a burg named Cando, North Dakota, couldn't make much of a mentor, but they probably never met Leo.

Harold

Harold Fitterer taught English and drama for many years at Mankato High School. He was built a bit like Al Capp's schmoos, well rounded in the middle. He was electric and magnetic. His high school plays became so popular that the English Department at Mankato State Teachers College (now University of Minnesota at Mankato) hired him to teach many English courses including English Methods.

"Your assignment for next week is to present a three-dimensional book report," said Professor Fitterer. "Choose one of your favorite books. This may be a bit different for you, but for this assignment you are the student and we are your classmates. Any questions?"

"What the heck is a three-dimensional book report?" asked Margaret, a seventh-grade reading teacher from Lake Crystal.

"Is it an oral report?" asked Fred, a composition teacher from Wells.

Fitterer feigned shock. Any occasion was an opportunity to become histrionic. "What? You have not been giving three-dimensional book reports?" He was Hamlet betrayed by his trusted Rosencrantz and Gildenstern. "Surely you jest. We have trusted you with the children of Minnesota all these many years, and now you play with my good intentions. "

"We still don't know what you're talking about," said Agnes, a ninth-grade teacher from St. Peter.

"Agnes, do you assign book reports to your students?"

"Of course I do," sputtered Agnes.

"How about you, Turk? Assign any book reports to your students?"

Turk, a seventh grade teacher from New Richland, snarled, "Naw, well, maybe one a year. I despised those damn things when I was a kid. Mostly I paid someone else to write them, so I hate to inflict the same agony on my students."

"Hmmmmm! Interesting, Turk. I'm looking forward to hearing more about your philosophy of teaching."

"What about you, Ed?" asked Fitterer. Book reports?" Ed taught five sections of British Literature to seniors at Eden Prairie Senior High School.

"Six or seven a year," said Ed.

"Wow!" said Fitterer. Six or seven a year? What kinds of book reports do you assign?"

"Sometimes they are written summaries. Some times they're oral. Most of the time it becomes a reading, writing, and speaking assignment." The Angel of Smugness lounged on Ed's shoulder, applauding his master.

"So," said Fitterer, "most of you have been using it the old fashioned, time-honored, this-is-another-boring-assignment technique to enrich your students' literary expertise? Is that right? You don't seem very excited to hear my idea."

"Agnes?"

Agnes ground her teeth.

"Margaret?"

Margaret stared and furrowed her brow.

"Fred?"

Fred's jaw muscles twitched. "To book report or not to book report? That is the question. Whether 'tis nobler in the mind to suffer/ The slings and arrows of a mad professor/ Or to stand against his sea of troubles and by opposing end them."

"Ah," said Fitterer, savoring the Hamlet challenge, "why, look you now, how unworthy a thing you make of me! You would play upon me, you would seem to know my stops, you would pluck out the heart of my mystery....S'blood, do you think I am easier to be played on than a pipe?"

"Touché," growled Fred.

"What the heck's going on here?" laughed Agnes, a fifth-grade teacher. "What's with the 'To being' and the 'stopping?' What's that got to do with anything? I didn't drive all the way up here from Wells to listen to babbling about "plucking out the heart' stuff? Now cut it out."

Fitterer sat on his desk and grinned, and grinned, and grinned.

We squirmed until Betty, a no-nonsense phonics purist from Minnesota Lake, asked, "Ok, so we're old-fashioned, but time's up, Mr. Fitterer. What the hell is a 3-D book report?" Betty had earned her nine-month county-school certificate in the 1930s, her two-year certificate in the 1940s, and was now in hot pursuit of her B.A. She had refused to give up teaching phonics for the "new method" of word recognition. She had also worn 3-D glasses in the 1950s to watch the creatures from dark lagoons creep toward her. She was done fooling around.

"You're right, Betty. 'The play's the thing to catch the king.' Whoops! Sorry, Agnes. Sometimes I can't help myself. Well, here it is. In your book report you must select some object or objects that are logically connected to explain any aspect of the literary work. You may explain a theme in the book, reveal the emotional and psychological state of a character, analyze the plot, or any other aspects of literary analysis which your students have done in their oral and written reports.

"In this assignment, however, you must use a symbol, your object of choice, to present your point. Remember the object is to be used as a symbol. There must exist some recognizable relationship between the object and your idea. You cannot use a toy car to symbolize the Joad's car in *The*

Grapes of Wrath. A car is a car, even if it's a toy. You cannot use water as a symbol of the Mississippi River in *Huckleberry Finn.* Water is water."

"Give us an example," groused Ed.

"Last winter I gave this same assignment to college day students, who were nineteen or twenty. I could tell that one of the students had completely forgotten to do the assignment. He drew a high number and after each presentation he looked at his watch, hoping he would not be called before the break. When I said, "Let's take fifteen," he dashed out of the room.

"He returned carrying a four-foot potted philodendron. I wondered if a friend had bought it or he had stored it somewhere in the building. I called his number. His demeanor had changed completely. He was ready. He carried the plant to the front of the room and set it on the table. 'I am using this philodendron to represent Pepe in John Steinbeck's short story 'Flight,'" he explained.

"Pepe grew from the dirt of the desert and the rocks. As this plant was once a seed, so was this boy once a seed in his mother's womb until he becomes a child of the earth. He struggles to grow until he thinks he is a man. He grows into a tall, thin stalk. 'He [had] a tall, thin head, pointed at the top,' just like this plant. Like this plant Pepe, too, wants to grow, to reach toward the sun. Pepe's dream is to blossom into a man.

"The sprouting leaves of the philodendron are thin and immature. To become mature, the plant must travel towards the sun. To become a man, Pepe must journey to town. The stalk adorns itself with leaves. Pepe adorns himself with his father's switchblade, his father's hatband, and his father's silk green handkerchief, which are all symbols of being a man.

"The knife represents both Pepe's power and prowess as well as the forces that Pepe faces in his quest to escape the forces of man and nature which strip us of our powers and reduce our humanity. Pepe's knife is a symbol of life's paradoxes. It symbolizes our strengths are our weakness.

"Pepe measured his manhood by his ability to throw a knife. He could hit a post from twenty yards. One day his mother sent him to town and he thought he was a man because men went to town."

"My student held the plant with his left hand," said Fitterer. "Then he reached into his pocket with his right hand, grabbed his switchblade, and snapped it open."

"He hurried home," continued the student, "and told his mother, 'After a few shots of tequila [I] got into a fight and flicked [my] knife. It went almost by itself.... I am a man now, Mama. The man said names to me I could not allow.'"

"His mother gave Pepe what she knew he needed to make a man's journey: a horse, a canvas water bag, black stringy jerky, his father's black coat, and his father's 38-.58 rifle and ten cartridges. They were like leaves sprouting from the philodendron. Pepe said good-bye to his mother, brother, and sister and headed for the high country. He knew the dark riders would soon be on his trail."

"Then," said Fitterer, "he told the end of the story. The dark riders chase Pepe up the mountain. They shoot his horse. Zip! The kid sliced off the top leaf of the plant. He loses his water bag. Zip, another leaf! His father's black coat. Zip! The knife. Zip! The rifle. Zip! Nothing is left of the philodendron but the stalk."

"'The second crash sounded from below,' read my student. 'Pepe swung forward and toppled from the rock. His body stuck and rolled over and over, starting a little avalanche. And when at last he stopped against a bush, the avalanche slid slowly down and covered up his head.'"

"My student set the plant on the desk. Zip! He sliced off the bare stalk. Now that's a book report!" shouted Fitterer.

"When I walked back to my office after class, I noticed a circular space in the carpet that matched the bottom of the philodendron plant that had once stood majestically in the foyer."

"Tom, this is preposterous," said Kathy. "This plan to overthrow the administration will never work, and if it does, you'll become assistant principal in charge of discipline. Horrors!"

4

Teaching

Student Teaching: A Parable

W E SOLD OUR SCRAP METAL, PAPER, AND POP BOTTLES to Mr. Krebsbach at the junkyard and headed toward the lumberyard. I ran toward the sand bins while Jim pulled his wagon. I climbed on top of the four-foot concrete divider separating the different grades of sand. The bins looked like three-cornered handball courts. Sand was piled highest against the back wall and sloped to the cement floor.

Plunging in 1944

"What ya waiting for?" yelled Jim. "Don't be such a chicken. Jump."

I hesitated and leapt toward the deepest sand. I missed my target. The toes on my left foot snapped as they hit the concrete. I clutched my foot and howled.

"Come on," yelled Jim. "Let's get the heck out of here. See that 'Keep Out' sign. Hurry up. Get up, will ya?"

I grabbed the side of the wall and pulled myself up on my right foot. "Give me a ride home," I pleaded. I can't walk."

"Aw, there's nothing wrong with you. Don't be a sissy. Besides you're too heavy for me to pull."

My foot throbbed. "Come on, Jim," I begged. "I need help. This is really tough walking."

"You can do it," he said. "You don't need any help."

I hopped six blocks uphill from the lumberyard to my dad's shop, begging Jim for a ride every step of the way.

The doctor set my foot in a cast and my dad made the only set of crutches in town for a nine-year-old.

My Rookie Year

THE BONFIRE

Like most first-year teachers, my job consisted of more than just teaching. I was also assigned the position of Senior Class Advisor. It didn't take me long to figure out why the position was vacant. My first major assignment was supervising the homecoming bonfire.

Back in the '50s, the homecoming bonfire was a religious ritual. If you were to look down from space on Friday nights from September through October, you could see these blazing funeral pyres burning near every high school in Minnesota.

Each inferno was an offering to the Great God of Football, a sacrificial flame to bless the boys armored in helmets, shoulder and hip pads, and brilliantly colored uniforms. Each participant in the struggle was identified by a number, so the worshippers could cheer for their native sons and scowl at the hostile intruders.

Girls wearing short skirts and waving pompoms led the frenzied mob in chants praising the valor of their warrior heroes. "Tony, Tony, he's our man. If he can't do it, Lee, can. Lee, Lee, he's our man, if he can't do it nobody can" until finally, "Team, team, they're our team. If they can't do it nobody can." Like the litanies chanted in the great cathedrals of Europe before Christian soldiers marched off to battle the infidels, these young goddesses proclaimed the splendor of their knights protected by plastic, leather, and a patronizing deity.

"Two, bits, four bits, six bits, a dollar," the cheerleaders yelled, "everyone for our team, stand up and holler."

Like any ritual worth its weight in wish making, football frenzy sought to drive the demons to pigskin destruction. Whether their foes were marching down the field or being pummeled into oblivion, the short-skirted beauties strutting their neatly choreographed dance routines chanted the same invocation: "Push 'em back. Push 'em back, way back. Push 'em back. Push 'em back, way back."

This wasn't football. It was religion. Opposing teams knelt and mumbled words seeking help from their purple and gold (whatever) ancestors, so they could knock the stuffings out of the rivals who challenged their superiority. The true believers screamed their dogma across the battle turf. "We've got spirit, yes, we do. We've got spirit, how 'bout youuuu?" If the opposition was not blessed with 220-pound linemen or fleet-footed backs, they probably had far few disciples asserting their superiority. Their chants seemed to evaporate in midair. Eventually the home crowd crowned itself victors, as the visitors eventually gave up the verbal battle. The home crowd mocked the puny response with "We've got more. We've got more!" Since so many participants in the ritual believed that football was life, the multitude reveled in the truth that those who can yell the loudest have the noblest cause and the purest hearts.

Tradition

For years the New Prague *Times* had used virtually every cliché to describe the punishment New Prague High School football players had inflicted on the other teams in the conference. "Friday night the Trojans whipped, out-played, discombobulated, outclassed, wiped the field with, beat, licked, thrashed, trounced, swamped, drubbed, routed, flattened, and knocked the opposition for a loop."

In the fall of 1953, New Prague had about eight hundred guys out for football. I was one of eighteen members of the Belle Plaine Tigers. The Trojans "pounded us to smithereens." Most teams dreaded the night they played New Prague.

In 1958 I was teaching for those same Trojans. New Prague scheduled Arlington as its homecoming opponent. The smell of blood was in the air. This would be no coffee party with prune-filled kolackys. The ritual strug-gle demanded elaborate ceremonies. Although the school board and administrators had hired several competent, experienced coaches to lead its warriors on the field of battle, they decided that a naive, inexperienced class advisor was competent enough to control the school pyromaniacs. I did not know when I signed my contract that in addition to teaching senior English, I would also be appointed bonfire supervisor.

The principal called me into his office and announced, "Tom, as part of your senior class advisor duties you are in charge of organizing the bonfire. We have had some trouble in the past years with kids stealing stuff. Make certain that doesn't happen again this year."

"What kind of trouble?" I wondered. "Who? Where? Help me out here! What dastardly rituals was I anointed to squelch? Were my reputation and my exorbitant $3600 salary in jeopardy?"

The bonfire committee and its henchmen met after school in my room. The good, the bad, and the ugly filled my room. Some sported their letter jackets, some combed their slicked-back ducktails, some rolled their ciga-rette packs neatly in their T-shirts, and some sat behind a stack of books. All social, academic, religious, and moral differences vanished as they gathered to plan the bonfire.

I stood in the hall and listened. "We'll show those sons-a-bitches from Arlington who can build a fire. Those Montgomery bastards tried to burn down last year's bonfire. We'll kill 'em if they show up this year. We gotta stay up all night and guard it."

Every general must have captains he can trust, people who will follow orders and act as if they were walking in the captain's shoes. Since school had only been in session for a month, I had little idea whose feet wanted to wear my shoes. However, during my first twenty-one years, my mentors had always told me that if I had one good friend, one person I could rely on, I would be fortunate. These same people had also informed me that "Blood is thicker than water."

How fortunate I was! I had my first cousin Pat in class. We had grown up sharing experiences on our grandparents' farm. I had often stayed at his farm and slept in the same room with him. We played baseball together. I ate at his parents' table. His mom, my aunt, played the piano and we sang Irish songs together. I was doubly blessed—I had one person I could trust and the same blood ran through our veins. If I had studied history more diligently in college, perhaps I would have learned that folks with the same blood running through their veins often enjoy beating the hell out of each other.

I cornered Pat outside the room. "Pat, you've got to help me," I pleaded. "The principal has warned me that what happened last year better not happen this year. No stealing, Pat. Promise me. You've got to help me keep these guys from pillaging the countryside. If they do, the principal will skin me alive."

"Don't worry, Tom. These guys are my buddies, and they like you. They won't do anything to make trouble," he replied. I heard his words but his Irish eyes were smiling. I should have known better.

I sat down with the thundering herd and they sketched out the territory to be scavenged for bonfire debris. "Me and Ken and Harold and the other guys from New Market will cover everything between here and Webster," ordered General Bull.

"Ya, and us guys from St. Benedict, we'll take that area, and Pat, how 'bout youse guys go west to Union Hill?"

"Ya," said Pat, my cousin, Attila the Irishman.

"And me and Dan can go out to Veseli, and den, da rest of dose guys from—" and so it went. Genghis Khan, Attila, and General Bull staked out every nook and cranny of the school district.

"By god, this is going to be the best goddamned bonfire ever!" they yelled. I cringed and wondered what that would involve.

"Now wait a minute," I said. "You guys have got to promise me you won't steal anything. Nothing. You can't even 'borrow' stuff. Just bring old boards, junk, nothing that's nailed down or valuable. Promise?"

"You got our word," said General Bull.

"Scout's honor," pledged Genghis.

"Nothin'll happen, Tom," swore cousin Patrick O'Attila.

The Huskers

I was teaching the differences between "lie" and "lay" when the principal's secretary knocked. "Tom, Mr. Kafka wants to see you, right now. He's really steamed."

He tapped his finger on his desk. Smoke still lingered in the corners along the ceiling and his eyebrows were singed. The dragon was angry.

"Tom, I thought I told you not to let those guys steal anything. I just got a call from Dr. Novak. He has a cornfield right next to the park where your hooligans have built their bonfire. Those kids stole the first two rows of corn shocks right out of his field. Get those kids out of class right now and get down there and husk his corn out of that bonfire."

"But I've got class and I'm right in the middle—"

"Never mind. Dr. Novak's mad as hell and he wants his corn. He says he's missing about fifteen bushels."

My students looked like maggots as they groveled in the debris. The corn shocks were covered with tree branches, barn boards, battered furniture, and a few outhouses. Some were so dirty their eyeballs looked like flashlights, but they were as happy as pigs at slopping time.

"God, look at this. I think it's old man B.'s outhouse. I bet he was surprised this morning."

"Ya, bet he had to take his toilet paper into the woods."

"Where the hell did all this hay come from? It's stickin' down my shirt. I'm startin' to itch like crazy."

"Hey, Pat, I heard someone borrowed your old man's flatbed wagon last night. Know anything about that?"

"Where did all this hay come from?" I asked.

Silence. I decided not to ask again.

"Hey, Mr. M., how many bushels did you say old Doc is missin'?"

"About fifteen."

"Well, we got about twenty-five bushels here," said Genghis, "so Doc ain't the only one missin' corn."

That night the sky above New Prague blazed in glory. It was truly the best damn bonfire the town had ever seen.

As I drove home, I noticed hay scattered along the road from New Prague to Union Hill. I learned later that my cousin and his buddies had stolen a haystack from his neighbor's field and pitched it on his dad's flatbed wagon. So much for oaths sworn in family blood.

THE KEYS TO THE KINGDOM

I owned one sport coat, which I wore to school every day. Each hour I walked into class, slipped off my coat, and hung it on my chair. At the end of the period, I slipped it on and headed for the next room.

My fourth-hour classroom must have been an architect's blunder. Unlike all the other rooms on the floor whose doors opened to the hallway, this room was five or six steps above floor level. It was an aberration, a structural misfit, but an appropriate dwelling place for several of the characters who inhabited it during their battle with British literature.

Sprinkled among the docile students were Tom R., Jack, Richard, Bill, and Tom J. I never really understood the meaning of *nemesis* until I met those guys.

Unlike classes today in which the students change courses every trimester or semester, the 1958 seniors met with me every day for the entire year. I was trapped and so were they. I taught all four sections of English 12, so there was no escape for any of us.

One winter day I walked up the six steps to my classroom, set my books on the desk, hung my jacket on the chair, and greeted my beloved students. I had just begun to expound on the virtues of the Romantic poets when the secretary knocked on the door. "You've got an emergency phone call."

I rushed down the stairs to discover that one of my favorite relatives had suffered a fatal stroke. My heart ached. I wanted to curse the gods, pound the door and scream, "Well, damn it all!"

Instead, I stuffed my grief. My students waited upstairs, their books opened to Browning and Wordsworth. What did I care if Wordworth's heart leapt "when [he] beheld a rainbow in the sky" or that "It was a beauteous evening, calm and free"? What did I care if Elizabeth Barrett Browning moaned, "How do I love thee? Let me count the ways"?

I walked back to my classroom and pulled the doorknob. Stuck. I pulled harder. Locked. I reached into my pocket for my keys. My jacket hung on the chair; the keys lay on the desk.

I watched them hoot and laugh. Most of the class just grinned but my nemeses smirked the smirk that only an embarrassed teacher knows. Jack and Tom R. were hysterical. St. Thomas J. stared at his book as if nothing unusual was happening. Dick looked bewildered.

"Damn it!" I muttered. As hard as I tried, I couldn't find the humor of being locked out of my own room. They knew my every tick and habit. The moment I had walked out they grabbed the keys from my jacket, locked the door, and waited.

They read my lips. No words, just lips and eyes silently commanding, "Get over here. Open this door." Their personal Marcel Marceau pantomimed frantically behind the glass door. Their faces applauded, "Bravo, Mr. Melchior! What a great performance! Encore! Encore!"

I threw up my arms and laughed. Jack grabbed the keys and opened the door. I laughed. They roared. We went back to daffodils, the ancient mariner, nightingales, and Grecian urns.

Jack Remembers: Forty-four years later I asked Jack Sticha about that first year and the lockout.

"We thought, 'Boy this guy is young.' We weren't used to having such a young teacher. We were used to the older teachers who had been there for many years. You were a novelty—someone young and green, someone we could work with and mold. We could sense you were a rookie.

"A lot of memories are blurry. I remember it to have been a really good time. I find it hard to believe I'd instigate something like that. Honestly, I can't remember if I took the key, but it was such a good idea. It was a lot of fun while we were doing it. While you were outside trying to get in, I had second thoughts such as, 'Maybe this is serious business here. We locked out our teacher. I thought about what could happen to me. I could wind up getting expelled. Someone could tell my parents.'

"You had this look of disbelief, a 'These students wouldn't do this to me' type of look. A 'Can this be really happening?' look. I was relieved at the end when everything turned out O.K."

CHURCH SCHOOL

I held my last-hour English class in the Methodist church three blocks east of school. I was not told this when I signed my contract, but I accepted the situation without question. "There's no room available last hour," the principal told me on the first day of workshop. "The church is just a few blocks away. You'll have to walk. We can't afford to bus you back and forth. Keep an eye on your students. Make certain you are back in time so they can catch the bus home."

I accepted the reason in good faith, but after a few days I suspected other reasons for wanting my group isolated from the rest of the students. My school, like most others, scheduled students using the rock crusher system. This class had many boulders.

One summer I worked for my brother-in-law who owns an asphalt plant. To blacktop the roads, Bituminous Materials, Inc., needed just the right texture of gravel to mix with oil that was then heated to create asphalt. This grade of gravel was generally found lying under a thin veneer of black dirt. The operation was then simple. Set up the asphalt plant, doze the gravel into a mountain, and push the gravel into several sifting screens. The finest grade slipped through quickly. Each screen separated various size stones until only the rocks were left and separated from the useful material. When the gravel was depleted, the rock crusher was wheeled in. The bulldozer now pushed ton after ton of stones and rocks into the crusher, which chewed up its food and spit it out.

Calculus, band, choir, college prep English and a few other electives were the "rock crusher" in my school as they were in most schools. The fine sand sifted through the first screen and fell into the advanced classes populated by the gifted writers, mathematicians, musicians and college-bound academicians. These students met third and fourth periods.

The pebbles and stones sifted through a screen with slightly larger openings and fell into the first period class. The large rocks refused to be sifted into any academic sandbox. Despite their protests, the crusher ground them up and exiled them to the Methodist Church to receive their daily dose of British literature. The crusher system of scheduling was not perfect. Gravel of every size somehow fell into every class.

Each afternoon I led my band of ne'er-do-wells and a few gentle souls to the church. Clutching our brown Harcourt, Brace copies of *English Literature*, we walked through the autumn leaves, winter snow, and spring rain. Never in the history of education were twenty-five teenagers more disinterested in walking toward Jonathan Swift, Byron, Shelley, Keats, and, the bane of them all, William Shakespeare.

The three-block trip took us about ten minutes. We kicked leaves, threw snowballs, and splashed water. Howard and Phil usually lagged behind, trying to make me think the smoke from their cigarettes was just the fog from their wintry breaths. The guys tormented and teased the girls who taunted them with more creative barbs.

Although I know they planned no evil, they all participated in a subtle work slowdown. In the fall and spring, they ambled along, gossiped, kicked stones, punched each other, and bragged about their beer-drinking escapades, and did everything possible to delay their encounter with the British literature. I was a young idealist, however, paid to educate the youth of the nation, and, by god, nothing was going to stop me from drilling the words of Andrew Marvell, William Blake, and Robert Burns into their adolescent skulls.

Most of the students humored me and struggled to fall through the screen, but most days ended in frustration. Then there was Bull, the biggest rock of all. There was no hole large enough to allow Bull to fall into the educational sandbox and no rock crusher strong enough to grind him up. He swore, spit, snarled, and simmered. He intimidated his teachers and harassed his classmates. When the urge moved him, Bull made my seventh hour purgatory in a church. He kept my fuse lit from the moment we set out on our daily odyssey until I had the crew safely returned to the high school where they dashed for the waiting busses.

Many a night I lay awake frustrated by Bull and the antics of his buddies. I had nightmares filled with Edgar Allan Poe-like plots to get my revenge. Perhaps I could lure him and the rest of my tormentors into some murky cellar under the pretense that I had hidden a keg of Hamm's beer that was waiting just for them. When they began their guzzling, I would wall them in.

CHICAGO TRIP

Each spring the New Prague seniors took a trip to Chicago. Again, no one told me that chaperoning this event was part of my duties as senior class advisor. Phillipa, Tom S., Tom's wife, and I were given the task of controlling 104 seniors. That meant each one of us was responsible for 26 teenagers. We took the train to and from Chicago. We visited the museums,

Waiting for the train to Chicago

the zoo, and attended *The Music Man*. Much of what went on, however, happened when we were not present. Although one of us "stood guard" at the hotel entrance, we couldn't stay up all night, nor could we know what happened behind closed hotel doors.

The Aragon

We spent one night at the Aragon Ballroom. We chaperones spent most of the night walking around, but we did sit down at a table on the second floor for a few minutes. We could see Dick long before he saw us. He was walking along very nonchalantly, examining the building and smoking a cigarette. Tom S. said, "Watch this."

Dick was looking at the ceiling and Tom walked toward him. Dick stuck his cigarette hand into his pocket, thinking Tom had not seen him. Tom blocked his path and asked, "How are you doing, Dick? What do you think of this place?" Dick wasn't much of a talker and tried to maneuver around Tom. His cigarette was smoldering in his pocket.

Tom moved when Dick moved, blocking his exit. Finally Tom said, "I hope that cigarette doesn't burn a hole in your pocket." Dick looked at Tom and said something like, "I won't do it again." Then he took the cigarette out of his pocket and threw it away. I doubt if it was the last cigarette he smoked on that trip.

One night three of the girls tried to sneak out to meet some sailors they had met at one of our tour stops. We stopped them at the door and they returned to their rooms, or so we thought. Years later I was talking with Rosie, who married my cousin, about that night. I mentioned the event and said, "Imagine what could have happened had you met those love-starved sailors."

"Oh, nothing happened, Tom. We waited until you went to bed and then we went out with them." I was learning what every teacher knows: we are usually the last to know.

Jack Sticha Remembers the Chicago trip. "I think I have to put the Chicago trip into some context. We were from a small town. I had never been out of the state. I think that was the case with many of us. That was a big event. We were getting out of town. It was the end of the year and we were going to graduate from high school soon and become young men and women. We were going to be out on our own. That was a time to start experimenting, to sow our oats.

"It seems trivial now but smoking and drinking were such a big part of the trip. Sneaking cigarettes was part of our ritual of independence. We didn't have booze on the train, but we would sneak into other cars or the bathrooms to smoke. We posted lookouts. We knew there were only two of you guys and 104 of us kids. We knew we had the advantage and that getting caught wasn't going to be a problem. There were some pretty innovative people on that train.

(We chaperones searched every suitcase before we left for Chicago. We also required the students to sign a letter acknowledging that they agreed to being sent home if they were caught drinking.)

The Poker Game
The game according to Jack: "The poker game started as an intimate, friendly game with four or five guys. It grew into quite an event. Of course the cigarettes were going pretty hot and heavy right away. Other people started coming into our room. Some joined the card game but there was perpetual activity in the room. We were playing when one of the girls said, 'Oh, oh, here come the teachers!' We weren't paying much attention. I was sitting on the couch, looking straight at the door.

"When I saw you, I don't know who was more surprised, you or I. Again I got this twinge of fear. I liked the situation but I got that twinge because there was smoke all over. I don't remember what I said. I think I put my head down. You said something like, 'I don't believe this. You guys better get this place shaped up.' When I looked up, you were gone.

"I was afraid of what could have happened, but I said, 'This guy is O.K. He's not going to bust us.' We pulled a lot of stuff we should not have done, but we realized you were not out to get us expelled from school."

The game according to me: When I opened the door, smoke billowed out. Jack was the first person I saw. He looked stunned and guilty. Everyone in the room looked like a trapped rat. No one spoke. I was stunned, as usual. I should have expected anything by that time of the year, but my students had a way of catching me off guard.

The truth is I didn't know what to do. I knew I couldn't send them all home. I certainly didn't want to expel them with only a few weeks left in the school year. I knew smoking was a violation of school policy and I was supposed to follow the rule to the letter. When I got to my room, I thought, that I should have done something, perhaps grounded them for the remainder of the trip. Would we ground everyone who was in the room? I couldn't tell who was smoking other than the poker players. I knew I could lose my job for not turning in the violators. I wasn't too worried, though, because I had already signed my contract to teach in Puerto Rico the following year. I think I did the right thing, but I'm not certain.

The Bill

I went to the check out counter to sign my bill. It was just a formality because the school was paying for the chaperones' rooms. My total included the cost of the room, but to my surprise there was also a charge for several mixed drinks and some beer. I argued that the hotel must have made a mistake. I later discover that the boys from New Market had ordered drinks and charged them to my room. Of course I didn't know that at the time, so I just signed my name and chalked it up to inexperience.

Padre Burton

In 1959 I accepted a teaching contract at Colegio San Antonio Abad in Humacao, Puerto Rico. There I met the most ingenious administrator I would work for in thirty-four years of teaching, Burton Bloms, O.S.B. San Antonio was changing from an agricultural school to a college preparatory high school. We would not have our first senior class until the following year. Benedictine monks associated with St. John's University in Collegeville, Minnesota, ran the school.

We were a little-known, small, private school tucked away in the middle of the island. Most of our students were very poor and supported by scholarships from the monastery.

To survive financially and academically, the school had to attract at least half its students from wealthy families. Most of these students attended the more prestigious schools in San Juan and other larger cities.

We knew one way to attract these students was to become an athletic power, to be so good that other student athletes would want to become part of our success. Because we had so few sophomores, juniors and seniors, we won few varsity games. We were creating no mystical athletic aura!

Padre Burton used a bit of creative administrative chicanery to advertise San Antonio Abad. He decided we would host an "under-five-footers volleyball tournament." No player over five feet tall could compete. Of course, every school had varsity and junior varsity teams, which practiced daily, but no one had an "under-five-footers team."

We had three advantages: first, many of our best players stood less than five feet, including Pedro Garcia, who was a phenomenal player; secondly, we began practicing for the tournament long before the invitations were sent to the other schools; and finally, General Burton decided to coach the the players he referred to as "my boys." The students worshiped him, and the Padre had honed his coaching skills working with students in one of the largest private schools in Mexico City. Burton drilled his team. They practiced diligently for two weeks.

Teams from almost every private school participated in the tournament, but Colegio San Antonio Abad swept through the First Annual San Antonio Abad Under-Five-Footers' Tournament. We were an unstoppable machine. Set. Set. Kill! Set. Set. Kill! Victory!

We sang, danced, chanted, and carried home our huge trophy—the first of many more to come. It wasn't long before Padre Burton's school was known throughout the island.

Good-bye Innocence

Part I: Mr. Band

In the eighth grade I began taking clarinet lessons. My idol was not Benny Goodman but the senior who played first chair in the high school band. I filled the air with sour notes and played a solo of misery for everyone who was forced to listen, but my idol was sensational.

I'm certain that Mr. De Leo, my band instructor, felt his lessons with me were his personal purgatory on earth. Whatever sins he had committed during the week would be washed away by having to listen to my weekly squeaking and squawking.

What made Mr. De Leo's musical purgatory so painful was that he was a virtuoso and a man of impeccable style. Only his students knew him as Mr. De Leo. To anyone in the Midwest who stepped onto a dance floor during the '40s and '50s, he was Guy De Leo. His Brylcremed, coal-black hair glistened under the stage spotlights. He combed it straight back, no parts or sweeping ducktails for Guy De Leo.

When he was directing his band in dance halls throughout the state, he wore his trademark white jacket and white shirt with ruffled cuffs. Many bandleaders wore slicked back hair and natty attire, but none sported a pencil-thin mustache like Guy De Leo. He looked like a cross between a Latin lover and western movie villain.

What agony it must have been for that talented man to direct his professional musicians at the Kato Ballroom on Sunday nights and then teach me on Monday mornings!

My band lessons were very much like going to confession. In confession the priest and I both hid in darkness behind the screen. I confessed my transgressions: "Bless me, father, for I have sinned." Band confession was different because I carried the object of my infidelity with me. Nervously I assembled its parts. I tried to accumulate enough saliva to moisten my reed and soften it for my musical confession. At least in church I never had to demonstrate my sins. All I had to do there was mumble them as quickly as possible, atone for my shortcomings with a few Hail Marys and Our Fathers, and slip out the door promising to sin no more.

This was not the case with clarinet confession. God sat right next to me. There's something completely discombobulating about having your personal god invade your private space, especially if your god has not had time to garb himself in his usual splendor. When god stayed up too late, imbibed a bit more than usual on evil spirits, and forgot to brush with Colgate or "cover up his tell-tale breath with Sen-Sen," I didn't want him sliding his chair six inches from mine.

I had come to expect an impeccably groomed, nattily attired instructor, wrapped in ruffled white purity. Sadly, a stubble field had grown up around that Clark Gable mustache. When my mentor nestled next to me, he reeked of cigarette smoke, cheap cologne, and ballroom sweat.

He leaned forward and tapped the music stand with his baton, glared at me, and commanded, "Play."

And play I did. I blew the most squeaking, groaning sounds that instrument was capable of producing. I created droning, howling half notes unheard by humans since the cavemen called their wayward urchins home for a good meal of raw mastodon.

I'm in the front, second from the left. Dad made certain my pants fit.

"No, no, no, no! Try it again— one, two, three, four. One, two, three, four. Again." Tap, tap. tap, tap. "C, c, c, c. D, d, d, d. Tom, did you practice?" Tap, tap tap.

"Forgive me, Mr. Pencil-thin-Mustache, but I did not practice." Tap, tap, tap tap.

"Ah, yes, and as your punishment, you will play in the high school band," he said. The band needed bodies to fill chairs. I was seated at the far end of the the clarinet players

I was a "bonus player." Any notes which I played were a bonus. I played only whole, half, and quarter notes. Whenever the music was peppered with eighth and sixteenth notes, I faked it. My clarinet and I were never upset or depressed because we played flats and sharps so poorly. They were not part of the bonus. With this philosophy, I seldom made mistakes. I played only "bonus notes" when those friendly whole, half, and quarter notes appeared on the page.

Part II: The Maestro

The master in chair one carried the entire clarinet section. Like typical eighth-grade brats we made fun of him outside the music room because he was quite heavy. No, we weren't mature enough to use euphemisms. We called 'em the way we saw 'em. The guy was fat. But could he play that licorice stick!

At the district music contest my music hero stood in center stage. He cradled his black clarinet, which looked like an ebony toothpick. His huge fingers easily covered every stop. When he began to play "A Carnival in

Venice," I could see those beautiful notes flow out of his clarinet—eighth notes, sixteenth notes, flats, sharps, and beautiful lilting runs. The notes curled about him. He played Ferris wheels, sideshows, merry-go-rounds, cotton candy, lovers, and con artists. He played blues and reds, bursting fireworks and a full moon. When he had finished dancing us through that Venetian festival, we cheered and yelled. We bonus players stared in awe at our hero. He was one of us, our hero, the musical wizard who modestly accepted his blue ribbon.

Part III: The Hawk

I played basketball on the B team that year, but when the varsity team entered tournament, I could not abandon my "gym rat" status, so I volunteered to become an assistant manager. My musical hero, the maestro of the clarinet, was the head manager. I was assigned all the menial jobs that he could pawn off on me, such as picking up dirty uniforms, jockstraps, and towels, but I got to sneak in a few shots before, during, and after practice. Sometimes I even got to touch the game ball and toss it to one of the varsity players.

On the night before the first tournament game, the manager and I had to pack all the equipment for the next day's game. We neatly packed the uniforms and warm-up jackets. By the time we had finished these jobs, I was tired, bored, and desperate to go up to the gym and shoot a few buckets.

We still had the tedious job of folding all the towels. I gave him my best eighth-grade whine, "Ah, I'm too tired. I've done enough work already. You finish these. I always have to do them."

"You stay here and fold these towels," he commanded. Back and forth we argued. Soon we were hollering at each other but I was not smart enough to know that a punk eighth-grader does not argue with a senior who is his superior. Soon I was reduced to my last line of defense, name calling, a strategy mastered by every junior high school kid.

"Do them yourself, Fatso," I yelled. Bam! He slapped me across the side of my face. That huge hand that caressed the clarinet, my hero's hand that was as big as my head, cracked me so hard my ear rang.

I staggered against the stack of towels. Tears streamed down my face. "You fat pig," I screamed. Crack! He smashed me again with his open hand. Pain shot across my face. My ear was numb.

Bull-headed and nearly hysterical, I screamed again. "You fat bastard. I hate you!" His hand exploding against my face sounded like a rifle shot, echoing from one corner of the locker room to the other.

Trying to hide my tears, I finally shut my mouth and folded the towels.

The basketball season ended and I gave up trying to play the clarinet. The music wizard graduated and my family and I moved soon after the school year had ended.

Part IV: The Awakening

Forty-eight years later I attended a concert with two of my teaching colleagues. We sat in separate seats and agreed to meet at intermission. I found them talking to a friend from their church. They introduced me and I shook their friend's hand, the same gentle hand that had created my magical carnival day in Venice, the same gigantic hand that had cracked me across the face again and again. He looked at me wide-eyed and exclaimed, "You're Tom Melchior?" He had buried me deep in his mind long ago, but suddenly there I stood the way he remembered me, a scrawny eighth-grader with curly hair, big ears and glasses. I knew we were both replaying that painful scene in the locker room. I could tell by the look in his eyes that he remembered my cruel insults and the beating he had given me. There were many days, months, even years when I didn't think about my head snapping back in pain, but I never forgot it for a minute.

Part V: Discipline

In 1959 Colegio San Antonio Abad was an all-boys school run by the Benedictine monks from St. John's Abbey in Collegeville Minnesota. I was a twenty-two-year-old German-Irish Catholic who had never traveled farther than Milwaukee, Wisconsin, to watch the Braves play baseball. I had talked with only one person of color in my life, a young black student from British Guinea, who worked next to me in the canning factory.

Colegio San Antonia Abad: Classrooms are located to the right of the bell tower.
Photograph from St. John's Abbey Archives, Collegeville, Minnesota

Some of the students at San Antonio came from middle-class families. Most came from poor families and most received financial help from the Benedictines. No one came from the rich families who sent their sons to the prestigious schools in San Juan.

Disciplining a school of cooped-up-boarding-school adolescents was far more challenging than teaching them geometry or English grammar. For both students and staff, corporal punishment was as acceptable and common as a lunch of rice and beans. If two guys fought on the playground, the headmaster simply said, "Juan, Felix, over here." They walked over to the good padre who said, "Bend over." Padre gave each a swat on the butt and sent them back to play.

All the classrooms were on the ground floor under the second story dormitory. The windows were Miami-style, crank-out louvered shutters. There were no screens. A walkway of red tile ran the length of the classroom section and the overhang from the dormitory protected the walkway from rain and the blistering sun. The classroom doors opened to the walkway and the walkway opened to the entire campus.

Padre X taught all the seventh graders. He was a stern, impatient taskmaster who had long ago forgotten about puberty, frantic hormones, and minute attention spans. Consequently, many of his students were found lacking in discipline. Almost any time I walked past his room, two or three students were kneeling on the red tile, heads bowed, reciting the rosary or some other prayers seeking atonement for their transgressions.

Physical punishment was as much a part of the curricula as Latin, English, algebra, science, or music, but I could not imagine hitting students or demanding they kneel for hours on a tile floor in the hot sun.

VI: The Bird

Emeraldo Rios was the magic bird of our varsity basketball team. He was left-handed, stood five-foot-eight, and weighed 120 pounds and when he touched the ball, his hands were soft as feathers. He flew down the court, danced through defenders and threw up shots that always seemed to find the basket and float through the netting.

Since we had no seniors in the school and the juniors were all average players, Rios was named the team's captain. He was a quiet kid and not the take-charge player one would think of as captain of any team, but Rios was different from most of the other players. He had lived in New York City and battled to survive in the city. He had seen cynicism bred from poverty and prejudice. He knew a world I had never seen.

Rios was polite, happy-go-lucky, and conscientious, and I loved coaching him and having him in class. Nothing ever seemed to rattle him. Each night the other "gringo" teacher and I chose an average third player and played Rios and two other varsity players three-on-three. We played tough, street rules basketball. He loved bumping and pushing his teachers and showing us gringo hotshots how to play the game.

Since I outweighed him by forty pounds and had fought the wars of high school and college intramural basketball, I pounded him whenever I got the chance. Since we were the teachers, we seldom admitted to even the most flagrant fouls and we seldom lost an argument. Rios never complained. He just smiled that smile that said, "Anything you can dish out, I have seen on the courts of the big city."

VII: The Hawk Returns

On the morning of our biggest game, we were discussing some topic in English class. The students and I were in a heated discussion, the class against the teacher. Rios made a sarcastic comment that for some reason upset me. I made an equally sarcastic comment and he made another. His smile disappeared, his face turned red, and fire burned in his eyes.

I felt like jumping over the desks to get at him. "Rios," I demanded, "please step outside."

In the hallway outside the classroom where all the students could see, I demanded that he apologize for his comments. Rios of the Streets smarted off and in a split second I slapped him across the face. "The Carnival of Venice" blared in my ears.

He smiled his "kid of the streets" smile and never said a word. He just stared at me and grinned. I told him to go anywhere but back into the class-room. When I walked into the room, the students just sat there and stared. I couldn't speak. My tongue shriveled and dried, my hands shook, and I felt as if I was going to vomit. I sat down and listened to my heart weeping someplace far away.

That afternoon the bird flew down the court, caressed the ball with his feathery touch, passed the ball to his streaking teammates, and fired shot after shot that snapped the net into a perpetual dance. He listened to me during time-outs but he never looked me in the eye.

I knew he would never forget his teacher slapping him just as I knew I would never forget that flabby hand snapping my head back in the locker room. He knew he had been wronged, and I knew I would never be as inno-cent as I was when I walked into my classroom that morning. I knew I could never be all that I wanted to be or all that I imagined I was.

I taught Rios for the next four months and coached him during the base-ball season. I left San Antonio Abad at the end of that school year.

Every hour I taught for the next thirty-two years, a fifteen-year-old Puerto Rican boy sat in a desk in the corner of my conscience, reminding me why I often tossed in my dreams. In my nightmares I heard the clarinet playing "The Carnival of Venice" in the background, punctuated by the sound of a hand slapping skin.

VIII: Last Chance

Approximately ten years ago my wife received a call from a young man who said, "Is this the home of Mr. Melchior, who taught in Puerto Rico?"

My wife said, "Yes, it is, but he will not be home for several hours."

"My name is Emeraldo Rios, and I was one of his students. I'm passing through Minneapolis and I thought perhaps we might meet for a few hours. Please tell him I called."

Emeraldo Rios, fourth from the left, and the Colegio San Abtonio Abad team

Montgomery High School, where I met the Dairy Queen

Dairy Queen

I flew home from Paris the day before the first day of workshop. I packed my suitcase, clock, and stereo and moved into Mrs. Strutnick's upstairs bedroom.

I overslept the next morning. I overslept on the first day of school. To make matters worse, I had never met anyone on the staff. The principal had signed me to a contract while I was still teaching in Puerto Rico. He had spoken to people who knew me and signed me sight unseen. Imagine what he and the superintendent thought when I was a no-show that morning.

As the clock ticked 8:10 a.m., I bolted out of the house and sprinted across the track and playground toward the high school. I raced up two flights of stairs and stopped outside the door. I gasped for breath, wiped the sweat off my face, straightened my tie, and walked into the staff meeting.

The second I walked into the room the superintendent, said, "And here is Tom Melchior who just returned from Europe." I waved and slid into the closest desk. Welcome to workshop. He introduced the other first-year teachers: Dave, biology; Jerry, girls' physical education; and Sue, junior and senior high English.

Throughout the day I worked at the usual workshop tasks I would follow for the next thirty-one years. I checked my class lists, recorded the names in my grade book, sorted and stacked textbooks, arranged the room, and prepared my first week's lesson plans.

About four o'clock one of the veteran teachers stuck his head into my room and said, "Tom, come on. We're going downtown for a drink." I was stunned. Teachers drinking! Teachers drinking in town! Teachers drinking in town at 4:15 in the afternoon during workshop! Where was I?

"I don't think so," I said. "I've got too much work to do here."

"It can wait until tomorrow," he said. "Come on. It's a tradition to take the new teachers to the Legion."

While the veteran teachers milled about, Dave, Jerry, Sue, and I took a table in the corner. Before we had time to ask, "Where did you go to college?" or "What's your home town?" the congenial bartender appeared."Welcome," he said. What'll ya have?"

"Give me a beer," said Dave.

"I'll have a Coke," said Jerry.

"Give me a rum and Coke with a twist of lemon," I said.

Sue hesitated. She frowned and fidgeted. "Do you have milk?" she asked.

"Yes, we do," said the bartender.

"Good," she said. "I'll have a glass of milk."

He grinned as he walked toward the bar.

I fell in love with her that first afternoon. In that dimly lit bar I drank my rum and Coke and watched her sip her milk. The room buzzed with chatter from colleagues guzzling every thing from Manhattans to Grain Belt, but she ordered milk and I was hooked for life.

Wanks

In the spring of 1968, I thought I would move away from the standard diet of adolescent literature such as *That Was Then, This Is Now* and *The Pigman* and sink our literary teeth into something that would stir up those teenage gray cells. I decided we would read John Steinbeck's *The Pearl*.

I knew those teenage brains had been spoon-fed pabulum which consisted of finely ground up literal images. What was, was. The word was the thing. A story about a teenager named Faith, was simply a story about a teenager named Faith. Having siblings named Hope and Charity was no more than the result of having weird parents.

To most of the students, a symbol was two big metal plates one of the kids in the back of the band smacked together at the end of "Stars and Stripes Forever." A metaphor was one of those things that blinked at the railroad crossing to warn everyone that a train was coming. Irony was something dug in the big open ore pits up around Hibbing and Chisholm, and a paradox was two guys that worked together at the local medical clinic. Figurative language was what Peggy Fleming skated in the ice during her compulsory routine.

I spent two days defining these terms. I covered the board with brilliant examples. I sang, I danced, I dramatized the differences between literal and figurative language. We put body parts on parade. I drew pictures of a "head band," "running nose," "toe nails," and "tongue lashing."

I told them the story about the Spanish Conquistadors who wanted gold and the Aztecs, who captured a few of the greedy guys, tied them spread-eagle to the ground, melted some gold, and poured it down their throats. "Now that's irony," I pontificated. "They wanted gold and they got it."

"See that piece of cotton with the red, white, and blue stripes and all those five pointed objects? We labeled that cloth hanging on the end of the stick f-l-a-g. Then we agreed that piece of fabric would become the symbol of our country. We could have tied Coke bottles and Pennzoil cans together and labeled them a 'flandsham,' but we decided on the flag instead. The object is a symbol because we agreed it was."

I threw out one brilliant example after another. Finally, we were ready to read the first paragraph of *The Pearl*.

Our discussions about the book's themes went nowhere. "Mr. Melchior, what the heck is Steinbeck talking about in this introduction?"

"Ya, what's all this stuff about allegory? And what's a symbol again?"

"You said this story is about us. No way. It's about this guy named Kino who lives in Mexico and finds a big pearl. I've never been to Mexico and my name sure ain't Kino."

"Me neither. I don't live in a hut near the ocean, diving for oysters for a living."

"What do you mean when you say, 'We all dive for pearls,' and 'Mother Nature demands we give our pearls to her'?"

How could Kino and Juan's story be their story as well? Day after day I struggled to draw parallels between their lives and the lives of Steinbeck's characters. Then I had an idea. I asked my ninth graders if they would be Wanks for a week.

"What's a Wank? Is this another one of your crazy ideas?" they asked.

The following article was published on May 1, 1968, in *Read: The Magazine for Reading and English*, American Education Publications, Xerox. (The names of the students have been changed.)

Meet the Wanks

It was announcement time at Metcalf Junior High School in Burnsville, Minnesota. Mr. Thomas Melchior, ninth grade English teacher, came on the public address system. "Some of my students will be doing a project in English. You will recognize them by the yellow basketball tops they'll be wearing this week. I am asking your cooperation in setting these people apart from the rest of the student body.

"They will be knows as Wanks. W-a-n-k-s. They have been told that they are not to speak until spoken to, drink only from the third floor water fountain, and eat last in the lunchroom. You may help see that these restrictions are observed."

The Wanks pose for Read Magazine, 1968.

That was all that was said. But a great deal more followed. The Wanks in their yellow basketball jerseys were spit upon, shoved against lockers, cornered in the halls, called names, and openly snubbed at social and sports events during the week.

Read: What was the purpose of your project?

Melchior: It began as an introduction to the themes in John Steinbeck's novel *The Pearl*. We are a suburban school close to Minneapolis and many of our students come from middle class or wealthy homes. They had little idea what Kino's life would be like.

I wanted them to begin to understand Kino, the poor Indian fisherman. I thought this could be accomplished by having the students be set apart by their yellow jerseys and be subjected to unfair discrimination. I really had no idea the student body would carry the idea so far. I was shocked—we all were—at how quickly some of the students jumped at the opportunity to be mean.

Read: How did the Wanks react to the persecution? Did they fight back or try to tell off their antagonists?

Melchior: No, we discussed this and agreed that since individuals such as Kino really couldn't retaliate, they couldn't either. This passiveness turned out to be the hardest part of the experiment. After the first day the Wanks realized that they had to have some defense. That's how their secret language came about.

Wank Talk

Melchior: We had studied that minorities frequently have an in-group language that binds them together and excludes others. Teenagers use slang expressions, which keep adults out of their world. We decided to see if such language would work for us. We developed a simple language code.

In place of "hi" or "hello," the Wanks substituted "Tra La La Boom De Aye." "Good-bye" or "so long" was replaced by "Last Train to Clarksville" (a popular song in the 60s). The principal was called "Rolls Royce," the assistant principal "Cadillac." All the teachers were called "Chevrolets."

Seventh graders were called "morts," eighth graders, "merts," and fellow ninth graders were called "glerts."

Most of the expressions were retaliatory remarks for insults made against the members of the class. 'Cut the apple' replaced 'Shut up.' "Simon and Garfunkle" meant "You're ugly." "Insect world" replaced "You're buggin' me." "You make me sick" was replaced by "The Mamas and the Papas."

The most drastic retort was "Yellow submarine," which meant "Take a long walk to the land below in which the fire never goes out."

Read: Did the language succeed?

Melchior: It succeeded almost too well. The kids who taunted the Wanks got really angry when they were answered in this code. One Wank girl was told, "You say that to me again and you'll get your head bashed against a locker." The nonwanks were very suspicious of the language and wanted to know what was being said. Suddenly they were on the outside and they didn't like it.

Read: Were the Wanks able to laugh off the persecution or did they take it seriously?

Melchior: The project was strictly on a volunteer basis, so any of the class members could drop out at any time. Some people dropped out the first day. But perhaps they got as much from the experiment as the kids who lasted the whole week.

One of the boys was taunted shortly after he left the classroom the first day. He punched the kid in the face, whipped off his jersey, threw it on the floor, and growled, "I'm not takin' anymore of that crap." After class Patty bent down to pick up some books from the bottom of her locker. A student walked behind her and shoved her into the locker. Several students spit on the Wanks. The Wanks were especially disturbed by the way some of their friends acted. They couldn't help taking the insults personally.

Read: Did all the students treat the Wanks badly?

Melchior: Oh, no! As a matter of fact, most acted as they do normally. A few students came up to me and said they couldn't take part in the experiment because they couldn't bring themselves to exclude the Wanks. These are the same students who would be concerned for anyone who was being treated unfairly. After school the day Patty was smashed into her locker, her best friend stormed into my room and read me the riot act. "You can't do that to these kids," she said. "I'm Marilyn, Patty's best friend, and I won't allow her to be hurt."

What a grand moment! Marilyn was in another one of my classes. She wrapped her arms around her books and stared at me. Time after time her glasses slid down her nose as she fired at me with both barrels. She pushed the glasses back and never missed a shot.

"When she paused to reload, I explained that I had no intention of hurting anyone and that Patty had taken off her Wank jersey. Then I said, "I want to tell you, Marilyn, that with a friend like you, Patty is a very lucky person. I tip my hat to you. Few ninth graders would have the courage to confront a teacher and speak out as articulately and passionately as you have. I'm proud of you.

Another Wank said, "I didn't like to be kicked and hit and pushed around. It wasn't fair. I really got the point of what discrimination is all about."

On the other hand, meanness toward the Wanks came from students who are generally unpleasant characters. This experiment gave them a chance to pick on a defenseless group.

Read: How did the Wanks feel when the experiment was over?

Melchior: One boy said, "I'm not as biased as I was before, but just wait 'til I get my hands on that guy who shoved me."

Generally, however, the students felt they understood much better what it was like to be different. At the end of the week, one of the Wanks commented about a student who had problems with weight and complexion. "I don't know how he can stand the ridicule. I'm going to try to stick by him."

One of the Wank girls mentioned a skinny girl in her physical education class who is picked on constantly. The Wank said she wouldn't pick on the girl anymore and would try to get others to stop.

Another Wank said, "I didn't like to be kicked and hit and pushed around. It wasn't fair. I really got the point of what discrimination is all about."

When we began the week, we didn't think about the experiment in terms of simply racial prejudice. Kino and Juana are attacked by their own people. However, the kids were called racial names.

Read: Would you please sum up the experiment?

Melchior: It was a valuable experience for all of us. We saw how quickly discrimination became persecution and that the basis for it can be as unfounded as a yellow basketball jersey or physical features.

We also learned that language is a very personal and powerful tool. It can be created and manipulated by anyone. It can hurt. It can isolate. It can be a means of defining one's identity and protecting that identity.

Read: If you had known then what you know now, would you do the experiment again?

Melchior: Yes, I think the experiment was truly educational. The Wanks learned about people—how they act and react, how they feel, and how they think.

I never did the Wank experiment again. As I think about *Read's* final question thirty-two years later, I'm not so certain I would say, "Yes." Fear walked beside me every moment during Wank Week.

Rae Ann remembers:

Thirty-three years after Wank Week, I contacted Rae Ann to ask her what she remembered about the experiment.

Rae Ann, grade 9

Being a Wank was very enlightening. It really opened my eyes. I don't remember *The Pearl* as well as the experiment. I never realized that people would treat others the way we were treated. Even though the experiment was artificial, it felt real. For us Wanks it was real for a week. When we started, most of us never realized what we were walking into. If we had, maybe we wouldn't have done it. Once I was in it I didn't want to quit.

One day I was late for the bus because we had to be last for everything. The bus driver was ready to go, so he shut the door. I had to walk home. He wouldn't open the door because I was a Wank. I suppose someone told him why I was wearing the yellow vest.

The next week when I wasn't a Wank, I asked him, "How come you didn't let me on the bus?" and he said, "Because of that experiment. You weren't supposed to get any special treatment."

I used our language, which made the other kids angry because they didn't know what we were saying. Having our language may have made things worse. They resented that and were offended by not knowing. They wanted to know what we were saying. Having our own language gave us power. It was a bond.

It hurt my feelings that a lot of my so-called friends who weren't Wanks treated me the way they did. They were my friends and all of a sudden they were my enemies. They became different. Perhaps I was more defensive. Perhaps they felt threatened or left out, but they certainly treated us differently. We didn't anticipate that reaction.

The experiment didn't change our friendships in the long run, but during that week the reactions of the people I was close to were really surprising. They seemed to enjoy making us go to the end of the line. I got the feeling they enjoyed watching us go through the ordeal. It gave them power over us. They dominated us and made us feel inferior. Someone I had been good friends with wouldn't talk to me. It was the first time I saw people being truly mean. I didn't think that was normal. I didn't want to know that.

After thirty-three years I remember that week more vividly than anything else in school.

Showdown at the Hanging Tree

Jerry Loftus was my student teacher in the spring of 1966. He was teaching Walter Van Tilburg Clark's novel, *The Ox Bow Incident,* to my last hour ninth-grade English class. The plot of the novel: Someone has been rustling cattle. Three strangers are accused and hanged by a mob of men. Shortly after the hanging, the real rustlers are caught.

Is This Story Relevant?

"I don't know what's happening," Jerry said, "but I can't get them interested in the key themes of the book. They're bored. They seldom volunteer and I end up doing all the talking. They can't seem to make the connections between the book and their lives."

"What do you want them to see?" I asked.

"We have just finished discussed the hanging scene and why the men acted as a mob and killed innocent people. I'd like them to discuss the ease with which we snap to judgment. I want to reinforce the idea that good people can, in intense moments, be swayed by emotions and not facts. I want them to make connection between what happened in the book and what's happening in their lives. They may not hang anyone from a tree, but we are all capable of rash judgment and 'hanging' others. Everyday someone is 'lynched' by gossip and innuendo. These themes certainly apply to teenagers. Got any ideas?" he asked.

We discussed several ideas and settled on a plan. We decided to dramatize our version of *The Ox Bow Incident.* We needed another player, so we asked Scott, a student in the class, to be part of our charade. He agreed.

The secretary's voiced blared over the intercom, "Mr. Loftus, this is Mrs. Stumm calling from the principal's office. Is Scott in your classroom today?"

"Yes, he is," said Jerry.

"Thank you," she said.

Three minutes later I charged into Jerry's classroom, shoved aside desks and plowed my way to Scott's desk. I grabbed him by the front of his shirt and lifted him out of his desk. I held him in front of me, nose to nose. "This is it, Scott. I've had it with you. I'm not taking any more guff from you."

As I dragged him out to the hallway, he yelled, "Wait! What's going on here? I didn't do nothin'!"

Once we were in the hall and out of sight of the students, I let go. I pounded my fist against the lockers and yelled, "What's the matter with you, Scott? Everyday it's the same thing."

Scott played his part and shouted, "Ow! Ow! Stop shoving me."

"Don't talk back to me," I yelled. Bam! I smashed the locker again and he continued his Oscar-winning performance.

When I had charged into the room, one of Jerry's students who took daily attendance was standing next to the door. Throughout this whole ordeal she continued to take attendance. While Scott and I were acting, she backed out of the room and hung the attendance sheet in the grating of the door, but she never looked at us. She could have blown the entire ruse.

We faked our act a few more times. Then I shook Scott's hand and he headed for the library to wait out the storm. Jerry paced back and forth in front of the room, feigning frustration and planning his strategy. "This is wrong," he said to no one in particular. "This is not right. This does not show proper teacher behavior."

The class was stunned. No one said a word. Jerry looked at them, "What do you guys think? Did you see what just happened in here?" No one answered. He pressed them a bit harder. He paced a few more seconds. "Do you think it's O.K. for a teacher to act like that?" I heard a few students mumble "no" and "no way." He paced again. Suddenly he whirled and asked, "Did you see that?" he shouted. "Did you just see Mr. Melchior charge in here, kick desks, and assault Scott?" Silence. No one moved. The novel was coming alive.

Jerry went to work. "Well, did you? Don't just sit there. Did you see him grab Scott's shirt and scream at him? Did you see him drag Scott into the hall? Did you hear him smash Scott into the lockers? Do you think that's right? What? You can't speak?" Students squirmed and glanced at each other, but no one spoke.

He changed his tactic and singled out students. "Bill, you saw it. Should we do anything about this? Should we report Mr. Melchior to the principal?" Bill looked at the carpet.

"Well," needled Jerry, "what do you think, Al?" More carpet gazing. "Andy, how about you? What would you have done if he had done this to you? What do you think we should we do about this?" Silence.

"Heather, talk to me."

"I don't know," she said. "I've had Mr. Melchior as a teacher for two years and he seems like a good—"

"What are you talking about?" asked Jerry. "Didn't you see what he did?" He stood a foot from her desk.

"What about the rest of you? Are you all mug-wumpers, afraid to stand up for your convictions?" Each time a student expressed doubt about the incident or shied away from acting, he returned with something like, "Should we simply let this pass? What about poor Scott? What if this had happened to you? Perhaps we should just sit here and read and pretend nothing happened."

"I think we should report him to the principal," came a voice from the back of the room. "What he did was wrong," snapped Ann. "No teacher should get away with treating students like that."

"What should we do, Ann?" prodded Jerry.

"I think all of us should go down to the office," said Ann. "We all saw and heard what happened."

A few people mumbled dissent but Jerry challenged them and they agreed to follow. Ann led the charge with Jerry a few feet behind. Every student followed although a few dragged along at the rear.

We could hear them coming. They walked into the office, shocked to see me with the principal. "Can I help you?" he asked.

Jerry nodded to Ann. Her voice trembled. "Yes, we, we—I mean the class and I—well, we want to report—ah, tell you—ah, what happened in class today." She was in agony. Her eyes darted back and forth from the principal to Mr. Loftus. She never once looked at me.

She told the story, her voice quivering. When she described hearing me shove Scott into the lockers, I said, "Wait, are you certain that's what happened?" I asked the class to follow me into the hall. I slammed my fist against the locker and yelled, "What's the matter with you? Every day it's the same thing."

"Oh no," they groaned. "We've been had. It was all a set up." They thought for a second and said, "Where's Scott? He betrayed us."

Mr. Lofts had no difficulty discussing the themes of *The Ox Bow Incident*. Today some of his students might say they never fell for our trap, but they were all there in the principal's office.

Jennifer and Carla remember: Forty years later I spoke with two of the students who were in class that day. Jennifer, who is now working in law enforcement, said, "I will never forget that day. I think about the lessons we learned about mob psychology, rash judgment, and human weakness. I've seen all this so often in my job." She told the story in detail and named everyone involved.

Carla said, "I thought, oh, no, not you too. I was just beginning to trust you and then all that happened. I don't remember anything that we were supposed to have learned. All I could think about was that you were just like everybody else."

Subversive Activities

In 1967 Neil Postman and Charles Weingartner unloaded a barrage of criticism and guilt on teachers throughout the nation in their book, *Education as a Subversive Activity.* We were accustomed to periodic flogging, but this was different. Neil and Charles stripped our egos naked and tied us to the rack. Then they stretched us with accusations that the future would shock us because we had shielded children from the real world and educated our students for obsolescence. They tightened the ropes and exclaimed, "You have used fear as your primary teaching tactic. You have alienated your students. You have destroyed creativity because what you teach is irrelevant."

Postman and Weingartner's first chapter found a new name for an old problem. They claimed education needed new, finely tuned "crap detectors" to help us examine whether or not we were mired in the muck of nonlearning. They claimed that there was crap here, crap there, crap everywhere. They claimed we were working with malfunctioning crap detectors rooted in antiquity.

"Why," they asked, "can't you see that you are perpetuating a system for educating students for a world which no longer exists?"

When they had stretched us as far as they wanted, they cut our ropes and rolled us to the ground to be pressed. We moaned as they lowered the rock of guilt. "Why are you creating illusions of reality?" they cried.

"Please don't torture us any more," we pleaded. "Our load is heavy enough. If we have sinned, we'll repent. Tell us how to change. What is an education for today's world?"

Our department reeled under the accusations. Postman and Weingartner challenged us to be subversive and abandon the old philosophy. The resurrection of Bloom's taxonomy staggered us. We were bombarded by the "new" this and the "new" that. We blinked and transformational grammar, structural grammar, behavioral objectives, and devious tools for evaluating our performance appeared.

Federally funded programs gave birth to Project Minnesota, Project Euclid, Project Nebraska, and on and on. The school district was so interested in the "New English" that they flew the senior high department head and me to Euclid, Ohio, to examine their program.

The message from *Education as a Subversive Activity* was loud and clear: Change. Be relevant. These Harpies screamed, "What are you guys teaching those kids? Why are you teaching that crap? You're doing it all wrong! What can't Johnny and Jane read? Why can't they spell? Why can't they write? What are you doing teaching that old Latin-based grammar? Dump all that intransitive and transitive nonsense. Why can't *there* be a noun? It's a place isn't it? Doesn't describing the 'surface meaning' and 'deep meaning' preached by Noam Chomsky make more sense?"

Our critics harped day and night. "Abandon sentence diagramming. Analyze sentence construction using the new language of transformational grammar. Doesn't determiner + adjective + noun + be verb + adverb + ing action verb + noun + preposition + determiner adjective + noun describe 'The hostile cat is voraciously devouring the catnip for lunch' more clearly than the old grammar?"

"Haven't you read the latest research in the *English Journal*?" our critics wailed. Research proves that teaching grammar, usage, punctuation and syntax do not make people good writers. It's all a waste of time."

"Revolution," sang the Beatles.

"Hell, no, we won't go," chanted the Vietnam war protesters.

"God is dead," thundered the throng from Haight-Ashbury to Harvard to the Hallowed Halls of Burnsville.

"Revolution," screamed the gurus of American education. "Time for a change," screamed the textbook industry. "Chuck out those old anthologies and sink thousands into the 'new math' and the 'new grammar,'" implored Harcourt Brace, Holt, Reinhart, and Winston, and the rest of the big hitters.

"Make learning relevant," Neil and Charles implored, and we bowed to the gurus and the seers who could see through the fog and lead us on to glory. Although we wanted to wave our own flags and march in a parade yelling our righteous indignation, the more we examined their appeal for subversive action, the more we were convinced they were right.

"New English" at Nicollet Junior High

In 1968 we revised Nicollet Junior High's ninth grade language arts curriculum to make it relevant. We were no longer just going to talk about communication. We were going to "do" English. Accepting our mission to become subversive, we followed the commandments prescribed by Neil and Charles: We would ask more questions and avoid giving the answers so freely. We resolved to listen more carefully. We would make the study of media an integral part of our classes.

For years we teachers had gathered our five flocks daily and taught "English," which was whatever we wanted it to be. Open the door, close the door, teach the lesson, open the door, and close the door. Forty-eight minutes to pound in the rules of grammar, mechanics, and usage. Forty-eight minutes to read *The Pearl*, *The Pigman*, *That Was Then, This is Now*, and other classic novels no longer than 150 pages set in twelve-point type.

Teaching as a Subversive Activity challenged us to examine what we were teaching, why we were teaching, and how we were teaching. While Bob Dylan proclaimed, "The times, they are a changing," we decided it was time to examine our philosophy of "We do it this way because we've always done it this way."

"Induction by Seduction!" was the cry. The faculty met for early morning sessions to learn how to induce learning. Each morning a professor from Mankato State taught us about behavioral objectives. Once we had determined what was worth knowing, we wrote individualized packets for mechanics, usage, grammar, and sentence syntax. We wrote goals: Each student must score at least seventy-five percent on each unit. We created two or three additional units for each item, so the students who fell below seventy-five percent could study and re-take each unit again and again. Our office was filled with mountains of individualized units.

Individualized Apostrophe Unit: Once the students had read the instructions about how to use apostrophes, they did the exercises and then checked their answers in the back of the packet. Cheating flourished.

When my four-year-old grandson was given the problem of solving a maze puzzle, he immediately bypassed the entrance and went to the center of the maze. He quickly followed the path out the entrance.

With thirty-five students on their honor, many found the answers first and zipped out of the maze. The only problem was that when they took the test, they couldn't solve the maze. Before long the individualized packets disappeared.

"Doing" English

"How can we 'do' English'?" we asked. "How can we involve our students in this creative process?" We split the year into two semesters. During the first semester we pounded the "old English" into the minds of our students. Forty-eight minutes of grammar, writing, and literature, five days a week. We split the second semester into two quarters and offered all ninth graders the choice of two electives. We offered electives in acting, newspaper, radio, and filmmaking.

First, we turned a storage room in the back of the library office into a radio station. We built a long desk and cut two holes into the top. We scrounged up two 33 rpm turntables and stuck them into the holes. Next, we commandeered a mike from the music department, and a few electronic wizards hooked up the mike and turntables to the school's switchboard.

We announced to the staff and student body that NJHS would broadcast every hour on Thursdays and Fridays. Students formed groups of two or three. The rules of the Nicollet Broadcasting System: During the forty-eight minutes of broadcasting, students must speak for two thirds of the program. Only one third of the program may be filled with music. All students must write the script, and all students must speak. No profanity. No vulgarity. All music must be approved. No thirty-minute jams by Jimmy

Hendricks and his buddies. All programs must contain school news, interviews, editorials, and other written assignments. All written assignments must follow the rules of standard English usage. The forty-eight minutes must be timed accurately, avoiding dead-air time. A final copy of the script must be presented and approved before each program.

Teachers and students who wished to listen to the radio programs called the switchboard and Maxine threw the switch.

In the newspaper class students studied editorials, news reporting, editorial cartooning, variety articles, sports reporting. They wrote and produced as many editions of their own work as time allowed. Many students wrote feature articles about school life for the local newspapers. Several students learned how to develop black and white photographs to accompany the newspaper articles.

In the drama class students wrote, directed, and produced skits and one-act plays for seventh-, eighth-, and ninth grade classes. A few groups performed for the nearby elementary school.

The fourth elective was film making. The school district bought several super eight-movie cameras and two projectors. Forty-two students crammed into my room, which became a writing studio, a film set, and editing room. Groups of students sketched storyboards for each film. Most of the movies, westerns, adventures, and mysteries, were filmed outside the school. The school paid for all the film, so we made certain every movie was scripted to the second. There were very few retakes. Once the film was developed, students edited each reel to create their final work of art.

At the end of the semester, students in the acting classes performed for all the students in language arts. The newspaper class published its final edition, and the radio class bid fond farewells.

During the final days of the semester, we conducted a film festival. Students showed their work to all seventh-, eighth-, and ninth graders who then voted for the best film, the best animated film, the best actor and actress as well as the best supporting roles, best editing, and other awards.

During the last hour of the final day of school, a day usually filled with water gun fights, paper tearing contests, and wild animal behavior, we gathered all the students for the Academy Awards Ceremony.

Rod Ellickson's jazz band rocked the joint as the students filed in. We made the Oscars out of old film, reels, broken camera parts, blocks of wood, anything we could find that related to the class. Then we spray-painted them Oscar gold. We stacked the golden trophies on the table, so the students could examine them as they walked into the lunchroom.

"Welcome movie fans," announced the master of ceremonies. "We are here today to honor our film greats. The first award will be given to the short film, which received the most votes." The band played a fanfare and we announced the name. The award winner walked to the podium and accepted the trophy. We made each presentation a major production.

After the final award we announced, "And now we will entertain you with a lip-sync by the Mamas and the Papa's. Mrs. K. will solo as Mama Cass." We grabbed towels and danced the twist like Chubby Checker while Mrs. K., who was six months pregnant, strutted her stuff.

For the grand finale we lined up like the Rockettes and danced as the words blared from the speakers: "Consider yourself at home. Consider yourself one of the family. We've taken to you somehow—" We climbed the bleachers and shook hands with our saints and sinners. Some laughed and some cried. A few would return to visit, but their lives as junior high school students ended when the last notes drifted toward the ceiling.

Assistant principals John and Burt and Principal Jerry help me lead the crowd with some fancy maraca shaking, hand clapping and guitar playing.

Bonnie gives the award. Kathy, Diane, and I cheer the victor.

Forty-two students in film making; Drawing by JiiJi Aaker

Mr. B.'s Bombers

Knock, knock, knock.

"Yes? May I help you?" I asked.

"My name is Heather and I'm from Mr. B.'s seventh-grade English class. He said he wants to challenge your class."

"What do you mean, 'challenge us'?" Are you talking about a spell-down? A vocabulary contest?"

"No, we want to challenge your class to a bowling contest."

"What? Is he serious? A bowling contest?"

"Yes, all the kids in our class want to challenge your 'gifted students.' We think we can beat you."

Mr. B. and I scheduled the bowl-off at the Savage Bowling Alley for four o'clock one Tuesday in December. Somehow we finagled a bus to take the two classes to Savage and to pick us up after our duel. I often wondered which budget the principal dipped into to finance our escapade.

The kids scrambled out of the bus and assaulted the bowling alley. "Hey, outta the way. Come on, girls. Stop messin' around. Lisa, think you can even lift a bowling ball? It's heavier than you."

"Buzz off, creep."

"Hey, I claim this ball."

"I got first dibs on it. Find another one."

"We got these two lanes."

"Don't you have any smaller shoes? These are way too big!"

"What are you, a munchkin?"

"Ah, stuff it, creepo."

"Boy, are we gonna whip you guys."

"I like this pink ball with all the sparkly stuff. Is it a ladies' ball?"

"It matches your blouse, Sandy. Go for it."

"Hey, Jack, you got muscles enough to lift that thing?"

"I'll beat your butt. That's for sure."

"OK, everyone. Quiet down, please."

"Hey, Mr. Melchior, can I get a coke and some chips?"

"Ya, me too. Me too, me too, me too, me too, me too, me too, me too, me too, me too, me too, me too, me too."

"OK, now that you're all hyped on caffeine and sugar, let's get organized," I said. "You have your teams. Now pick out your alleys. Remember one of Mr. B.'s teams bowls against one of mine. One person from each team keeps score. Everyone checks the score. Don't ask Mr. B. or me to settle any scoring disputes. And remember, the busses will be here at 5:30, so we must be finished by 5:20. Have fun."

In what became known as the First Battle of Savage Lanes, Mr. B.'s Bombers faltered badly and lost by several hundred pins. Taunting their victims, the victors paraded their score sheets around the lobby as if they had won a world championship.

The moment we stepped onto the bus, the students gossiped about boy- and girlfriends, chatted about sports, and worked on homework. A few die-hard winners tried to stir up Mr. B.'s team, but no one was interested. By the time we arrived at school, several were sleeping.

February
Knock, knock, knock.

"Hi, Heather, what can I do for you?"

"We want to challenge you to a rematch. We think you were just lucky last time, and we're out for revenge."

"Just a second, Heather. Class, Mr. B.'s class thinks you were just lucky last time. Do you want to accept their challenge for the Second Battle of Savage Lanes?"

Mr. B. and his class caught us completely off guard. When they took off their winter coats and sweaters, every student was wearing a T-shirt with Mr. B.'s Bombers written across the front in magic marker. They cheered, "Bombers, Bombers, that's our team. Think you can beat us? What a dream!"

The Bombers meant business. They kept a running total of all four contests. Guzzling Cokes and chomping on Snicker bars, they moved from one game to the other, cheering on their teammates. By the sixth frame of the third game, the Bombers gave up hope. They suffered another ignominious defeat in the Second Battle of Savage Lanes, losing by more than three hundred pins.

May
Knock, knock, knock.

"Hi, Heather, how've you been? How are the Bombers doing? Ready for summer vacation?"

"Hi, Mr. Melchior. I'm pretty good. Mr. B.'s Bombers want to challenge you guys one more time."

"Bowling again?"

"Naw, we want to play you in softball, using one of those big sixteen-inch balls."

"Just a second, Heather. Class, Mr. B.'s Bomber's wants to challenge you to a softball game with the big ball. Do you want to accept the challenge?"

With two victories under their belts, my students decided it was their turn to psyche out the Bombers, who were grasping for a final bit of glory. They wrote Melchior's Marauders across the fronts of their tee shirts with bright magic markers.

The Bombers were practicing when the Marauders made their appearance. Mike Lindquist, the best trumpet player in the school band, led the team into battle, blaring out an heroic fight song. We marched out single file, lining up from the tallest to the shortest. We strutted, waved banners, hooted and catcalled to the Bombers.

By the third inning the Bombers were buried. They had no more luck with the sixteen-inch softball than they did with the sixteen-pound bowling ball. They bobbled ground ball, muffed easy popups, overran fly balls, and rarely made an accurate throw. The Marauders blasted line drives and circled the bases at will. By the fifth inning the Bombers had fallen apart. We claimed victory number three.

The next morning I noticed someone sitting in a chair in front of Mr. B.'s room. His legs were sprawled out and his head hung as if he had been sleeping there all night. When I walked a few steps closer I recognized Mr. B.'s handiwork. He had stuffed a pair of sweatpants with rags. Pinned to the pants legs were two tennis shoes. Mr. B.'s Bomber T-shirt was pulled over a sweatshirt also stuffed with rags. Pinned to the shirtsleeves were two gloves. He made the head out of rags and topped it with an old baseball cap. From a distance his work looked very much like one of his students taking a nap. Pinned to Bomber's shirt was a large sign that read: TEAM FOR SALE.

Nicollet Junior High School logo
Drawing by Ollie Kaldahl

Composition

Teaching Writing

Once I left elementary school I never wrote another narrative until I began teaching. No stories about what I did during the summer. No fictitious accounts about how I made the major leagues with my blazing fastball. No anecdotes about dating, working, or defeating dragons.

I attended two high schools and every minute in English class was spent reading literature or doing grammar exercises. In my senior year we studied British literature and underlined phrases and clauses in *Keys to Essential English*. Four years later after I had received my B.A. in English, I fell into the same trap and taught seniors British literature and used *Keys to Essential English*. Underline, fill in the blank, and write the correct letter on the blank. Nothing had changed.

Nowhere on my undergraduate and graduate transcripts is there listed a course on how to write or how to teach writing. I did take a course entitled Rhetoric during a summer institute at Boston University in 1965. We spent most of the time listening to the professor extol the virtues of formal rhetoric. We went to listen to Noam Chomsky analyze surface-and deep-structure sentence meaning. All that erudite theory, however, didn't help me when I returned to teach junior high students that fall.

Of course I did write papers in many of my undergraduate and graduate classes. Facing the daunting task of analyzing some of Descartes' ideas, I plagiarized the life out of several books and threw together a seventeenth-rate exposition. I analyzed poems, explored Odysseus' reasons for defying Poseidon, and examined other esoteric topics. In graduate school I compared the style of William Dean Howells with that of William James. I analyzed the symbolism in Ibsen's *An Enemy of the People*, and I compared the intellectual differences between the gifted and the rest of us.. In my composition final in a graduate program designed to prepare me to become a better secondary English teacher, I summarized my tasks as the stage manager for the college production of *All's Well That Ends Well*.

The directions for each writing assignment were always the same: "Write a paper about—. Make certain it is well written." Never once during all those semesters did anyone ever say, "Now here are some hints about how to write a good paper." They could just as well have said, "There's a lake. Jump right in and swim like an Olympic champion."

The Other Side of the Desk

During my first year of teaching, I taught like most of the other Pavlovian graduates. We analyzed literature. We wrote expositions about the meaning of poems, the reasons why Macbeth became obsessed with power, and how Jonathan Swift used satire to shame his Englishmen into feeding the starving Irish people.

I broke the spell the day I announced to my college prep seniors, "The heart of good writing is showing and not telling. You must provide details," I pontificated. "If you are describing someone, I should be able to pick that person out of a crowd because you have shown him to me. Details, details, details. Show. Don't tell."

I then walked around the room and placed one soda cracker on each student's desk. "Now, these crackers are like people. Although they have much in common, each is unique. Write a paragraph in which you describe your cracker. Then we will mix five or six of the crackers together. You will read your paper and the rest of your group should be able to identify your cracker because you have described it in great detail."

What wailing and gnashing of teeth! What teacher character assassination! At the end of the assignment, most of the students ate their crackers. Jim K. was one of the students in the class of '58. The last time we met we shook hands, exchanged polite formalities, and talked about our kids. Then he looked at me for several minutes. "What?" I asked.

"I still can't believe it," he said. "You had us write about a damn cracker!" Forty-one years later he was still complaining about the assignment.

In the 1990s a tidal wave of composition books flooded elementary and secondary classrooms. Textbook publishers figured out what many elementary and secondary writing teachers had discovered long ago: You can't get someone to bake a cake by simply demanding that you want a good cake.

One day I came to class with a baseball and flipped it to one of the eighth grade girls. "Throw me a curve ball," I demanded.

"I can't"

"Come on. You can do it. Give it a try."

"I CAN'T!" she exclaimed!" squirming in her desk.

"Why not," I asked.

"I don't know how."

"Sure you do," I insisted. "Everybody can throw a curve."

"I CAN'T THROW A CURVE! NO ONE EVER SHOWED ME HOW!"

"Well, this is how you do it. Hold the ball like this. Place you thumb here, your index finger here, and your middle finger here. Then—."

When elementary, secondary, and college teachers, and textbook publishers figured out that teaching a student how to write a composition was the same as teaching an athlete how to throw a curve, the writing process was born.

The Writing Process (The Simplified Version)
I. Pre-writing: Do a lot of stuff that helps you think of a topic.
II. Organize: Make certain what you write has a beginning, middle, and end with lots of stuff in between.
III. Write.
IV. Edit. Clean up all the writing "zits." Read the paper aloud and give it the tongue test. If your words make your tongue happy, then you probably have something worth keeping. If your tongue isn't happy, perhaps the paper needs some work. Make certain that your paper contains at least five sentences that you would invite to Prom. Write at least ten words to which you would tip your hat. Peer Editing: Con some of the smart guys into reading your paper.
V. Polish and Present.

A Composition Allegory
Pre-writing
"Dad, what do you think about us making some maple syrup?" asked Paul, age thirteen:

"What do you mean?" I asked.

"I saw these guys on television tappin' maple trees and makin' maple syrup. We've got maple trees just like that. Can we try it?"

Organization
We bought several dowels four feet long and one inch in diameter. Then we cut them into four-inch lengths. Paul cut a notch at the end of each so he could hang his buckets. We drilled a hole down the middle of each piece of dowel.

Next, we gathered every gallon ice cream bucket in the county. We found our old, blue-enameled canning kettle buried under years of lost treasure in the basement.

Paul drilled holes in the maple trees, using my dad's twenty-five-year-old hand auger and drill bits. Then he pounded in the wooden spigots and waited for the woods to awaken.

Write
The spring sun melted the snow and turned the floor of the woods to mush. The sap surged from the roots to feed the bark and bud the leaves. On its way up the tree, some of the sap found the spigots. We stood on the deck in the spring silence and listened to the first drops of maple sap tap, tap, tap, on the bottoms of the plastic buckets. The Melchior Maple Syrup Company was in business.

Paul drills and Marty supervises.

My wife couldn't stand the chaos, so she got into the car and visited her friend in town. That was a mistake.

We set up the boiling operation on the kitchen stove. Our cauldron was the four-gallon canning kettle. The old kettle may have thought we subjected it to bubbling hell when we canned tomatoes, but that was nothing compared to Paul's torture.

Paul and his brother Marty, age ten, slipped and stumbled through the melting snow and gooey black dirt, gathering buckets of sap. They tromped mud across the family room carpet and the kitchen floor, tracking in soggy leaves and dog poop. With each step they splashed a bit of their precious elixir over the lip of the buckets onto the carpet.

For the next three hours we splashed, dumped and boiled; boiled, dumped and splashed. "Boil, boil, toil and trouble, cauldron burn and cauldron bubble," I chanted, just to make my sons think I was concocting more than pure maple syrup.

Whenever the sap boiled down and we could see the maple syrup forming on the bottom of the kettle, one of the bucket brigade dumped in more sap.

Finally they maple trees gave up. We had emptied every bucket from every tree we had tapped. The three of us stood around the stove watching the sap disappear and the brown syrup begin to congeal on the bottom of our cauldron.

Just then my wife walked in. "My, God," she screamed. "Look at this place! What have you guys done?"

We had turned the kitchen into a tropical Rainforest. For more than 180 minutes we had sent hot steam to the far corners of the forest. Rivulets of water ran down the window. It looked as if it were raining inside the house.

The walls were sweating from the workout, and tiny streams worked their way down the birch cabinets.

"You've ruined my kitchen. Look up there. The wallpaper is ruined."

Sure enough. The wallpaper was so sopping wet it had begun a slow, pasty slide down the wall.

The Final Draft

We sat at the table and stared at the pancakes steaming on our plates. Paul cradled the tiny cream pitcher that held the precious syrup. We passed the pitcher to each other and poured the pure maple syrup on our pancakes. We ate in silence and grinned, thinking nothing we had ever eaten tasted so delicious.

Cookie Compositions

My sophomore Honors Composition class was a disaster. We were halfway through the semester and the students were still turning in papers that were stinking up my desk. It would have taken a new potion of Oxy 323 to clean up all the writing zits. Forget about the quality of their ideas.

Their compositions were ugly. I constantly reminded them that their papers ought to be attractive. "Marty, look at your paper. Would you ask it to the prom? It's wearing worn-out tennis shoes and its two front teeth have been knocked out."

I threatened, I joked, I feigned heart attacks. Nothing worked. Billy ripped out his composition, leaving a third of his masterpiece still wired to the notebook. Martha, more concerned about how she looked than about the beauty of her paper, absentmindedly blotted her lipstick in the lower corner. Andy's contribution was patriotic. He wrote the first American flag paper I had ever seen. One line was written in red ink, the next in blue. Red, blue, red, blue.

"God bless America and all composition teachers," I sighed.

Half of Angela's paper was written with fiery passion. Unfortunately, the passionate part was a love note, which she had written on the back of her English assignment.

"Where's your paper, Tony, and where is your book?" I asked, falling into the old trap.

"Don't you worry, Mr. Melchior. I've got it right here." He reached into his back pocket and grabbed his "polished" composition. What had once been a sheet of smooth, white paper was now a two-inch by two-inch square reeking of french fries. He unfolded his masterpiece with the tender care of a gold miner sharing his secret map of a treasure in the Sierra Madre Mountains "There you are, Mr. Melchior, just like you asked."

It was time for action.

The Contest

"Could I have your attention, please," I announced."Halloween is next Wednesday. We are going to hold the First Annual Halloween Writing Contest. Since we have been working on exposition, you are to begin with a thesis and then support that thesis with well-organized support.

"Here is your thesis: Ladies, you are to explain why you should be chosen Witch of the Year. *Witch* in this case refers to a shrew, harpy, or battle-ax—someone with a "witch-like" disposition. Gentlemen, you are to explain why you should be chosen Warlock of the Year—someone with an equally irritating and disgusting personality. You may use both fact and fiction. Your task is to show that your recent obnoxious disposition, irritating idiosyncrasies, careless hygiene, and odious personality entitles you to wear this year's crown. All papers are due on Monday.

"Each composition must contain a minimum of 200 words. Organize your argument and provide specific supporting examples of your dastardly actions. Proofread carefully, edit your rough draft, and type your final copy. Make certain your paper is as zit free as Snow White's complexion. Do not wrinkle, fold, or mutilate your paper. Please do not use it as a napkin or Kleenex. When you place it on my desk, make certain it is as pure as a senior's soul.

"I will select five witch and five warlock semi-finalist papers that present the most convincing arguments, and then we will have a Halloween read-off. After I have read the papers, you will choose the winners, who will receive their prizes. During this time I shall treat you to cookies and hot apple cider."

The night before the great event, I selected the ten best papers. Then I asked my wife, "How can I make cookies that are half-baked?"

"What do you mean?" she asked.

"I want to bake cookies that look terrible, are pock-marked, have gooey insides, but still look good enough for the students to eat."

"Take a few of those Pillsbury cookie rolls and cut them. Lay them on a cookie sheet and place them close enough so they run together. Then bake them for a few minutes less than the directions require."

I pulled those golden brown cookies out of the oven. They looked wonderful. Instead of individual circles, the sheet was one massive cookie. I stuck a toothpick into the center and drew it out. Perfect. Gooey dough clung to the toothpick. I then cut the cookie-lake into squares and baked them for a few more seconds to seal the sides. I then placed each square on a napkin to hide the surprise inside.

"Look at these horrible cookies," I said to my daughter, who was also a sophomore. "I can't wait to see my students' reactions when I pass them out."

"Dad," she said in all her sophomore wisdom, "those cookies won't even faze sophomore boys. They'll eat anything."

I placed the cookies gently on the back seat and loaded the gallon jugs of cider, paper plates, and napkins. I made a quick stop at the bakery and headed for school.

The Cookie Composition Countdown

I read the ten papers and the winners received their certificates for the all-expense-paid tour of beautiful downtown Savage. "Now as I promised," I announced, "we are going to celebrate this writing contest with cookies and cider." Since the class was the period before lunch and many students never ate breakfast, they salivated at the mention of cookies and cider.

I knew I could never control my laughter if I passed out the cookies, so I asked a few students to pass them out while I poured the cider. As I poured, I watched the students' reactions. My daughter was right, of course. Most of the boys wolfed down the cookies in great gulps. A few of the girls picked up their treats, pressed them, smelled them, checked to see if anyone was watching, and slid the half-baked cookies under their napkins. A few bit into the cookies and stopped. They spit out the cookie as quietly and politely as possible. The guys chomped away.

I stood up, looked at the class, and said, "I'm really disappointed."

"Why," they asked. "What's the matter?"

"I know those cookies are terrible. But some of you are eating them anyway and some of you know they are awful but you said nothing."

"Ya, they're really bad," they whined. "What's the matter with them?" By now even the boys were feeling sick. Some squeezed my revenge and the insides dribbled out onto their desks. "You tricked us. You deliberately fed us those rotten things. What's the big idea? Teachers aren't supposed to do that kinda stuff."

"So did you like what I gave you? Well, those cookies are just like the papers you have been turning in for me to 'eat.' They were half-baked, half-done, pathetic excuses for the real thing. I didn't do my job and I tricked you and you don't like it. If I tried to feed you another one of my cookies, you wouldn't accept it. My friends, that's what is going to happen in here from now on. You better bake your compositions well, or I'll say the same thing to you as you have said about my cookies. 'I'm not eating any more of that garbage.'" I walked over to the closet and took out four white bags filled with huge chocolate chip, peanut butter, and oatmeal and raisin cookies that I had purchased at the bakery. I held up a huge M&M chocolate chip cookie. "See this?" I said. "This is a real composition. This is the only kind of cookie I will accept from you from now on."

The baking improved dramatically for the remainder of the semester.

In 1944 at the age of eight, I was already a "superb" letter writer, mastering mechanics, spelling, and coherence. My Uncle Art was serving in the Navy and I thought I could put his bike to good use. I didn't get Art's "bick."

Grading

I penciled in the last dot on my computer grading sheets and walked down to the main office. I laid the sheets on the stack with hundreds of others. Another semester was history.

I walked into the hall and stepped into the horde of students moving to the gym like an agitated river. On the last hour of the last day of the term, we were sending yet another black and gold team off to battle. Students who have just finished two days of testing are ready to party.

Instead of sitting in my assigned seat across the gym in the sophomore section, I sat on the first row of bleacher seats next to the exit. I planned to slip out early to prepare for my Monday classes.

He slipped into the small space next to me just as the cheerleaders pom-pomed onto the court. The pep band hit their first notes. The students jumped up and sang the fight song. As we were sitting down, he leaned toward me and said, "Mr. Melchior, I just gotta tell you I loved your class."

I was stunned. Just minutes earlier I had penciled in his grade of F. For twelve weeks he rarely scored above D-. He failed the final exam miserably. Out of more than two thousand points he averaged about fifty percent. There was no question in my mind that he had learned little if anything.

Instead of replying, "That's great!" or "I'm glad to hear that," I thought of the F and blurted, "Really?"

"Yeah," he yelled two inches from my ear, "I thought about signing up for it, but everybody said it was so hard, being an honors class and all. I'm not much of an English student, never get much above a C in the regular English classes."

The Bravettes ran onto the floor, knelt, and touched their foreheads to the floor. They swung into their Rockettes can-can routine and the kids cheered. The sophomore boys in my section stood on the benches and tried to whistle, but they were salivating so badly from ogling the girls whirling before them they could barely manage a tweet.

"Yeah," he yelled, "everybody said it was so hard, all that writing and tons of reading, and all those Greek names and stuff. But then some of my friends said, "Yeah, it's tough but we really like it."

The Bravettes pranced off the floor and the cheerleaders began their favorite yell. They were led by one of the math teachers, who yelled, "You guys over there, you yell 'black.' You junior and seniors over here, you yell 'gold.' OK, now let's hear you."

The teacher grabbed the mike and looked at the students. They knew the yell. They were hyped and conditioned. "I say 'black.' You say 'gold.'"

"Black," screamed the sophomores.

"Gold," screamed the juniors and seniors.

"Yell when I point," he demanded. "Now let's hear you! I say 'black,' you say 'gold.'"

"Black!"

"Gold!"

"Ya, well, I decided to take it anyway, so I signed up and I'm glad I did."

"Again. I say 'black.' You say 'gold.'"

"Black!"

"Gold!"

"Tell me what you learned."

"I say Burnsville. You say 'Braves.'"

"Burnsville!"

"Braves!"

The band played its favorite jazz piece, a four-minute drum battle.

He leaned toward me. "It seemed everything we studied was speaking about my life. I loved all that Joseph Campbell stuff about how life is a journey and how we all go through the rites of passage and face the dragons of life. That's like my battle with drugs. They're my demon. I'm Luke Skywalker trying to find myself, battling the dark side. That was cool."

"What else?" I asked.

The cheerleaders circled the gym again, and executed several of their gymnastic routines.

"I loved all that stuff about archetypes," he continued, "and how they are found everywhere—in our dreams, in movies, books, poems, and music. I really liked the day we went to the Walker Sculpture Garden."

The coach walked into the center circle to talk about the big game. "I want to thank all the other coaches who have done such a great job. I also want to thank the guys on the scout team. They have really—"

"Tell me about your favorite sculpture."

"No problem. *Prometheus and the Vulture*. I'm both Prometheus and the vulture. That sculpture was about life, about the power of good and evil. I hope Prometheus doesn't lose his strength. I hope I don't lose my power."

"I also want to thank the Bravettes, the band, and the cheerleaders. Thanks for your support. I want to tell all you guys—"

"Of all the stuff we read, what did you like best?"

"Mmmmmm, that's tough. I liked *Gilgamesh*. I want to have a friend like Enkidu and I think most of the kids my age want some answers about whether there is life after death. *Antigone* was great, especially the second one, the one written during World War II."

"The one by Jean Anouilh?"

"Yeah, that one," he said.

"And now I'd like to introduce the sophomores on the team. Please hold your applause until all the guys are down here. Terry Johnson—"

"Why did you like *Antigone*?"

"Cuz it made me think about stuff like is there anything I would die for? Why'd she die when she discovered her brother was a bum? That seemed so stupid. It made me think about tyrants. Creon was a maniac. At the end I was so confused about who was right that my head ached."

"Our juniors were led by Buster Malloy as well as—"

"I was really depressed by all the irony stuff we read, but I guess that's part of life. Even though I read the poem about those hollow guys a dozen times I never understood it until we discussed it in class."

"Now let's hear it for the seniors who are playing their final game. First our co-captains—"

"You mean 'The Hollow Men' by T. S. Eliot?"

"Ya, that one. We got a lot of hollow people today, and I liked that part about 'Here we go round the prickly pear at five o'clock in the morning.'"

"OK, now let's give them a big hand and send them off to victory," yelled the coach.

The pep band played the Burnsville fight song. The students sang, clapped, and stomped their feet to the rhythm. Then they stormed down the bleachers and out the exit next to us.

He didn't move. "You know, I thought I knew all the stuff but I really choked on the tests, especially the essay questions. I had ideas but I felt as though the clock was squeezing them to death. Well, I gotta go now, Mr. Melchior, but I just wanted to tell you I thought it was a great class. See you in the halls."

A few students were hanging around the hall as I walked back to the office. Some were playing "gotcha," a few were stuffing their backpacks with books, and a several couples were stocking up on a bit of lovin' to tide them over until their 5:00 date.

The lights in the office were dim. I walked over to the mountain of computer grade sheets and dug around until I found mine. I took the secretary's pencil out of her cup and erased the black dot next to the F. I penciled in a new grade and passed him on his way to fight new dragons.

Old Man

Teachers probably handle stress and frustration as well as most people who work with a room full of squirming, hyperactive elementary students. Most secondary teachers maintain their sanity while teaching five sections of junior high school students whose bodies have become Barnum and Bailey hormonal circuses or 150 high school students, wandering somewhere between "be cool" and "get a life."

Old Man out for a stroll

Some teachers maintain balance by jogging or walking. Others torture themselves with more punishing exercises. Those afflicted with severe cases of frustration drown their sorrows at the local wailing bar and grill. Others gather with their colleagues to atone for their shortcomings at the Church of the Inadequate or the Temple of It's All My Fault. Here they flog themselves because Jimmy and Judy didn't pass. They put on their teaching sackcloths and hair shirts and offer penance for failing to motivate all one hundred and twenty of their charges to academic excellence.

Old Man saved me. Before he became Old Man, he was just a piece of rubber. My brother-in-law bought the mask and wore it to a Halloween party. He walked in the front door of his friend's house, greeted the partygoers, and walked out the back door. I borrowed the mask sometime in the early '70s and never returned it. Old Man lived in my desk drawer in the English office.

Usually I coped with the stress and frustration of teaching quite well. One day, however, something in me twitched. I couldn't keep the beasties down. Perhaps it was the day the principal placed a note in my permanent file stating, "It was observed that you were correcting papers during a department meeting on attendance policy," not that we even had an attendance policy.

Perhaps it was the day I was notified that I had the second poorest record for turning in my daily attendance sheets.

Perhaps it was the day another letter went into my file because "It was observed that you were swimming during your lunch period."

Perhaps it was the day we had to evacuate the building halfway through my major exam.

Perhaps it was the day I had to break up a fight between two screaming, swearing senior girls, sprawling on the carpet, trying to gouge each other's eyes out.

Perhaps it was the day one of the wrestling girls sued the school and me because of my failure to prevent the fight, which endangered the child blooming within the girl's womb.

Perhaps it was something as simple as correcting compositions for more than three decades.

I opened my desk drawer and took out the mask. I walked over to the coat rack and put on someone's trench coat. Then I found a yardstick to use as a cane. I pulled on the mask. I walked into John Silver's class, mumbling, "Those damn kids. What's the matter with kids today anyway?" I hummed as I shuffled to the window that overlooked the parking lot. The kids watched, bewitched by this strange intruder. I stood by the window and stared at hundreds of student cars. "Look at all those cars," I snarled. "Not one more than a year or two old. Then look at the cars in the teachers' parking lot. Pieces of junk."

"That's what's the matter with kids today. They're spoiled. They say they have to work to earn money to go to college. Bah! What a joke! They stay up all night flippin' burgers at MacDonalds so they can buy these hot cars and fancy clothes. Then they whine because they are too tired to study and that school starts too early. So some quack psychologist claims these poor babies need to sleep longer in the morning because their biological clocks are out of sync. What a crock! Then some mugwumping legislators pass a bill to start school later so these cry babies can work even later." I turned, glared at the class, and walked out. When I had blown off enough steam, I returned to the English office to attack another stack of themes.

Dracula or Wolfman appeared only when the moon was full. Old Man came to life only during my second hour prep. Soon my colleagues recognized when my moon was full. "It's time for Old Man," they'd say and I would begin the ritual: put on the trench coat and free Old Man from my desk drawer.

One day after a frustrating meeting with the administration, Old Man decided to invade the holy of holies—the administrative offices. He wanted to pay a visit to one assistant principal in particular. Old Man relished the thought of treading on the sacred administrative carpet because this victim had never met him and would have no idea who was berating him.

I walked into the administrative office, carrying the mask in the rolled-up trench coat.

"Is Mr. B. in his office?" I asked his secretary.

"No, he's in the conference room. All the principals and counselors are having a meeting."

"You mean ALL the principals and ALL the counselors are meeting right here behind this door?"

"Yes, they're all in there. It's a very important meeting. They gave very specific orders they are not to be interrupted."

How often I had explained to my students what Cyrano de Bergerac meant when he said, "There are things in this world a man does well to carry to extremes." Many people have questioned the value of studying literature. "Tom," whispered Cyrano, "this is a time for extremes."

A middle-aged English teacher, who danced the one-two, one-two educational fox trot like a champion, entered the men's room. Old Man, who treated educational bureaucracy, gibberish, and hierarchy with brash irreverence, shuffled out, psyched for show time.

I knocked on the door and stuck my head into the *sanctum sanctorum.* Every head looked up. Every hand holding a pen froze in midair. Jaws dropped. Eyes widened. What a glorious sight! No one said a word. No one moved a muscle.

I walked in, examined the room, and rapped the yardstick on the table. I pointed to the sink behind them and broke into a current country western hit: "I'm goin' to hire a wine-o to decorate this room, so you won't have to ramble and you won't have to roam. I'll take out the dining room table, put a bar along that wall, and a neon sign that lights the way to the bathroom down the hall."

They looked on in disbelief. They screwed their mouths into fake grins, the kind we all make when we think something is humorous but we don't know why. Soon the muscles in our mouths ache after a few minutes of such labored mirth.

I stared at them for a few seconds. Silence. Pencils were still frozen in midair. I walked out, slammed the door, and sprinted up the stairs.

"O frabjous joy!"

My Opening Farewell

After I had retired, I taught two fall sections of English 85 at Normandale Community College. All students who hoped to complete a college degree were required to pass Composition 101. Students who had failed their way through high school or who could not pass the basic skills test to qualify for English 101 had to prove themselves in English 87, a basic, non-credit class focusing on writing simple paragraphs. Students whose writing skills were so deficient they could not qualify for English 87 were assigned to English 85, the most basic of all non-credit courses.

The conversation in English 85 was peppered with "He don't," "I ain't got none," "They seen," "I'm goin' with he and Sally," and "Me and her went to town."

Many English 85 students were teenagers who suffered from academic mononucleosis. They caught the virus in elementary school and the plague followed them into my classroom. This disease caused them to fritter away their pre-college educational careers, where they had skipped class and avoided homework. This lethal virus followed most of them into my classroom. It became my task to cure them of their illnesses.

Several students, however, spoke English as a second language. Ironically, they spoke English too well to qualify for the English as a Second Language program but not well enough to qualify for English 101.

Several students in their late twenties and early thirties took the class to make career changes or improve their skills to qualify for better positions in their companies. English 85 also drew people in their late forties and early fifties who wanted to earn the college degree they were unable to pursue when they were young.

Students in my second fall session were Mary and Jane, eighteen-year-old girls from a nearby high school; Bill, a young man who wanted to start his own bicycle repair business; two teenage au pairs from France; four recent immigrants from Cambodia and Japan; Sam, age thirty, Angie, age thirty-five, and Tony, age thirty-three, all seeking career changes; Betty, forty-something, who wanted to enrich her life; and Bart and Burt, twenty going on, who weren't certain why they wanted to go to college; Charity, Jackie, Todd, Bud, and Christine who were in Ignominious 85 because their parents had said, "You go to college or else!"

For the first several class sessions we followed the curriculum religiously: "What's a noun? Define adverb. Draw one line under the subject and two lines under the predicate. I, we, he, she, they, and who are nominative pronouns. What's a clause? How could you tell an adjective clause if you saw one walking down the street? How do you show that Billy owns a cap? What makes a verb regular? What makes a verb irregular? Should an irregular verb eat more bran flakes?

"Your dog doesn't understand you because he knows his usage. Say, 'Lie down,' and he'll obey. You're making a schizophrenic out of that semicolon. Every apostrophe you write is paranoid.

"No, 'When I visited my old Aunt Tillie in Nashville last summer during the guitar-picking fest,' is not a sentence. It doesn't make any difference how many words there are; it's still not a sentence. Yes, 'Go,' is a sentence." On and on we went with grammar-speak.

After several weeks I said, "To heck with the course description. You guys need to learn how to put some sentences together into a paragraph or two. For next week I want you to write a paragraph and tell me about something that happened to you. Pick an event and show the action. This type of writing is called a narrative. Tell a very short story. Don't make it up. Write about something that really happened to you."

I realized at that moment I was singing the same writing anthem, which I had sung for years. After reading dozens of books about writing, I had come to the conclusion that the single most important skill was "showing, not telling." Hundreds of students had heard the song. "Don't tell it. Show it. Use specific action verbs, which create a vivid picture in the reader's mind. Don't use is, are, was, were, be, or being, because they don't show any action. Even Liza Doolittle in *My Fair Lady* sang, "Don't talk of love. Show me. Show me now."

The next week the students brought their masterpieces for Show and Tell. "Would anyone be willing to read?" I asked. Bill volunteered.

"I have always had a dream to own my own bicycle shop," he read. "Ever since I was a kid I have loved bikes, not Harleys or them kinda bikes, but bikes you can pedal, you know, like the ones that have one speed or maybe fifteen speeds. Those fifteen speed bikes can really go, but you got to be really careful because there tires are so thin unless you get a mountain bike which are pretty expensive, maybe even three hundred dollars, but you can go just about any place with them. But they break down, to. Thats why I want to own my own bike shop. thats it. thats my story."

Silence. I tried to think of something positive to say about Bill's non-narrative. "Thanks, Bill, you certainly showed your passion for bicycles. Bill has broken the ice. Who would like to be next? Thanks, Angie."

"I took this class because I need to improve my righting to get a raise. If we go to school the company pays for it if we get a C. My boss is drivin' me nuts so I gotta learn to write good so I can transfer to another department. My friend, she works in billing, they get more money then I do 'cause they got more responsibility, although I don't know how she can be so smart she never even graduated. I think she got a GDE or GED or something like that, whatever that is. So thats the reason I want to learn better grammer."

"Thanks, Angie. Let's hope by the time this quarter is over you have that job in billing."

"Jackie, would you read your paper, please."

"Ah, I couldn't get it done. I had to work a lot this week."

"Bud, how about reading us your paper."

"Sorry, but I couldn't think of anything. Nothin' ever happens to me. I lead a very boring life."

I stared at my hands. They never used to be so wrinkled. I counted the second hand ticking on my watch. Why had I, a happily retired teacher, ever decided to inflict such pain on myself again? "Hmmmm!" was all the furor I could muster. After years of cajoling and scolding, "Hmmmm" seemed more fitting than feigning anger and indignation.

Mary and Jane sat on the far side of the room, trying to shrink. "Mary, would you please read your paper."

"Ah, OK, One day my mo-, my mo-, my mother and I—" Her hands began to tremble; the paper shook. She looked at me and her eyes began to roll. She gasped for air.

"Mary, are you O.K.? What's the matter?"

Suddenly she melted and slid to the floor.

"She's hypoglycemic," screamed Jane. "I don't think she ate dinner or supper today. Her blood sugar is way out of whack."

"My wife's hypoglycemic," I said. "Here's some money. Mary, can you walk? We've got to get you up to the lobby. They're selling apples and fruit juice there. You've got to eat something right away before you pass out."

"I'm O.K. I'm O.K. I can stand up. Just let me get something to eat." We stood her up and she wrapped her arm around Jane's neck. They took my money and headed for the lobby. The rest of us took a break.

Ten minutes later Mary sat in her desk, munching on an apple.

I called on forty-something Betty. I knew she wouldn't let me down. Unlike the "kids," Betty had lived. She had forty years of stories to tell.

"I want to tell the story of my first boyfriend. God, was he a loser! One night he came to pick me up...."

"Finally someone is going to tell a story," I thought. "Now they'll get an idea of how to do this assignment."

"Well, when he knocked on my door—what a jerk this guy was. He still lived with his mother. What a pill she was! She worked as a waitress at a strip joint down on Hennepin Avenue. She smeared on lipstick and dressed like she was twenty-two, mini-skirts and vinyl boots. This guy was Mama's boy, thirty-five and still living at home. When he knocked, Oh, I have to tell you what he said to me on our first date. He wore white pants and...."

I walked to my car after class, moaning the same old song teachers sing every time an assignment bombs, "What did I do wrong? Everyone tells stories. I ask them to write a story and they wander off on those wild mental safaris. They can't write three sentences that stick together. But when we take a break, they go out into the hall and tell story after story, filling in the most intricate details."

Farewell

The next week I made certain I arrived early. Before class I conspired with Sam and Marie, one of the French au pairs, and they agreed to play along with whatever I had planned.

At the beginning of class, I put the students into groups of two and set them to work finding adjective clauses. I slipped into the men's room, put on my overcoat, and slipped on the mask. I stuffed fruit and candy kisses in my pockets. I wrapped myself in a log chain like Jacob Marley. Then I grabbed my walking stick and inched my way down the hall to my class.

Old Man stood outside the door and sang, "Oh, I'm looking for a sweetheart to take to the Normandale Spring Dance. Where, oh, where is my sweetheart?" Of course the students couldn't see him but the room became very quiet. He shuffled into the room singing, "Do ya wanna dance and hold my hand, tell me that I'm your lover man? Oh, baby, do ya wanna dance?"

He walked toward Tony and whacked his desk with his ruler. It cracked like a rifle shot. "You better start hitting the books, lad," Old Man growled.

"Well, here are a couple of beauties," he sang as he hobbled toward Charity and Jackie. "Say, baby, do ya wanna dance? How about both of you going to the Spring Dance with me?" He threw a chain over his shoulder.

"How about a few kisses, my beauties?" He reached into his pocket and offered them several Hershey's kisses but they shrieked and fled to the far corner of the room.

Next Old Man turned to Bart and Burt, who sat in the back of the room. "What are you two buzzards looking at?" he snapped. He walked between their desks and shoved them apart. Then he fell on his knees and raised his arms to the heavens. "Oh, powers on high," he prayed, "please watch over these two rascals. I fear they are on their way to composition damnation. They don't do their homework and they need special guidance. Look down on them and zap them with some academic electricity." He grabbed each by the shoulder and pulled himself up. Bam! Bam! He cracked their desks with his ruler.

"How about you two?" he said to Marie and Nicole.

"Non, non, non, monsieur. Non, non, non, s'il vous plait."

"Say, are you making fun of me? What's this 'sill vooo play' stuff? Can't you speak English?"

"Non, monsieur, we are from France!"

"Ho, France, you say. Debout. De bout. You know. Stand up. Now, chantez La Marsiyea."

"Quoi?

"Chantez. Chantez. 'La Marsiyea,' Old Man shouted. "You know, your national anthem."

"Oh, oui, 'La Marseillaise,'" said Marie.

"Ya, that's what I said, 'La Marsiyea.'"

They sang, "Allons enfants de la Patrie. Le jour de glorie est arrivé. Contre nous de la tyranie. L'ét—"

"O. K., O. K., that's enough," he yelled. "How about a kiss?"

They took the chocolates. "Merci, monsieur."

Old Man spotted Angie, cowering in her desk. "Ah, dear heart, how about a kiss? Angie reached out and took one of the kisses. "And how about you, my angel? Do ya wanna dance and hold my hand, tell me I'm your lover man, oh, baby, do ya wanna dance?"

Angie frantically slid her chair away from Old Man. He whipped out the banana and pointed it at her. "Stop!" he shouted. "Stop in the name of the law or I'll fill you full of vitamins."

He turned to Mary and Jane. He tried to lasso them with his chain. "How about you two? Do you want to go to the dance?"

They backed away, screaming, "Nooooooooooooo waaaaaaaaay!"

Fearing that Mary would have another hypoglycemic panic attack, Old Man turned to Sam, who had agreed to Old Man's shenanigans but had no idea what the old fella had planned for him.

"Say, buddy, what's the big deal with you?" he shouted. He hovered over Sam, tapping the desk with the ruler. "What are you staring at?" ⸱

He grabbed a fistful of Sam's shirt and pulled him to the floor. He towered over Sam like St. George ready to spear the dragon. "I told you that you had better start hitting the books and I mean it. What do you think this is, a junior high school?"

Then he speared Sam again and again right in the armpit, the way they did in those seventeenth-rate swashbuckling movies from the forties. Sam played his role perfectly and slumped to the floor.

Old Man looked at the class. He walked toward the door. "What a pathetic group! Doesn't anyone here want to go to the spring dance with me?" He looked at Marie. "What about you, Frenchie? I'll get you a green card so you can stay here in the good old U. S. of A."

"A green card!" she shrieked. "Oui, monsieur, I'll go! I'll go!" She sprinted toward Old Man and leaped.

He caught her in midair. She wrapped her arms around his neck and he carried her out of the room, singing, "I'm so glad, my dear, ya wanna dance and hold my hand. Oh, baby, baby, baby, are we gonna dance."

The next week every Composition 85 student turned in a vivid account of what had happened the night the dirty Old Man visited their class.

The Visitor

I had one quarter, nine weeks, forty-five days to teach the early American writers, including Ralph Waldo Emerson, Henry David Thoreau, Nathaniel Hawthorne, Edgar Allen Poe, and Herman Melville (*Moby Dick* alone would have taken us the entire quarter). Thomas Paine, Benjamin Franklin, and Thomas Jefferson also wanted their patriotic masterpieces read. Ann Bradstreet, Cotton Mather and a few minor essayists and poets demanded equal time, too. Tucked away among these writers was an excerpt from a sermon by Jonathan Edwards, the noted Puritan preacher.

I zipped through the political writers and forgot about Ann and Cotton. Jonathan Edwards's sermon, however, piqued my interest. Perhaps it was all the "fire and brimstone" stuff I had heard as a kid. Perhaps I just wanted to see how my students would react to another "This is soooooo boring" piece of early American culture. Perhaps I just wanted to have some fun.

Reverend Melchior Storms the Pulpit

A few days before I delivered Edwards' sermon, I visited the assistant principal and planned the caper. I arranged the desks in a circle and placed my podium between two desks. The students, used to sitting in their customary pews, walked in and shook their heads. "Sit anywhere," I said. "Today we are going to listen to Jonathan Edwards's famous sermon, 'Sinners in the Hands of an Angry God.'" I began to read the way I envisioned a pulpit-pounding Edwards speaking on Sunday morning, July 8, 1741. (He barely spoke above a whisper but I needed drama. I read from selected passages of the sermon and added students' names.

"There is nothing that keeps wicked men [like you students] at any one moment out of hell, but the mere pleasure of God. The bow of God's wrath is bent, and the arrow is ready on the string; and justice directs the bow to your heart, and strains at the bow; and it is nothing but the mere pleasure of God, and that of an angry God, without any promise or obligation at all, that keeps the arrow one moment from being drunk with your blood."

I saw the handle on the door turn. He slid into the room dressed in a Franciscan monk's habit. The hood draped over his face and he looked like a specter from Edwards' vision of hell. A few students sitting across from the door saw him. I stared them down and turned up the volume.

"The God that holds you [Angela Jones and you, David Anderson] over the pit of hell, much the same way as one holds a spider, or some loathsome insect, over the fire, abhors you, and is deadly provoked."

My hooded colleague moved toward the circle and stood about five feet from the nearest student. Everyone saw him but no one spoke.

"His wrath towards you [juniors] burns like fire; He looks upon you [Paul Smith and you, Beth Tikalsky] as worthy of nothing else, but to be cast into the fire; He is of purer eyes than to bear to have you in His sight; you are ten thousand times more abominable in His eyes than the most hateful venomous serpent is in ours."

The monk eased closer and stood only a foot or two behind two students. They squirmed and hunched over, but they didn't turn around or speak. I tore into the sermon. "You [materialistic sons and daughters of suburbanites] have offended Him infinitely more than ever a stubborn rebel did his prince, and yet it is nothing but His hand that hold you from falling into the fire every moment. It is to be ascribed to nothing else, that you [Andy Swenson] did not go to hell last night; that you [Kim Baker] were suffered to awake again in this world, after you closed your eyes to sleep."

He moved closer, this time standing no more than an inch or two next to the student. The student scrunched down. The monk had invaded his sacred space. The students looked up, and I pounded the podium.

"There is no other reason to be given," I ranted, "why you [Jeannie Hanson and you Brett Barnes] have not dropped into hell since you arose this morning, but that God's hand has held you up. There is no other reason to be given, while you have been reading this address, but his mercy; yea, no other can be given why you do not this very moment drop down into hell."

The monk laid his hand on Brett's shoulder. Brett stiffened and I roared, "O sinner, consider the fearful danger you are in! It is a great furnace of wrath, a wide and bottomless pit, full of the fire and wrath that you [weekend partiers and cigarette smokers] are held over in the hand of that God whose wrath is provoked and incensed as much against you as against many of the damned in hell."

He removed his hand and Brett's shoulders slumped. He eased toward the door.

"You [slackers] hang by a slender thread," I hissed, "with the fire of the flames of divine wrath flashing about it and ready every moment to singe it, and burn it asunder."

No one saw him leave the room.

I continued with fire and brimstone. "He and you have no interest in any Mediator, and nothing to lay hold of save yourself, nothing to keep off the flames of wrath, nothing of your own, nothing that you have done, nothing that you can do, [nothing, nothing] to induce God to spare you one moment."

I never told them who the mysterious stranger was, and if they are reading this today, they are still scratching their heads.

Study Hall Supervision

Study hall supervision was a blight on my school day. On the first day of each new semester, twenty-five to thirty strangers walked into my room for study hall. They were a mixture of sophomores, juniors, and seniors. Students who chose five classes from our seven-class day had two study halls. Students who chose six classes had one.

They didn't select me as a study hall supervisor. The computer read their schedules and sent them to me. Unlike students in my academic classes, I matched their names with their faces and never learned much about them. Each day they walked in and slid into their designated seats. The studious ones attacked their assignments and never squeaked during the entire period. Some stared into space dreaming about who knows what. Those who caroused into the wee hours joined the exhausted who had worked the night shift. They nestled their heads into the crooks of their arms and dropped off to sleep. Some simply laid their heads on the desk and fell into a dead sleep. Spittle drooled from their mouths and formed a pool on the desk.

A few escaped to the library to study, goof off, or rendezvous with loved ones. Some signed out to see the nurse, counselors, or other teachers. A few worked on the yearbook or the school newspaper. Others had passes that were probably forged.

After I had signed all the passes, the bathroom exit began. At some point I realized how ridiculous that daily ritual had become. The school required a bathroom pass, so each student had to approach the desk and recite the standard question, "Can (sometimes "May,") I go to the bathroom, please?" How embarrassing! How must that have looked to anyone from the non-school world? Sixteen-, seventeen-, and eighteen-year-old students lined up in front of me to ask if I would allow them to go to the bathroom. How many times had I sprinted for the men's room without asking their permission? Where else in the world but school did people ask permission to answer nature's demands?

Finally I couldn't participate in the farce any longer. I made two small passes, which could fit into any pocket. "From now on," I announced, "please don't ask me for a bathroom pass. Take one off the desk and slide silently out the door. If you decide you want to use the bathroom at Burger King, that's your problem. I have never said, 'No, you can't go to the bathroom and I'm not about to start now.' Again, don't ask. Just take the pass and go."

The final five minutes of study hall supervision jangled my nerves. Students stormed back into the room from pass-land. Sleeping students wiped the drool from their mouths and mopped up the ponds on the desks with their shirtsleeves. The docile bookworms had enough quiet and yearned for action. The bored squirmed and the travelers were restless. It was "We've-been-good-now-let-us-unravel time." I couldn't think of anything to keep them quiet during those final minutes.

One summer I thought of a way to calm the tumult at the end of study hall. I filled two notebooks with trivia questions. I had the foresight to plan for those last five minutes, but I didn't have the vision to create a game like Trivial Pursuit, which appeared several years later.

On the first day of study hall, I announced, "At the end of the period, we are going to play a game to test your intelligence. I will divide you into two groups. The three rows to my left will be known as the Spider Spit Team. The three rows to my right will be called the Bat Breath Team. I will ask six questions a day. Spider Spit, you will begin. If you cannot answer the question, Bat Breath, you will get a chance. Whether or not you answer correctly, Bat Breath, you will get the next question. It is possible for one team to win twelve points in one day. The first team to reach fifty wins a fabulous prize.

"Do not blurt out the answer. Talk it over and select one person to answer. You get only one answer. If the other team blurts out the answer, you get the point. Mary, you're on the Spider Spit Team, so you keep track of Bat Breath's points. Andy, honored member of the Bat Breath horde, you keep the Spider Spit's score.

For the first day or two the students played somewhat hesitantly, humoring me as if I were someone from the cuckoo's nest. I watched the clock and established a pattern. As soon as the second hand indicated three minutes remaining, I began the questions.

"First question: No talking please. What does the suffix -osis at the end of psychosis and mononucleosis mean?

"Question two: Where did the Los Angeles Lakers play before they moved to Los Angeles?

"Number three: "Who said, 'Give me liberty or give me death'?

"Number four: Who were the first two men to climb Mt. Everest?

"Number five: What is the name of the mythical city buried beneath the ocean?

"Number six: How many feet are there in a mile?"

After a few days the action heated up. The Rip Van Winkles woke a few minutes earlier. With five minutes left in the class, the pink passes were stacked on my desk. Soon I forgot about watching the clock. If I forgot about the clock, someone said, "Mr. Melchior, it's time for the game."

I rewarded the winning team with bags of tiny candy bars. It didn't take long to discover which team had the intellectual firepower. To keep the games close, I loaded the questions and made certain both sides earned their sugary prizes.

During a fire drill I told Jim W., a business teacher, about my game. He said, "I've got a great idea for you."

At the end of study hall the next day, I asked Linda if I could speak with her for a few minutes. Linda was a member of the Bat Breath team, but she had never shown any interest in playing the game. "Linda," I said, "I need your help. The boys are getting cocky. They think they know everything about sports. Every few days I am going to ask an impossible sports question. At the end of the period I will give you the answer for the next day's question. Will you play along with me?"

She smiled. The imp was free. "Sounds like fun. Will we do that every day?"

"No," I said, "we want to keep them guessing." I gave her the first answer.

A few days later I said, "Ok, gang, here is the last question for the day. During World War II what pitcher played despite being seriously disabled? He played in the American League."

Silence. I repeated the question. A hand shot up in the back of the room. "Linda?"

"Three-fingers Brown. He played for the St. Louis Browns," she said in a voice a bit louder than a whisper.

"Correct," I said. The students said nothing and rose as the bell rang.

"Question number six," I said a few days later. "What St. Louis Cardinal was nicknamed for his hometown?" Silence. I repeated the question. Still silence. "His name refers to a liquid and a turn in the road,"

The hand went up in the back. "Linda."

"Could that be Vinegar Bend Mizzell?" she asked. She was good.

Several of the boys turned and looked at her.

Three days later the game was on again. "Today's final question is from the world of sports. It's a tough one, but you guys should know this one. This player was known as the Louisville Colonel and he—"

"Pee Wee Reese," shouted Linda. "He played shortstop for the Brooklyn Dodgers."

This time the gawkers turned all the way around in their chairs. A few said, "Wow! Does she know everything about sports?"

I asked fairly simple questions for a few days. I let a week pass. and then threw another ringer. "Today's last question," I announced, "has two clues: He stunned the golf world at a young age by winning several championships and then he became famous for designing world class golf—"

Zip! Up went the hand. "Linda?"

"That would be Bobby Jones."

My colleague teaching in the next room heard the groans. Linda tried to act as if her answer was nothing special, but I know she heard, "She's really somethin'. Does she know everything? What does she do, study the sports almanac?" The guys scratched their heads and fretted. Linda basked in glory.

Several weeks later, I asked another difficult question, but I had not given Linda the answer. "What was the name of the Minneapolis Lakers' center who led them to NBA championships during the early 1950s?"

A moment of silence. No answer. All heads snapped around and stared at Linda. She shrugged her shoulders.

"Geeeez, she's human after all," exclaimed Tony, who was fed up with being outwitted by a girl. "There's something she doesn't know. Wowie!"

We didn't wait long to strike back. "Here's the final question for today. The state of Texas has many college football teams, including TCU, SMU, Texas A&M, and UT. There are four points for this question. Answer as many as you can. Spider Spit, it's your turn.

This was serious stuff. Four points. The Spider Spit jocks put their heads together. Finally Tony said, "I quess the only one we know is UT, the University of Texas."

"Ok, Bat Breath, any answers? Everyone looked at Linda. "TCU stands for Texas Christian University. I think SMU stands for South Moravian University. No. Make that Southern Methodist University, home of Doak Walker." The room was her stage and she was giving an Academy Award-winning performance. "I'm not certain what A and M stand for. Perhaps it's Aeronautical and Mechanical. No. I think it's a land-grant school, so it must be Texas Agricultural and Mechanical."

We shucked and jived for the entire semester. They never caught on. Linda became my Queen of Sports Trivia.

Freedom

"I can't wait 'til I'm out of here. I'm going to Madison (University of Wisconsin) and have kegger parties. I can't wait 'til I'm free," said one of my high school students.

1958, St. John's University, Collegeville, Minnesota

My favorite college English professor was one of the first people on campus to read Albert Camus' *The Stranger*. Usually Prof urged us to read everything, but he passed his copy of the book to only a few brilliant students. Existentialism became the buzzword in world literature classes. The writings of Soren Kierkegaard, Jean-Paul Sartre, and Camus became the focus of classroom discussions.

I went to Prof's room on the ground floor of Benet Hall to ask him about the book. He stared at me for a few seconds and then changed the subject. I tried again to steer the discussion back to Camus, but each time he stared at me and squirmed uneasily in his chair. I left without an answer when the silence between our words told me he was finished.

I tried to figure out what had happened as I walked to my room. "What the hell's going on here?" I asked myself. "I'm in college. I'm old enough to drink beer and be drafted. I'll read the damn book if I want to." I read *The Stranger* and understood Prof's silence. I was not prepared for the journey.

I was a misfit in Camus's theater of the absurd. I could not envision a world so wasted and decayed. My world was filled with light, youth, passion and promise. I rejoiced in life. How could one become so completely alienated from people, nature, and God and even himself?

Jean-Paul Sartre used the phrase "condemned to freedom" to describe the existential man who would spend eternity in a world with no exit. I could recite the lines, retell the plot, name the characters, but I could not comprehend the existential world and the characters who lived there. How could one be "condemned to freedom?"

Fall, 1962, Burnsville Junior High and High School, Burnsville,

The three fourteen-year-old eighth grade boys wore leather jackets, greased their hair, and smirked as they walked. They were rebels tucked into time between the dead James Dean and the hippies to come. They hooked their thumbs in silver studded belts and swaggered down the hall. Students parted like the Red Sea as they made their early morning rounds. They ducked out of the building whenever possible to grab a smoke.

They tolerated me as they doodled the minute hand forward, ogled the girls, and slicked back their hair. They disregarded my invitation to master the fundamentals of grammar. They didn't read because they "didn't wanna." They did nothing because they "didn't wanna" and proclaimed their independence with "You can't make us. What do we need this stuff for anyway? I ain't never gonna be no English teacher."

In mid-September, a ninth grade boy shot himself and left a suicide note. He said that three eighth graders had been extorting money from him. Each morning they met him at the bus and demanded payment. They threatened him when he did pay and roughed him up when he couldn't or wouldn't pay.

Rick had suffered in silence. Not one teacher was aware of what was happening as the busses pulled in each morning. If some students knew, they never told us. Our school was only six years old. Most of us teachers were in our early- or mid-twenties. We were filled with idealism, but Rick's suicide destroyed our innocence.

Although I did not know Rick, I still felt guilty about his death. But I knew the extortionists and I flogged myself for not seeing the tragedy unfolding. If only I had—

Fall, 1982, College of St. Catherine

Twenty years later I was invited to the College of St. Catherine to speak to a group of students who dreamed of becoming teachers about why students fail and why the fire within dies. At eleven o'clock the night before my presentation, I was still tossing and turning, trying to answer the question myself. I closed my eyes. A line of light shot across the darkness. A second line streaked parallel to the first. Things like this happened to me often, so I paid attention. I knew I was getting help. Suddenly, Asterisk popped in between the lines.

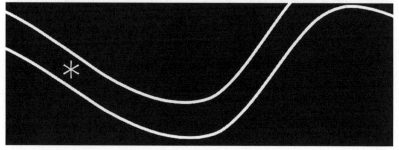

He floated between the lines. At first he panicked. He pawed the air. "Who put me in this jail?" he screamed. "I want to be free. Get me out of here!" There was no end in sight! He was trapped by lines.

Suddenly he became weightless and drifted like a blown feather. He flipped a few times, stood on his head, and somersaulted back and forth. He stopped pounding his fists against the lines.

Faintly, the opening notes of "Ode to Joy," from Beethoven's Ninth Symphony filled the air. The lines undulated and he floated with the melody. The chorus sang Schiller's words,

O friends, no more of these sounds!
Let us sing more cheerful songs,
More full of joy!

The music swelled and the lines looped and twisted with each invocation to joy. Asterisk strained to understand the words.

Joy, bright spark of divinity
Daughter of Elysium

He slid along the lines. The music eased his pain and wiped away the dark images pounding in his mind.

All who can call at least one soul theirs,
Join in our song of praise:
But any who cannot must creep tearfully
Away from our circle.

"Join, join, join," the words rang in his ears. "No," he cried. "I call no soul mine. I will not join. I will not be circled. I want to be completely free. No soul calls me his to keep." He slammed his fists against the lines.

Asterisk pushed the top line, stretching it like a rubber band until he shot through into space.

The line healed immediately and he drifted freely. "Oblige me not!" he exclaimed. "I shall bind nothing and nothing shall bind me."

The music called
>All creatures drink of joy
>At nature's breast.
>Just and unjust
>Alike taste her gift.

"I need none of her kisses or the fruits of her vines. Nothing touches me," Asterisk screamed. "I am free of nature's laws. I will not be trapped by beauty." But the lines beckoned him and the chorus sang,

>You millions, I embrace you.
>This kiss is for all the world.

Asterisk wavered. He reached for the music. He pulled back and cried, "No, your embrace and your kiss demand my soul. I will not be owned!"

The lines danced whirled and the chorus claimed,

>Brothers, above the starry canopy
>There must dwell a loving Father.
>Seek Him in the heavens;
>Above the stars he must dwell.

"Must dwell?" I asked. "A loving Father?" I hesitated. "But what—" The music thundered. The lines circled him and squeezed him into the center. He gasped for breath and pushed away. "No," he screamed, "I want no lines, no boundaries, no constraints, no dogma, no rules. I want to live out here with no-things.

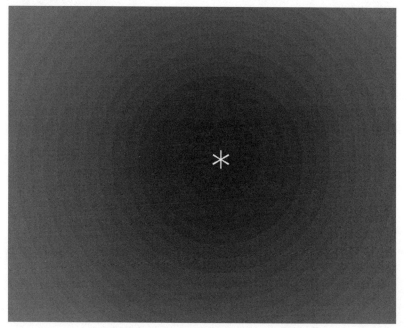

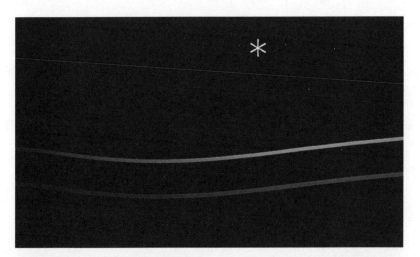

The music faded. The lines dissolved. He drifted freely in the darkness.

The next day I told my dream to the students in the education seminar. "What do you think the dream meant?" they asked. "What does your dream tell us about teaching, about those students who live outside the lines?"

"I think the dream tells me that you and I will have students in our classes like Asterisk, who live outside the boundary lines of family, school, nature, students who live outside moral and ethical lines. They often rely on their own personal experience for meaning. They refuse to look outside themselves. When they turn inward, they find a wasteland. Reason nourished on nothing is impotent. They are alienated and estranged, paralyzed by fear. They are condemned to freedom.

"In my last year of teaching I had a senior boy who seldom showed up for study hall, and when he did, he slept. The next time he came to study hall, I picked up my attendance records and sat in the desk next to him. 'I think you're bound for a bit of trouble here with all these absences,' I said. I looked at his arms which were dotted with cigarette burns. Healed pockmarks scarred each arm. Some burns had scabs. Others festered with pus. That day's burns were raw.

"Why are you doing that?" I asked. He looked at me and grinned. Then he put his head on the desk and dismissed me. The next day I gave him a copy of a poem by Stephen Crane from *Black Riders*:

> In the desert
> I saw a creature, naked and bestial,
> Who squtting on the ground,
> Held his heart in his hands,
> And ate of it.
> I said, "Is it good friend?"
> "It is bitter-bitter," he answered;
> "But I like it
> Because it is bitter,
> And because it is my heart."

He looked at the poem for several minutes, set it aside, and laid his head on the desk. He dismissed me unceremoniously. On the way out he handed me the poem and said, "What's that got to do with me?" He didn't wait for my answer. He was free.

The Slows

I don't know when the "slows" began, probably four or five years before I retired. They sneaked up on me, insidiously. My energy drained drop by drop like intravenous feeding gone berserk. I was never free of nausea and fatigue. My stomach boiled and my head floated. At first I thought it was caused by my morning diet of coffee and donuts. When I lectured, my body stood in one spot and my words echoed from a voice four feet away.

I fought through my first period class and slept with my head on my desk during my second-hour prep. By the end of the day, I was exhausted and left school as early as possible, lugging my homework with me. I limited my correcting to five or six papers a night and tried to finish them before supper. I went to bed at 8:30 and by 3:00 a.m. I was wide-awake. This happened for two or three nights in a row until I was so tired I could sleep through the night. Then the cycle started over again. The slows got slower and slower.

I went to the doctor for my annual physical. He wrote me two prescriptions and said, "Make an appointment to see me in a week and we'll discuss the results of your physical."

I asked the pharmacist about the medication, and he said, "One is for your stomach and the other is an anti-depressant." I was stunned. An anti-depressant! Did the doctor really know I was depressed or was he guessing? Depression. Me? Impossible! Couldn't be!

I asked my wife if she thought I was depressed and she said, "Without a doubt."

"How can you tell?" I asked.

"Easy," she said, "you don't sing anymore. You've been singing ever since I met you, but I haven't heard you sing for a long time. I hate to tell you this, but Meg (our sophomore daughter) said, 'The kids at Burnsville get the best of Dad.'"

"What the heck does that mean?"

"It means you give all your time and energy to teaching and have nothing left for us," she said. "You leave here at 5:30 a.m. and get home at 4:00 p.m., but then you shut yourself in the den. After supper you go back to the den and then to bed."

I returned to the doctor a week later. "You prescribed an anti-depressant," I said. "Why? Are you telling me that something emotional has triggered this psychological plunge?"

"No," he said, "I'm telling you that something has caused a chemical imbalance in your system. Perhaps it was the sinus and knee surgeries. I don't know what caused it, but I do know you are depressed."

"How can you tell?" I asked.

"I can tell by looking at you," he said. "You need to see another doctor."

"You mean a shrink?" I asked.

"Call it what you will, but you need someone who can help get you through this," he said.

I tried fighting the slows without medication. I couldn't even say the word *depression*. I was fifty-four years old. One day I walked through the door full of gusto and the next day I couldn't find the door handle. Each day I became more and more depressed. I fought. God, I fought, but I felt the way I did when I was a kid and I dreamed the German Army was chasing me. At first my feet flew, but soon they became heavier and heavier until I froze in place. I finally admitted the doctor was right and found someone who could help me.

A few days later I pulled into the parking lot at school, opened the door, and sang my favorite Joe Raposa Sesame Street song as I walked toward the school. "Sing. Sing a song. Sing it loud. Sing it long." I walked down the hallway to my room singing, "Sing of good things, not bad. Sing of good things, not sad."

At night I turned off the lights in my room and sang all the way to my car. I passed students and teachers who turned their heads and watched me Sesame Street to my car. I sang the song until I retired.

I told my students my story. If everyone else could tell I was swallowed by the "slows," certainly they could see something was out of kilter. I gave them the best I had under the circumstances, but they will never know what I could have given them. I knew, however, and I could not convince myself even though I told myself, "Don't feel guilty. It's not your fault."

I don't know if I did the right thing by telling them, but I think I did. I wanted them to know that my depression had cheated both of us, and if they had seen my struggle, I wanted them to know the reason why.

For the next few weeks students came in before and after school or stopped before or after class to tell me about their battles with depression.

"I'm going through the same thing and I'm only sixteen. I want to tell you why I fall asleep in class."

"I want to tell you why I'm so hyper."

"Do you have trouble with anxiety?"

"What medication are you on? What are the side effects? I've got dry mouth all the time. It tastes as if I'm eating aluminum foil."

"I'm taking this or that medication."

I answered their questions as honestly as I could. We were no longer teacher and student. We were just people battling one demon and it felt good to fight together.

5

Seemed Like a Good Idea at the Time

Breaking Up Is Hard to Do

THE EVENT AS KATHY REMEMBERS IT: "I WAS STANDING IN my room preparing for the next period. The kids were passing and it was pretty crowded. Two guys, big kids, squared off right in front of your room. At that time women weren't supposed to do anything. We were supposed to call the men. I had stuff in my hands—scissors and rubber-cement bottles. I hollered for you. I don't know where you were, in the library or in your room, but I hollered for you. Then, of course, you came. I dropped a bottle of glue. That got all mixed up in this thing because people thought a kid had thrown it and that people were cut with glass. There was glass and glue all over, but no one got cut.

"You tried to break up the guys. You grabbed one of them from behind. I was still holding all that junk, so I was no help at all. The kid that you didn't grab pasted the one you held. It was as if you were holding one kid so the other kid could paste him."

The event as I remember it: The two ninth graders were well-built guys. They certainly weighed more than I did. I grabbed the kid from behind and wrapped him in a bear hug, pinning his arms to his side. I can still see the other's guy's fist just before he punched the guy I held. Bam! A free shot to the jaw!

I just grabbed the first guy I saw. It seemed like the best thing to do. Everything happened so fast. The kid was a sitting duck. His father sued the school and me. He accused me of not knowing how to break up a fight. He certainly was right about that. He said I should have gotten down on one knee between the boys, held out my arms toward them with my palms up, and said, "This fight is over." The case never went to court.

The principal told me the insurance company met with the father and settled the case. "In minor claims like that one," he said, "the insurance company may have paid a settlement or they may have refused to pay.

I broke up several fights in the following years, but I never grabbed anyone from behind and I certainly did not get down on one knee, hold out my hands, and declare that the fight was over. I did, however, think before I got involved.

The Curse of Edgar Allen Poe

I spotted the old kerosene lantern at the other end of the flea market and bought it for three bucks. What a find! Just what I needed for my unit on Edgar Allen Poe! I took the lantern home, cleaned it up, put in a new wick, and wrapped a black cloth around it, so I could open the cloth just a bit and let out a sliver of light. Perfect. I was ready.

That fall my classroom was in the corner of the library. It was a window-less cubicle isolated from all the other classrooms. Students had to wind their way through the bookshelves to reach the room.

I set the lantern in the far corner of the room and said, "Today we are going to read and discuss 'The Tell-tale Heart' by Edgar Allen Poe. Would you please sit on the floor in this corner?"

They grumbled and squawked. "Jeez, this is just like grade school."

"I can't sit on the floor in this skirt."

"I thought this was English class, not phy. ed."

"This better be good."

"What the heck are you up to today, Mr. Melchior?

"Is this another one of your weird ideas?"

"What's that lantern for? Are you going to rub it and free a genie?"

"Bill," I said, "would you please turn off the lights? We need just the right atmosphere for this story."

We sat in the dark for a few seconds and then I lit the lamp but kept it covered. I had just enough light to read. "True!-nervous, very deadly nervous I had been and am; but will you say that I am mad? The disease had sharpened my senses—not destroyed—not dulled them."

They fell under the spell of Poe's words. No one complained. No one moved. I read on. "He had never wronged me. He had never given me insult. For his gold I had no desire. I think it was his eye! Yes, it was this! One of his eyes resembled that of a vulture-a pale blue eye, with a film over it. Whenever it fell upon me, my blood ran cold; and so by degrees—very gradually—I made up my mind to take the life of the old man, and thus rid myself of the eye forever."

I read on. "Each night I quietly opened the old man's door and stuck in my head.... And then when my head was well in the room I undid the lantern cautiously.... I did it just so much that a single thin ray fell upon the vulture eye."

Cough! Cough!

At this point I separated the black cloth. "I undid it just so much that a single thin ray fell upon the vulture eye." A ray of light split the darkness.

Cough!

Cough! Cough!

Cough!

I continued reading. "I had my head in and was about to open the lantern, when my thumb slipped upon the tin fastening, and the old man sprang up in bed, crying out—"'Who's there?'"

More coughing. Still more coughing.

"Mr. Melchior, we can't breathe."

"I can't stop coughing."

"Me either."

"I'm dying. I need air."

"Me, too," echoed throughout the room.

"Bill," I said, "will you please turn on the lights."

A thick, oily black fog rose from the lantern toward the ceiling and then drifted down like chimney soot.

By this time all my students were coughing and wiping tears from their eyes. I opened the door and they charged out. The smoke billowed out behind them. They looked like coal miners coming out of the shaft after a day of digging.

Shut-eye

"Hey, Mr. Melchior, guess what? I learned a new isometric exercise. It's one of those levitation exercises that will make you feel as if you're floating on air. Want to try it?"

"Sure. What do I have to do?" I asked.

"OK, just stand here against the book cabinet and push your back hard against the cabinet. Now close your eyes. Now hold out your arms and tighten your muscles. Make your arms and wrists real stiff, and pretend that you're pushing down. OK, now really tighten your muscles."

Click. click. He snapped one handcuff around my right wrist and the other to the cabinet handle.

"Hey, how's that for a real levitation trick?" Bob laughed.

The class went bonkers. "Geez, Ward, you're crazy. What the heck are you going to do now?"

Many of the students looked shocked, but I knew that inside they loved watching me squirm.

"Great trick. I feel lighter every second. I'm levitating toward the ceiling now," I laughed. "Now get me out of here."

"Heck, no," he smirked. "Last hour we locked Mr. Plotnik to the blackboard and kept him there all hour. It was the best math class we've ever had."

In a split second I realized Bob, the master trickster, had not committed the perfect crime. The cabinet had two doors. One door opened toward the corner of the room. No escape. The other opened outward toward the doorway.

I swung open the cabinet door, stepped into the doorway, and reached for the all-call buzzer that connected each room to the principal's office. I held my finger on the button and said, "OK, Bob, you have five seconds to unlock me or I'll press the buzzer. Mr. McCoy will be up here before you can say, 'Bob Ward is history.'"

Click. Click.

I never again shut my eyes during class.

Scars

Pat and Mike are identical twins. They played high school baseball for me for three years. I could not tell them apart. They blocked the bills of their caps the same way. They wore their uniforms the same way. They sounded like one voice. The only way I could tell them apart was that Mike batted left-handed and Pat batted right-handed. If I needed a left-handed pinch hitter, I couldn't look at one of them and say, "Mike, get in there and get us a hit," for fear that I may be looking at Pat. So I looked at the field and called for one or the other.

Pat and Mike Ryan

I seldom started one without the other. Certain things in life just seem as though they ought to be. Having one in the outfield and the other on the bench was a violation of natural law.

They didn't start many games during those three years. We always seemed to have outfielders who hit better or fielded better, but the twins were a coach's dream. They never missed practice, they were never late, and they were the first players on and off the field. The never complained about having to run during situation drills or grimaced when asked to lay down a sacrifice bunt.

Pat and Mike let the rest of the world talk. They sat together on the bus and listened and laughed at the antics of their teammates. They always greeted me with a smile and "Hi, coach," but they seldom spoke more than that during an afternoon of practice. They were great competitors and two of the finest people I know.

One Saturday during their senior year I scheduled our team to play in a weekend tournament. The game was to be played quite far from school. There were no busses available, so I had to find transportation for the team. We carried a roster of sixteen players. On Friday noon I could only find one other person to drive. I knew we couldn't carry sixteen players and all our equipment in two cars, so I made what I thought was my best choice—I cut the roster. I can't remember how many guys I cut, but Pat and Mike's names were not on my list.

That night their dad called and asked me to explain why I had not included his sons on the roster. My body queezed the way it always does when I screw up. I began to explain my predicament, but the words were hollow. My heart pounded. He very politely explained how much baseball meant to his boys and how hurt they were by being cut. I stammered, trying to get out of my mess. "I think I've made a great mistake," I said. "Tell them to be at the school tomorrow at ten o'clock. Come hell or high water, I'll find someone else to drive." I did and everyone made the trip.

The next day I apologized to Pat and Mike and the other players I had cut. Pat and Mike smiled and said, "Oh, that's O.K, coach, no big deal."
I had been well-schooled in how not to treat students and athletes. I was twenty-five and should have known better. By doing what was expedient instead of what was right, I scarred them. When they rub those wounds, they'll think about high school baseball and their coach. My scar is just as tender as it was forty years ago.

Pat or Mike Ryan, Mike Norton, Mike or Pat Ryan

Some Races Cannot Be Won

When I was a kid, I read nearly every word in *Sport Magazine* from the feature articles to the comic strip showing how I could change from an eighty-pound weakling to a muscle man. I, too, could be like Charles Atlas and stop bullies from kicking sand in my face. *Sport* was my Gospel. I believed everything I read.

In one issue I read an article about Harrison Dillard, a track star from Baldwin-Wallace. Dillard is the only man to win an Olympic gold medal in both sprints (1948) and hurdles (1952). In 1948 when I was twelve, Dillard was the best low hurdler in the world. In the trials for the 1948 Olympics, he hit several hurdles and did not qualify to race in his specialty. However he won the gold medal in the 100-meter dash.

I can still see Dillard's picture in *Sport*. He hovered over a hurdle, right arm reaching ahead, head flat down, right foot slashing across the center of the hurdle, left arm and leg dragging behind. I had yet another hero. Between 1947 and 1948, Harrison Dillard won eighty-two consecutive hurdle races. I took third place in the only hurdle race I ever ran.

In the eighth grade I joined the track team because we didn't have a baseball team. We trained with the varsity team on the field across from the school. I had never jumped a hurdle in my life, but there was something dazzling about seeing the Saturday Movie Tone newsreel of Dillard flashing down the track, gliding over those hurdles.

Unlike Dillard, who had to clear many hurdles in his Olympic race, I had to jump only three. Since we had no hurdles coach, I relied on Dillard's photo. I tucked my cheek against my shoulder, reaching out, stretching out, and gliding inches over each hurdle. One race sparked illusions of grandeur for which I would pay dearly.

In the spring of my sophomore year, I played baseball for Garden City High School, but on the day of the track team's conference meet, the coach asked me if I would like to ride along to the meet, which was being held at Mankato State Teachers College.

During the meet Coach K. said, "We're short a guy in the 440. Would you like to run?"

"What's a 440?" I asked.

"Just once around the track. I think you're in pretty good shape. We really need a runner."

"Just once around the track," I thought. "Only 440 yards. The team needs me. I ran a race once. I'm in pretty good shape. If I win this race, I could help the team win the meet."

I borrowed a uniform and track shoes from another player. "You can't pace yourself very much in this race," advised Coach K. You have to sprint hard to have a chance to score."

Before I had time to think about his words, I was lined up with guys from other schools who had trained two months. The starter pulled the trigger and I took off. I led at the first turn. I sprinted down the straightaway. On the second turn I had the inside lane. As I raced toward the finish line, the stadium slowly tilted to the right and then to the left. Black holes spun in my eyeballs.. Colors flashed by. I drifted into darkness and plowed face first into the cinder track. End of track career!

I couldn't become a track star, so I became a teacher. The race runs in the same direction.

I was much safer with the baseball team. Garden City High School, 1951: The day we took this photo it was 35 degrees. Front row left: Fred Kelley, Darrell Hohenstein, John Harkins, William, "Butch," Gardner, Larry Dermody, Tony Wendlendt, Second row: Elwin Mc Grew, Dean Putrah, Tom Melchior, Earl Reid, Dave Forrey, and Coach Luckemeyer

Spittin' in the Snow

For two or three days, blizzards swept January winds around the junior high. Mountains of snow towered outside the C entrance. Down one flight of stairs and out the door to the Arctic. After the blizzard a foot or two of fluffy white snow capped the mountains. Then the temperature plunged. For three weeks the thermometer hovered around twenty below zero.

On my way to school one morning during this Arctic blast, I played my usual mind games. "Now what can I do today to add some pizzazz to today's reading, 'To Build a Fire' by Jack London. The day before I had outlined the characteristics of naturalism. "Now, students," I said, "the naturalists wanted to depict the conflicts between humans and nature as realistically as they could. Humans and nature were equals. They followed Charles Darwin's motto: 'Only the fittest survive.'"

The students added these characteristics to the list of the other -*isms* we had studied during the fall semester and grumbled. "So, Charles Darwin sailed around the Galapagos Islands in the Beadle, taking notes about which iguanas and turtles were the fittest. So, what's the big deal about that?" they asked. "Don't tell us that humans and nature are equal. We could go down there and wipe out every single thing on those lava heaps."

Every day these ninth graders lived Darwin's *Origin of Species*. They knew they were "fitter" than the seventh and eighth graders. They ruled the halls and the lunch line. The guys with the brightest feathers strutted proudly before their worshipers. The Aphrodite goddesses ruffled those feathers with a tight sweater or a few come-hither glances. In this maelstrom of natural selection, everyone knew who would end up getting stuffed into a locker or getting his bare butt snapped with a wet towel in phy. ed.

I pulled into he parking lot and walked to the C entrance. The second I saw the snow mountains, I knew that Jack London would live again that day.

They filed into the room chattering, giggling, suspecting nothing. The bell rang and they groaned when I wrote *naturalism* on the board.

"OK, class, today we are going to read Jack London's famous short story 'To Build a Fire.' London's protagonist is a naive, young prospector seeking his fortune in the Yukon. His only companion is his dog. Like all great writers, London is a master of creating setting, so before we begin reading, I think we need to get into the mood.

"Follow me. We're going to go outside for a few minutes. It's not 70º below zero and our spit won't freeze before it hits the ground, but it's a good way to get ready for this trip to the Yukon."

"What?" they whined. "Are you serious? It's twenty below out there!"

"Oh, come on. You're exaggerating. We're only going to stay out a minute or two, just to get a taste of winter."

"Can we go to our lockers first to get our coats?"

"Do you think London's character went to his locker? Let's rough it. Come on, you guys. Toughen up." I used my best "survival of the fittest" psychology.

I led the way. "Follow me down the stairs and out the door."

Grumble and moan! It took about two seconds for nature to humble my fittest. Most huddled close to the door " Mr. Melchior, I'm freezing!"

"It's colder'n hell out here!"

"I'm gonna catch pneumonia and die, and it'll be all your fault."

"Jump around," I yelled. "Clap your hands. Stomp your feet. Get that blood circulating. It's only twenty below. That's a long way from seventy. Spit. See if it freezes before it hits the ground."

"Gross," they screamed.

"Please, Mr. Melchior," they pleaded. "Let us go in."

Teachers know that some students welcome any excuse to get out of school and avoid work, even if it means freezing off their tushkies. A minute in the cold means one minute less in class.

Although most of the class hovered near the door shuffling their feet and assuming the "Minnesota Hunch" position, a few reckless renegades romped off to butt their heads against snow banks or play King of the Hill.

"God, Mr. M., we're dying out here."

The chorus swelled. "Yeah, come on. Let's go in."

"OK," I said, "I think we've had a good dose of naturalism." I never saw a group so happy to go to class. They sat in their desks and shivered.

"That was so great," I lied. "Now we're in the mood for London's story."

"Where's Jim?" someone asked.

"Oh, my god," I thought. "Perhaps Jim had taken off for the mall. Perhaps he was lying out there freezing to death! Where is Jim?" I asked. "Did anyone see Jim?"

"The last time I saw him he was standing on the top of one of those big snowdrifts diggin' for his shoe," said Frank.

"What do you mean, 'He was digging for his shoe?'" I asked.

"Well, he was wearing loafers and just for the heck of it he kicked one up into the air and it sank into the soft snow on the top of the hill. Then we played some King of the Hill, and I guess the shoe got buried."

I panicked. "Will a few of you guys help me find that shoe?" I asked. "Jim could be—"

The door opened and Jim walked into the room, an icicle carrying a frozen loafer.

Dear Sister—

A Letter from My Daughter
My daughter was a fourth-grader in the Catholic school. Sister X had the students correct their own papers. She then called the students' names and they announced their scores which she recorded in her grade book. The following is a letter from Mary M. to Dear Sister and all teachers who think it's a good idea to save a few minutes by having students give their scores out loud.

Dear Sr.

Yesterday I told you that I had -0 wrong but I really had - 6 wrong. I didn't want the class to know that I had so many wrong. I am sorry that I cheated. I want you to put in your score book I have -6 wrong.

Love,
Mary M.

6

Mentors and Minotaurs

Thomas Patrick Moore

IF I COULD CHOOSE A MENTOR TO GUIDE MY MIND AND spirit, I would look for someone who could be all things to me—saint, sinner, musician, counselor, confessor, sculptor, gardener, and friend. I would choose someone who could give me a balanced sense of time, place, and identity. I would choose someone who has given and taken from life's cycles, someone whose body and soul have burned with creative fire. I would choose Thomas Patrick Moore, my grandfather.

Thomas Patrick takes a break before playing his favorite Irish waltz in C.

Someone who had never met Tom Moore might be tempted to argue that a farmer with only an eighth grade education could never satisfy my need to have a mentor who could write the poetry of life. Some might argue that I would be a fool to choose Tom Moore instead of one of the world's great intellects. Some might wonder how a man whose feet were so firmly planted in rich black soil could become a great poet.

If a poet is someone who captures a vision of life and if a poet can pluck truth from every hiding place in the mind and spread it out for the world to see, my grandfather was a poet laureate. Although Thomas Patrick Moore never wrote a line of poetry in his eighty-four years, my heart is filled with his poems.

In the early April mornings he wrote his sonnets, his free verse, his soliloquies, and his epics. He was my Odysseus, traveling through his sea of rich, black earth, turning back the gleaming fields behind his favorite team of horses. He wandered year after year through those fields, plodding behind his plow, stoking the dream-fires in his imagination. How many pages can a man write holding leather reins and walking twenty years in a narrow furrow?

I want him to teach me about those fertile fields—the womb into which he planted the seed of grain and the womb into which he planted his dreams.

I need him to teach me how to love the land. I need the earth-poet in him to show me what I should feel and smell when I take a fistful of dirt into my hands. I want him to reach down into his field, scoop up a handful of earth, crumble it into my hands and say, "Here, Tom, feel this. Take a good whiff of what we were and what we will become."

I need the poet in him to tell me if his heart races when he plants seeds in the spring and harvests the fruit of these tiny miracles in the fall. I want to ask him if he feels the cosmic power of planting life, if he feels the seeds sprouting in the earth, pushing toward the sky.

I yearn for him to say, "Here, lad, husk this cob of corn," in the same brogue his father brought from Ireland. "Now shell the kernels, boy, until you have nothing but the naked cob left in your hands. Everyone knows the corn is pure gold, and today the cobs are ground-up, good-for-nothing stuff, but for years we burned them to keep warm in the winter."

I need to hear his stories—stories that philosophers and academicians in ivory towers have translated into ponderous prose and erudite syntax. I need to ask him questions: "Why do you walk through your wheat field and rub the grain in your palms? What music do you hear as you milk the cows or watch the birth of a calf or a litter of sleek brown pigs? What do you dream about while you are cultivating corn? What do you feel when you look into the eyes of your favorite team of horses and stroke their soft lips? What are those gentle words you say to them that make them open their mouths so willingly and accept the steel bit that harnesses them to hours of dragging a two-bottom plow?"

Every fall he followed his team of horses, walking through row after row of corn. Snapping the cob off the stalk, he raked the cob across the metal hook on his leather glove and stripped off the husk, year after year, acre after acre, cob after cob. I want to ask him what books he wrote in his mind as he husked that corn.

I need my grandfather to speak earth poems—poems that sing the songs of creation, the mysteries of life and death, and love of the land. I want to know how this man who never heard Chief Seattle's speech about the sacredness of Mother Earth discovered that he and the earth are one body, one spirit. As my mentor he could tell me about the yearning to plant seeds and the joy of birth. He could teach me how to grieve the destruction of the land and the loss of a child.

Tom Moore was born on March 5, 1885. He died on March 4, 1976, one day short of his ninety-first birthday. On the day of his funeral, I told my children to pay close attention because they were going to see something they would probably never see again. Grandpa was buried in St. Thomas, Minnesota, thirty yards behind St. Thomas Catholic Church, where he was baptized, received his First Holy Communion, confirmed, married, and laid to rest.

Grandpa Moore sitting in his granary with my children: Marty, Meg, and Paul.

My Grandfather Never Understood

My grandfather never understood
   health spas,
      but he knew his earth.
One spring morning smelling of re-birth
   he led me through barn doors
      into his magical kingdom.
We climbed hayloft stairs,
   sidestepping drowsy cats
      and scaled mountains of sling-hauled hay.
I chewed dry sweet clover
   and he pitchforked matted alfalfa
      that defied unwebbing and exploded
         into dust clouds as it hit the floor below.
Frenzied barn swallows flitted from mud nests
   hidden by rafter shadows.
      Pigeons flapped frantically
         toward cupola light.
Below, each stall burst into life
   as thrust after thrust of hay
      swished down from above.
When he finished, sunbeams,
   slivering through barn walls,
      sliced through dancing alfalfa dust.
I followed his bib overalls
   down the loft steps
      into a world of steamy, chomping animals.
Gauzed in the hazy morning light,
   he stood between Flossie and Dolly,
        singing his love song.
Each horse accepted the bridle bit, and
   nuzzled the gentle hand
      which guided the cold steel over their tongues.
Over each he threw a web of leather straps, and
   metal rings—a harness,
      smelling of sweat and time.

In one sweeping arc he flung me
   up on Flossie's back, and
      I clenched tufts of coarse, black mane.
He wrapped the leather reins
   around each hand, and

marched us into the spring morning.
He harnessed his team
   to a single tree,
      silver-steel plow.
Before him on that April morning
   stretched acre on acre
      of black earth spiked with corn stubble.
He set me down behind him,
   and with a flicked rein and a clicked tongue
      his horses drove the steel into the earth, and
         curled two glistening, ebony furrows.
Hour after hour I walked
   in my grandfather's furrowed path,
      skipping often to match his footsteps.
No, my grandfather never understood
   health spas, but
      he knew his earth.

Thomas Patrick Moore

Saturday Matinees

When my son was fourteen, we biked to the town where I had lived until the end of the eighth grade. While we biked, I reminisced about my youth.

I expected many changes during those thirty years since I had left town, but I was dismayed to discover the Legion Theater had become The Yarn Basket. The large blue and gold American Legion sign had disappeared from the marquee. The *Now Showing* and *Coming Soon* display cases had vanished.

Gene Autrey from a 1940s penny arcade card

I stood in front of The Yarn Basket and recalled how we memorized the movie posters for that day's feature as we lined up all the way back to Hank Paul's Skelly station. When the theater manager unlocked the door, we stormed the concession stand, stuffed our pockets with candy, and bought the popcorn that had tantalized us as we stood in line. Then we dashed for the best seats.

When we were six, seven, and eight, we sat in the front row, close to that gigantic screen inhabited by swashbucklers, whiskered desperadoes, and men who rode horses named Champion and Trigger. Once the theater darkened and the matinee began, we never stopped moving. We squirmed, changed seats, extracted melting Hershey bars from our pockets, hurled insults at the nearest group of girls, and made trip after trip to the concession stand.

We roamed freely in the open space between our seats and the screen. We fought every fight, memorizing the details of each scene which we would enact the following week in our secret clubhouses or on the trails around the lake. Once we knew the plot, we could strap on our rubber guns, change the names of our bikes from Schwinn to Champion and Trigger, and float through hours of Hollywood illusion.

When we were nine, ten, and eleven, we abandoned the front rows and moved to middle rows, closer to the concessions and the action in the back row. The girls were not so far away and they were the victims of far fewer insults.

Those Saturday matinees at the Legion Theater were filled with fantastic characters. Our heroes snatched us from the real world and thrust us into places like Transylvania, Iwo Jima, Guadalcanal, and the Bar X Ranch.

Scrunched up on the floor and peeking between the seats, we watched mesmerized as the new moon transformed Lon Chaney into Wolf Man and Bela Lugosi into a vampire. We applauded the marines and John Wayne. We cheered as Gene and Roy restored justice to the West.

Somewhere in the Yarn Basket flitted the shadows of my youthful heroes: heroes with pearl-handled six-guns, clean-shaven faces, steely eyes, and faithful dogs and sweethearts; heroes who wore Yankee pinstripes with the numbers 3 and 4 on their backs; heroes whose integrity never wavered; heroes who used might for right; heroes who never compromised.

Roy Rogers from a 1940s penny arcade card

I knew that Ken Maynard, Lash LaRue, Red Ryder, Gene and Roy were good and just. Villainy was never confused with goodness. Scoundrels always lost. Never then did I face the dilemma of choosing between right and wrong, between good and evil. Black and white Saturday matinees were part of youthful security.

Youth gave us the priceless luxury of black and white values. No one wanted to be the guy who plotted against Ken, Lash, Red, Gene, or Roy because that meant being knocked off a galloping bicycle, rolled down a hill, and pummeled for our wickedness.

Standing outside The Yarn Basket, I tried to find the words to describe to my son that walled up in that building were memories of my youthful innocence. Locked inside was my childhood love affair with Margaret O'Brien and my dad's uninhibited laughter at the antics of Abbott and Costello. The words of my heroes echoed in the rafters. I knew if I could climb up there, I could find a world where all my questions would be answered.

It's difficult to recall a black and white world when I now live in a world filled with many shades of gray

Gus

Small towns possess magical powers. While I crisscrossed every inch of Gaylord on my Schwinn, bounced, pitched, and punted my way through the seasons, stole my first kiss, and worshiped my heroes, the town brewed its magic potion in my mind. Like an alchemist it mixed my childhood experiences in a wonderful concoction that I could drink again and again when I grew older.

I knew every place in my town—the Green Lantern, Lake Titloe, Tip Top Cleaners, and the Merc. They were the nourishment for my brew. I went to the Green Lantern to hover around the pinball machine with my buddies, Lake Titloe to catch bullheads, and the Merc(antile) to get orange crates for my rubber guns. I stopped at the Tip Top Cleaners to nag my dad for a buffalo head nickel or an occasional Mercury dime to buy an ice cream cone or comic book at Renner's Drug Store.

I was just fourteen, done with grade school and ready for the senior high when my parents announced, "We're moving. We sold the Tip Top Cleaners and bought a house in Garden City, just south of Mankato." The alchemist put away his potions. No more memory brewing to be done here. Just "We're moving."

In the back of my mind I knew we would return someday and my buddies and I would win championships in every sport for the honor of Gaylord High School, After all, I had sung vigorously with the cheering fans, "We are loyal to you Gaylord High, to the purple and gold, Gaylord High." It never occurred to me when we drove out of town that I would never throw another ball or shoot another basket with them again. In fact, the only time I ever saw one of those childhood friends was at his funeral.

Arriving

Our 1951 silver-bulleted Studebaker fought the looping curve on Highway 169 before dropping into the valley of Garden City. We turned left across from the only two businesses in town, Crane's Hardware and Gray's Market.

One block east we pulled up in front of our new home, an old wooden-framed, one-story, leaning structure that could have housed hermits or eccentric old spinster sisters in a Hawthorne novel. Seeing our new house was a lot like having your date's father turn on the porch lights just as your lips touch the luscious lips of the girl you love for the first time. Surprise! It's just an illusion! It's not what you thought it would be!

Fourteen-year-olds don't ask why they're moving or how much the new house costs. I discovered years later that the house cost $3000. I'm not certain if it was Huck Finn who said, "It didn't cost nothin' and it was worth it, too," but that line certainly applied to our broken-down place.

I had no idea that fewer than 100 people lived in town and that there was not one fourteen-year-old among those 100. Years later I discovered that the words describing Moses as "a stranger in a strange land," would pop up again and again in literature, almost as often as I would find myself that stranger in a strange land. No longer could I call my buddies together for a pick-up game or bike over to the school on Saturday morning and know that a red-hot game of half court would be waiting for me.

My new alchemist demanded much higher payment for his service, and his brew was bitter sweet. My entire family worked feverishly to fix up our house. When Dad was not driving back and forth to work long hours in Mankato, he was sawing, hammering, painting, or crawling under our house, repairing pipes and trying to figure out a way to prevent them from freezing during the winter.

My job was to tame the jungle around the house. The grass was knee high and every variety of undesirable weed lived in undisturbed serenity. Around the entire corner lot, a fence made of square pickets jailed us from our few neighbors. An orange maze of tiger lilies smothered the fence.

I tore out the picket fence and thinned the tiger lilies as my mother directed. I plunged the foot-wide push lawn mower into the snarled grass again and again. Cut, rake, cut, and rake. Clear a five-foot-square area. Burn the grass. Whack the weeds with a hand scythe. Rake with the old iron rake, Cut, rake, cut, rake, pick up the pile and burn. Our house was shaded by towering basswood trees, and since it was fall when we moved, the fallen leaves made the War of the Great Grass Cutting more challenging. In a matter of weeks the place where the "new family" lived looked pretty good.

The Sacred Place
Just a few blocks down a grassy road east of our house was the ballpark. It was nothing like the fenced, finely groomed park in Gaylord. The Garden City ballpark was part of the fair grounds, but Mother Nature had sculptured this park. Fairground buildings ran parallel to the baseline from home to third base, pinching the entire field toward the Watonwan River, which paralleled the base path from home to first and then bent left, a natural right field fence.

The lay of the land shaped the outfield. A gigantic oak about 100 feet past third base claimed part of left field. Huge limbs stretched into the playing field, knocking fly balls unceremoniously to the ground. Screeching blasts destined for home runs in other parks ricocheted off the limbs or tore off leafy branches that spun down like toy propellers.

The outfield had no fence. It simply dropped off as if Mother Nature had stuck her tiny pencil in one of those silver compasses used by geometry students, stuck the ice pick end into home plate, and drawn the outfield arc. Then she decided that center field should begin a gradual slope toward the river and cut through right field. Along the right field line, relatives of the baseball-gobbling oaks in left field sank their roots along the right field foul line and knocked down line drives hit their way. The right fielder needed sprinter speed to run down line drives and nab them before they bounced into the river and floated toward New Orleans.

The infield was horrible. Every infielder who survived the season should have been given a Purple Heart. Ground balls bounced erratically. Every hop was a bad hop. The infield either made great players or reduced them to gun-shy basket cases, who fought every ground ball. Major-league players would have demanded renegotiated contracts and knee-to-chest jock straps.

The backstop screen began behind first base, twisted to arc the batting area, and ended at a wooden post behind third. Foul balls pulled over third base headed for the fair grounds. Balls sliced over first were pulled like magnets toward the river, and balls fouled straight back zipped over the fence like bottle rockets.

Each hitter became automatically two inches shorter as he stepped into the batter's box. Two good-sized foxholes had been scratched out over the years and no amount of fill or tamping could prevent guys from digging their spikes into the soft ground and shrinking each hitter.

The pitcher's mound looked nothing like those finely manicured mounds on which major league prima donnas survey their kingdoms. The infield gradually sloped up to what might have been the approximate regulation height. The pitching rubber wavered a bit from age.

Gus

Unlike other aspects of the ballpark, which suffered from lack of a devoted lover, the pitching mound had Ray (Gus) Gustafson to fill its gouges with clay, tamp the clay flat, and manicure the mound to his liking. The pitching mound was Gussie's sacred place. Here he performed his magic, and what a magician he was!

Gus was my hero. He seemed about seven feet tall, but he probably stood three or four inches over six feet. He looked a bit like Ichabod Crane decked out in a baseball uniform. Gus was thin with hundreds of joints and miles of arms and legs. When he started moving all that loose stuff around, hitters cringed. Gus was a flamethrower. He threw bullets, aspirins, and white lightning. He could "bring it." Gus threw smoke, headache tablets, and buzzers.

Ray Gustafson

Fastballs exploded out of those whirling arms and legs and sliced off a piece of the outside corner. Before they knew it, batters were muttering obscenities and throwing their bats in frustration. Many were happy to get back to the bench where it was safe.

Proper decorum dictates that pitchers with class should not laugh at their conquests. I don't think Gus liked anything better than zippin' a called third strike past a hitter. But Gus had "that look." You could never tell if he was squinting from the sun, clenching his teeth in pain, or stifling a grin. I had seen that grin too often to be fooled. He just stood on the mound rubbing the ball, waiting for the next victim.

One of the reasons Gus was my hero was that he was the only other person I knew who loved throwing a ball. I'm not talking about people who like to play catch or pitch. I'm talking about a guy who loves the touch of the seams and the smooth leather, the snap of the wrist, and the white blur that wants to rip off the other guy's glove. I loved to play "burn out" with my friends, and I didn't lose too often, but I never challenged Gus. Bruce Springsteen knew what Gus and I knew: "He could throw that speedball by you, make you look like a fool."

Heroes are usually older. They have mastered their skills. Anyone knows that to be a good baseball player, you've got to listen to your older heroes. Now when you are fourteen or fifteen, anyone who is older than you is "old." How old was Gus? How should I know? I just moved to town. All I knew was that he graduated and was a local hero.

Gus loved to experiment with different kinds of pitches. I was often his guinea pig. To help Gus perfect his repertoire, I rode my bike down the lane to the park. I slipped a handkerchief inside the catcher's mitt. The mitt wasn't one of those fancy ones they have now, the kind that looks like a first baseman's mitt. This was a genuine pud, a stuffed donut with a pocket in the center. No one caught Gus's fastball one-handed with a pud.

I put on the catcher's equipment. Gus warmed up a bit, each pitch picking up speed. After a few pitches he turned up the speed. He threw lightning! Pitch after pitch knocked the mitt off my hand. Then he grinned that "oh, I'm in pain" or "the sun-sure-is-bright" grin. The master was giving the kid lessons in how to pitch.

Soon it was time for Ewell Blackwell. Blackwell, who played for Cincinnati, terrified right-handed hitters with his side arm delivery called

"The Whip." Gus set those arms and legs a whirling, stepped half way to third, dropped his shoulder and fired blazers that started down the middle of the plate and screwed into the inside corner. Imagine having to stand up there four times every Sunday and try to hit bb pellets shooting off the top of the grass. When he had the "whippers" down, he worked on his infamous knuckle ball. I couldn't catch that dancing devil. I swatted at it and walked back to the backstop to retrieve every pitch.

Years later when I was teaching, I asked the students to select an object which knew them well, an object which had been through the battles of growing up with them, an object which was a symbol of their personality. The next task was to write about themselves thorough the point of view of the object. I often wonder what Gussie's glove would have said about him.

Gus had the most unique baseball glove I have ever seen. It looked as if a shoemaker had laid two pieces of leather together and cut out a glove that had a thumb and two big fingers. The first and second fingers fit into one section and the ring and pinkie fit into the other. Then he sewed some webbing between the thumb and the first big finger. He tied the two big fingers together with rawhide. The glove was flat and had virtually no padding.

It folded neatly into Gus's back pocket or sailed like a Frisbee to its designated place between innings. Like its owner, it paid no attention to style and never yearned to be a flashy, expensive model, but there was more to this glove than met the eye. Gus was ambidextrous. He could throw better left-handed than many players could with their dominant arm.

Most pitchers must either spin 180 degrees to throw to second base or jump and twist both feet and their body clockwise and then throw to second. In both cases the runner can take a generous lead off the base. Not with Gussie, they couldn't. He stood on the mound, slyly slid his left hand out of that flat piece of leather, gripped the ball, and fired to second. With the second baseman or shortstop standing close to the bag, runners stuck to second like taffy in a molar.

Everyone who played Garden City hoped that by some miracle Gus wouldn't pitch that day. But Gus pitched every Sunday, and batting averages dived like the butterflies in the hitter's stomachs. Those zipping fastballs, diving curves, fluttering knuckle balls, and the hated Blackwell sweep were Garden City's team. Without Gus on the mound, it was an even shoot-out. He was the pitcher. That was his job and he loved it.

Gus could also whack that "old tomato." Years later I watched Ted Williams sweep his arms, snap his wrists, and rifle towering shots into the heavens. I had seen that swing when I pitched batting practice to Gus.

Gus's goal was to hit fly balls over the giant oaks down the right field line and then stand back and admire each one. Gus could "hang 'em out to dry," too. I never felt sorrier for a tree than I did those old oaks down the right field line. Gus tore frozen ropes into those old fellas till they groaned.

Gus virtually disappeared from my life during the school year. He ran the Standard Station at the other end of town. Not far on my old Schwinn, but fall threw me into school and football. Then basketball season flew past, and soon we were jogging down the fairground's road to prove that baseball can be played in freezing rain and bone-chilling winds.

About that time I started hanging around the Standard Station, probably tormenting the hell out of Gus, but he never sent me packing. Every morning Gus' mom brewed pots of coffee, and the bakery sent over the rolls that drew the world's greatest bullshitters ever assembled in such a tiny space. Players and fans stopped in to replay Sunday's game. Local farmers stopped to fix a tractor tire, tell a good joke, or eat cinnamon rolls. Anyone heading north or south fueled up at Gussie's Standard. Full service. Wipe everything. Check all dipsticks.

"Oil's down."

"O.K., Gus, throw in a quart." Gus was firing fastballs. Ripping shots into the oak. Playing the station game like the master of the mound. Hustle in. Make change. Fling a few zingers at his buddies and dash back to the pumps. "How ya doing? Fill 'er up?"

I never drank coffee and rarely had money for the rolls, but I didn't have to pay a cent to suck in what could best be described as a cross between a Marx Brothers' movie and a Pentecostal confession. No one escaped the biting barbs. These people had no secrets. They couldn't keep from telling them if one should slip into their lives. There were no psychiatrists, counselors, or mental health clinics in town. People just brought their pain, joy, and recent transgressions to the morning revival meetings. After the poor victim had been sufficiently barbecued for his sins, hooting and belly laughs absolved him of his sins, at least for that day, anyway.

After the crowd had left, I hung around the garage and watched Gus change oil or fix flats. I putzed around with a few tools, just waiting until Gus had finished every job. He knew why I was waiting. Finally he took one of his blue oil rags or a handful of paper towels and taped it into a ball. He grabbed the broom in the corner and the game was on.

The hitter stood in the closed end of the garage and the pitcher outside. The rules were simple. Hit it off the ceiling—out. Rap it into the garage floor—out. Rip a liner off the windows or wall—out. You must hit it this far to get a single, here for a double, this far for a triple, and anything rapped outside was a homer unless you caught it. Hitting one of Gus's smokin' rag balls with a broom head one-foot square was like swatting bats in the dark I never won, but I didn't care. We were "playing the game." Life always asks, "Did you win?" It seldom asks, "How's playing the game going?" The only critics were the wrenches, oil cans, tires, and other residents of Gus's garage family. Any adult watching us would have said, "Look at those two guys, acting like kids, playing ball with a broom!" But what joy! What fleeting joy! When your alchemist says, "You are no longer a child. You must get serious about brewing an adult potion," there are no more broomball games on the schedule.

During those two years we lived in Garden City, I spent relatively few hours with Gus. But when you are starving, and someone hands you food, you never forget him. When you're a kid, naive, disjointed, and starving for something you can't even name, broomball in a Standard Station garage with your hero is food from the gods.

Field of Dreams

I've seen Gus one or two times in the past forty years, but I think often about him and that oak-lined field. Every kid should be so blessed to play in such a sacred place, such a memory maker. I chased balls into the river up to my knees, hit those water soaked balls with real wooden bats, threw batting practice for hours, and walked among my heroes. What a blessing to play under those oak trees, watching the ball ping pong back and forth and then diving to catch it as it dropped lazily to the ground. Never again would I play on a carpet of acorns that crunched and popped when I walked on them. Sometimes I'd grab a handful and pepper the old tree.

I played on college fields and dozens of the best amateur diamonds throughout the state. I played in the old Class C minor league Rox Park in St. Cloud and the park where St. Paul Saints played on Snelling Avenue. I even played on two fields in Puerto Rico, but nothing compared to that old fenceless park down by the fairgrounds.

Every kid needs a hero, and for a few short months Gus was mine. I'm certain he never thought of himself as anyone extraordinary. His life changed the day his father burned his arm on a school bus muffler. When he died from an infection, Gus's dreams of going to college vanished. Gus was given the responsibility of running a business and supporting his mother and sister. Those few hours we spent in Gus's garage, whacking a cloth ball with a broom, freed both us from the Furies. I was just a kid, free of feeling alone, free from worrying about my family and how long my dad would stay sober. In that gas station garage, the only thing that mattered was the whoosh of Gus swinging the kitchen broom at one of my cloth fastballs and the hootin' and hollerin' about whether the ball was a single or a double. Every kid needs a hero. Every kid needs memories like these.

High School

Making a Difference

On May 27, 1954, we filed into the gym together, listened to the speakers, enacted the necessary ritual, and headed out into a spring thunderstorm. Tonight we'll sit around and tell stories about those good old days—some of you recapturing twelve years of school together, others of us who popped in here and there will recall bits and pieces.

Our stories will be different, slanted by what we remember and how we feel about those days. Were they truly the carefree days of youth? We won't tell everything. We will guard what was embarrassing, threatening, humiliating, and fearful. What a reunion it would be if we told all those stories!

Some of us have maintained friendships over these forty years while others of us renew acquaintances or perhaps for the first time, we share stories with classmates who are still strangers.

Although I loved school, over the years I have often thought Paul Simon sang it best: "When I think back on all the crap I learned in high school, it's a wonder I can think at all." What did I learn? What information can I remember from those hours of studying? How did those "formative" years affect my life? I have forgotten much, but I do know that the people who taught me influenced my life.

Last year I retired after years filled with thousands of teenagers, reams of papers, stacks of literature, textbooks preaching the dogmas of grammar, usage and rhetoric. I had no idea when I was a seventeen-year-old senior that I would spend so many years teaching students who were forever young. Teenagers immersed me in their ever-changing jargon, bebopping, duck tailing, hula hooping, mind jangling, and soul searching. I had no idea that I would be one of the fortunate whose profession would become my passion.

High school sought to prepare me to live in the literal world of chemistry formulas and physics problems; the world of yes and no; the world of what was and what wasn't; the somewhere world where people stopped you on the street and asked, "I have to meet a train. At what time should I be at the station? One train is coming from New York, where it's 6:00. It's carrying forty passengers and a twenty-member tuba band. One third of the time they travel twenty miles per hour and two thirds of the time they travel almost fifty miles an hour. What time will they arrive in Minneapolis to meet the train from San Francisco, which left the day before yesterday, broke down twice, once for thirteen and one-half minutes and the second time for ten minutes and seventeen seconds? They were averaging fifty miles an hour until they unloaded a herd of cattle outside Denver."

High school prepared me to answer questions such as, "What's the formula for hydrochloric acid? Would you credit or debit Acme Trucking? What did Archimedes discover in his tub? What's the past perfect form of *be*? A week never passes without someone asking me to explain which way their gears rotate or how much horse power is exerted by Belgian draft horses pulling a sled loaded with five hundred pounds of rocks. One day a man said, "I would like to know what you know about the natural resources in Guam. Please fill in these blanks." Once a very crotchety lady at the coffee shop demanded I take her true-false test about the meaning of Shakespeare's *Hamlet*.

What influenced me most were not facts and the treasures of the empirical world. What influenced me most were my teachers. They helped form my character, my vision, and my values. They helped shape my philosophy of life, my philosophy of teaching, and they did it by what they said and what they did and by what they didn't do or didn't say. I didn't realize all this at the time, but they wove themselves into the fabric of my character.

I believe in the power of stories. Chemistry analyzes what we are composed of, but stories reveal who and what we are. We are our stories. When some asks us, "Do you know Bummer?" We answer, "Sure, we know him. We went to high school together." If the person is really interested in Bummer, we tell all the Bummer stories we can remember. We know Bummer through our Bummer stories. We probably ran out of Bummer stories when we parted after graduation. Now we admit we really know only the Bummer of high school. We remember only shadows of the person we dated for the prom or sat next to in history.

These are several of my stories from high school. They are as vivid as the day they happened and they have dramatically affected my life. Your stories will be different from mine. We will both tell the truth, but your truth and my truth will be different. In the movie *Radio Flyer*, Tom Hanks is talking to his sons about truth. He tells them, "History is in the mind of the teller. Truth is in the telling." This is my history, my truth.

I learned something about teaching the morning I walked through the homeroom door into the sanctuary where the class of 1954 had gathered to begin its junior year. I was a newcomer, an outsider. Every head turned to look at the skinny kid with glasses.

I don't remember who the homeroom teacher was, but I remember being waved to a seat in the back of the room. I have never forgotten the empty feeling of being a stranger in a strange land, the feeling that I could never again be what I once was or return to that safer place. I didn't realize the blessings of this terror at the time, however. Years later I taught in a school of 2000 students. When strangers from strange lands walked into my classroom, I remembered the looks on yor faces.

When I grew wiser, I took these strangers aside, shook their hands, and asked them about the land they had come from. I talked about the size of the school and told them what we were doing in class. Then I introduced the strangers to the class and found someone like LeRoy or Janet and made a seat available next to those persons of kindness.

So, you see, I learned something from that unremembered teacher during those first moments in my new school. You were there, too, players in my story, but often we don't realize we are playing a role in someone else's story. At sixteen we think the whole world focuses only on our story.

For the first few months of the '53 school year, my dad and I lived with my grandparents. Dad worked at the Model Clothing Store. My mother, sister, and two brothers stayed in Garden City until my dad finished building our house.

During those weeks the physics classroom became my personal Garden of Gethsemane. Physics and mathematics were a mystery to me. I had no background and no interest in the class. I took it because someone said, "You need that for college," which was for me, of course, a lie.

Mr. Physics

Mr. Physics was my Nero of science. He was the first person to introduce me to passive educational tyranny. He taught me how the lethargic tyrant can fiddle away while the spirit of his student burns to cinders.

I can still see him sitting on his throne, which sat elevated on a platform, one leg thrown over the other, turned away from the class, slouching behind his desk. Disdainfully, he looked down on his subjects. The barrier of space between tyrant and subject spoke the unspoken.

I never once believed that this person who taught with so little passion saw me as more than eleven letters in his grade book. Those eleven letters had been uprooted twice in two years and spent the summer running a dry cleaning plant in St. Paul. I was a kid who didn't want to leave his friends, never wanted to enter that new school, and I certainly didn't want my life filled with physics anxiety. I needed to be more than eleven letters, but he never made an effort to see me.

I got an F in physics that first grading period, the only one I ever received. I deserved that F. It was embarrassing and humiliating. What could I do with an F? Talk it over with my aging grandparents? Take it to my dad who was isolated from his family and fighting his own demons? Call my mom who was lonely and isolated? Bury it?

I'm trying to find the positive in the negative here, to see how this failure influenced my philosophy of teaching. What happens when I write F on my student's report card? I know that F may mean the end, but I also know F may be the beginning of something as well. I have not forgotten my F and the feeling of failure. F's give birth to fear or resolution.

I never once believed that Mr. Physics saw me as anything more than someone occupying a desk, a stupid kid defiling his sacred class. Never once during my six weeks of frustration did he ask, "Hey, Tom, what's happening here? What's the problem? Got any questions I can help you with?"

Never once in his physics and chemistry (another class I needed for college) did I feel as if I were anything more than formula, a task to be analytically observed, and a problem of force, movement, and matter to be solved with a slide rule. He never lit the flame of science within me, but I do owe him a debt. He introduced me to "I don't-give-a-damn educational tyranny." I met other teachers like Mr. Physics. I earned my F, but I think if "we" had been more involved, he and I, things would have been different. I did fail students, and I thought about mine every time I did.

In physics and chemistry I was Theseus walking through the dark labyrinth, expecting to find my Minotaur lurking behind each page of my textbooks. In the myth the king's daughter Ariadne helps Theseus by giving him a ball of string which he unravels as he travels into the depths of the unknown. At the end of the labyrinth, Theseus steps into the Minotaur's filth and suffocating stench. In the midst of this wasteland world, he kills the monster with his bare hands and follows the string back to Ariadne.

By the time I encountered Mr. Chemistry, I had met my Ariadne, my classmate Mary S. She was not a king's daughter, but she was a person of royal spirit. She unraveled her ball of knowledge with kindness, patience and humor. Many hours before and after school we sat at her kitchen table and she filled the twisting pathways of chemistry with light and helped me defeat my Minotaur.

Mr. English

Each morning as soon as the school door was unlocked, two eighth graders and I went directly to visit Mr. English in the library. We read the sports page and chatted with him about whatever was happening.

I thank Mr. English for showing me that kindness has a place in teaching and for not dwelling on my weaknesses. This became evident during one of our weekly vocabulary lessons. He gave us five words a week and we were to know them by Friday. "Tom, you take the next one," he said.

"Ka-litch," I said confidently, emphasizing the second syllable.

"I'm afraid you forget the accent mark above the final *e*," corrected Mr. English. The word is pronounced cli-shay with a long *a* in the final syllable. For the remainder of the year, any worn out expression uttered in class was greeted with, "Isn't that a 'ka-litch' and a hoots of laughter." It's quite easy to become a *ka-litch*. The classroom was Mr. English's stage and every reading was presented with passion. I can still hear him playing the role of the three witches who greeted Macbeth. How he loved phrases such as "When's the hurly-burly done?" and "Anoint thee, witch! the rump-fed ronyon cries." He seemed to know everything about the lives of the authors we read, including the juiciest gossip. He informed us that Lord Byron once fired two pistols in his bedroom.

When I was sixteen and seventeen, I wasn't ready for the great writers. Studying the Romantic poets and Shakespeare was not the same as studying geography or history. I lived in the literal world. I could fill in the blanks with *what*, but I never bothered with *why*? I knew little if anything about symbol or metaphor. I had not lived enough to fully appreciate the wisdom that filled his classroom each period.

Ironically, I used the same grammar and rhetoric book my first year of teaching. Although I had done the exercises religiously as a student, four years later I recognized only the cover of *Keys to Good English*. Behind the green and white cover outlining the key lay the world of sentence syntax, proper usage, and correct grammar. For the remainder of my teaching career, I thought about how to "make that stuff stick."

"Memorize great poetry," preached Mr. English. "Memorize. When you memorize these wonderful words, they are like precious gems which are yours for as long as you live. They will become your friends. You may call upon them whenever you wish."

Wordsworth was one of Mr. English's favorite British poets. "The world is too much with us/ Getting and spending we lay waste our powers/ Little we see in nature that is ours. For this, for everything, we are out of tune," exclaimed Mr. English. His explanation of the poem may have been my first lesson on materialism and ecology.

Like most British literature teachers Mr. English required us to memorize Macbeth's words

> Tomorrow and tomorrow and tomorrow
> Creeps in this petty pace from day to day
> To the last syllable of recorded time
> And all our yesterdays have lighted fools
> The way to dusty death. Out, out, brief candle!
> Life's but a walking shadow, a poor player
> That struts and frets his hour upon the stage
> And then is heard no more. It is a tale
> Told by an idiot, full of sound and fury,
> Signifying nothing.

I taught *Macbeth* during my first year and like my mentor, I required my students to memorize the same lines. Many years passed before I understood the lines. As a high school senior my life didn't creep along. I knew little about the ravages of time. I was a naïve innocent who never hung out with "idiot[s] full of sound and fury" nor did I know they existed. I looked forward to everything, not "nothing." Time has added flesh to Shakespeare's words.

Teaching gave Mr. English the opportunity to perform several times a day. I knew that each class would be a command performance. Once each

year he turned the stage over to any senior who wanted to participate in the class play. He cast the roles, directed the construction of the stage settings, and molded us to his liking. Watching him direct was like watching a tragic-comedy within a tragic-comedy. He cast me as Mr. Parcher in Booth Tarkington's *Seventeen*. He decked me out with a bowler hat and a mustache. To help me fit the role, he stuffed a pillow under my shirt. Many of the characters in the play were made-up with black faces. When I look at the photographs of the black-faced characters in our production, I realize we did indeed live during a time of innocence.

Mr. Parcher presents a gift to our illustrious English teacher, who also directed our senior play, Seventeen by Booth Tarkington.

I don't think Mr. English had any interest in sports, but he came to most of our games. I was thrilled to see him in the crowd. He is one of few teachers I remember attending our games. No matter how well we played or how poorly we played, he greeted me in the library the next morning with "Good game last night."

I visited Mr. English often during my college years and my first years of teaching. He loved to talk about his collection of books, movie magazines, stamps, sheet music, and rare coins. His most valuable collection was the red-covered grade books that stood near his piano, a grade book for every year taught. "You're in there, Tom," he said, "every assignment, every quiz, every test, and your final grades are also listed there."

At first I thought they were just one of many items he had gathered over the years, but I knew that we were more than just numbers to him. We were his students. We were the fire of his life. I thank him for passing on a bit of that flame to me.

Coach Basketball

Twenty-three-year old Coach Basketball was one of the most instrumental people in forming my philosophy of teaching. I'm certain he thought he was doing the right thing, but more than any other person in my high school and college education, he taught me how to use humiliation. He taught me how to use fear and shame to destroy self-esteem. He taught me how to use power to intimidate.

During practice the night before our first game, Coach Basketball called us down two-at-a-time to receive our game uniforms and our silver warm-up suits. Guys came up from the locker room wearing their game uniforms, shot buckets, and generally horsed around. Two more guys were called down. Finally I was the only guy left on the floor without a uniform. He called me down alone.

I can still smell the damp, musty locker room. I can see the plaster chipping off the walls. I can reach out and touch the rows of green lockers.

Coach Basketball called me into his office, shut the door, and told me to sit down. This man I had met only a few weeks earlier when practice began towered over me. I sat and my 6' 3" first-year coach stared down at me. Behind him lay my uniform and warm-up suit.

He said, "Some of the guys think you are getting a little too cocky— Some of the guys say— Some of the people downtown are saying— I've heard—."

I became sick to my stomach. I could feel myself shrinking. "Who could "those guys" be?" I wondered. "Cobble? Dave? Moldy? Lefty? Growler?" Those guys were my friends.

His words pressed down on me. I gasped for breath. My heart pounded. I began to sweat. I stared at the floor. His litany of accusations echoed in my ears, hovered over me, and squeezed my head. The words grew smaller and dissolved. They sounded as if they were moving farther and farther away. The words changed into fear. I don't rember the sounds stopping.

Red blurred before my eyes. He held my uniform in front of my face.

I dreamed about that day for years. In my dream I confront Coach Basketball and challenge his accusations. I storm upstairs. I scream, "OK, you guys, what the hell is going on here? Did one of you say—?"

In my dream I put the uniform into my locker, pull on my pants and coat, and walk out the side door of the school into the cold. I walk home, numbed by his words. My joy for the game slips away with each breath of winter night.

Of course that was a dream. I put on my uniform and joined the guys on the court. I felt alone, heartsick, isolated. I was not the same kid who walked down those stairs. I would never be that person again. In my dream, I never played again and I never told anyone why I quit, but I didn't quit. I played. I played because I loved the game. I played because I knew he was wrong. I played because I believed those guys were my friends.

That season I seldom took a shot, drove for the basket, passed or dribbled without thinking, "Should I have done that? Will some of the people downtown think—" Sometimes I played with joyful wildness, free of the curse. Then I remembered and the haunting began again. Coach Basketball never said a word about it again. I never discovered if what he said was true. I was a kid. He was Coach. What coaches said was gospel. Perhaps what he said was true. Perhaps someone was saying—. It's difficult to see the real you, especially when you are having fun.

This all happened nearly fifty years ago, but just retelling the story still makes nauseates me .

Mrs. Music

Mrs. Music taught my mom and dad in the 1930's. Later she taught me with the same pizzazz and gusto. She knew I loved to sing even though I couldn't read music or tell B flat from B plus. She knew that sooner or later I would end up singing the melody with the sopranos, so she blessed me by putting me next to Pat. If a heavy metal concert were playing on his right side and jackhammers were tearing down the Empire State Building on his left, Pat could sing the tenor harmony and never miss a note. I just followed Pat and hoped he was never sick.

When we practiced solos or ensembles, Mrs. Music tucked us into every nook and cranny of the school. Then she made the rounds helping each of us. She sang the music for me to mimic. She knew that such magic would occur between the notes on the page and my ability to sing them correctly. When I botched things up, she patted me on the back, sang it again, and said, "Now, you sing that again." No frustration. No bitterness. No quitting.

I cherish the moments we spent practicing for concerts in Mrs. Music's house. I didn't know it at the time, but what I cherished most is what she taught me about loving her students and loving her job. She was tough as nails and could growl better than most of my coaches, but she loved us and music so much that nothing could suppress her passion to teach young people to sing. Her classroom was the choir room in school and her living room at home.

Coach Football-Baseball

Coach Football-Baseball was a ferocious competitor. At 5' 8" he played line backer at Minneapolis North and carried his football career to Gustavus, where he also played baseball. Gustavus played an unbalanced line and so did we. Gustavus used it to gain national acclaim. We used it to gain ignominy. The only thing unbalanced about us was our talent.

Many people say he was difficult to play for, but I disagree. We called him "Growler" and growl he could. When we lost to Montgomery, 46 to 19, he wrote the local paper's game summary, which began, "The Belle Plaine Tigers were mere kittens last Friday night." He had every opportunity to "ream us out." Lord knows it must have pained him to see his warriors falter again and again, but he vented his fury with the help of the subs. Today coaches demand that their players wear their helmets at all times. This was not the case in 1954. The substitutes lined up their leather helmets along the sideline, and when we faltered badly, Coach booted them in frustration. The subs scurried to line them up again for our next fiasco.

During one game I called a pass on third and just a yard to go for a first down. The play fizzled and we had to punt. "Why the heck did you pass with so little to go for the first down?" he growled.

"Jeez," Coach, " I said, "you know I can't see the down marker. I had no idea we were that close." What can you say to your myopic quarterback? He just shook his head and walked away. He seldom shed his snarly face during football games because he was always right in there with us during our humiliating losses. We won half our games, but it seemed as if we were the weekly scapegoats for other teams.

Our baseball team was much better and we won most of our games. Only years later when I coached high school baseball, did I understand the torture I inflicted on the poor man. I usually ran the count on the batters to 3 and 1 or 3 and 2. I bounced a few into the dirt and sent a few high pitches off the screen. Of course the walks often resulted in cheap runs.

During one of my typical outings, Coach paced back and forth, firing stones at the dugout wall. My mother and aunt were sitting in the stands, horrified that their poor Tommy was getting abused. They didn't realize that pitch after pitch I was gnawing away the poor guy's sanity. All he could do was encourage me by yelling something like, "Throw strikes now. Make 'em hit the ball." I knew he was doing a lot of grumbling that I couldn't hear. I knew just how he felt. We won the game 3 to 2.

I played town team baseball with coach for three seasons. He was an excellent fielder, a great pivot man, and a fearless hitter. He stood with his left foot on the front line of the batter's box. "Why do you stand so close to the pitcher?" I asked him.

"I want to hit that curve ball before it breaks," he said. "I don't care if I'm closer to the pitcher. I want to challenge them."

After high school my teammates and I went our separate ways, but we came home for the holidays. During Christmas vacation we tried to find some janitor, administrator, or teacher who would open the school and let us into the gym. The only person we could count on was Coach Football-Baseball. We could always depend on Growler to open the door.

Gene O'Brien

Gene O'Brien moved to St. Paul from Richmond, Wisconsin, when he was eleven. He and his brothers developed their baseball skills in the St. Paul parochial school leagues. He attended Cretin High School and in 1939 Gene enrolled at St. Thomas, where he starred in football, hockey, and baseball.

In December of Gene's junior year, the Japanese bombed Pearl Harbor. He and twenty-five fellow Tommies signed up for the Marine Corps Reserve. Reserve members were assured that they could finish college before being drafted.

During his junior year he signed a baseball contract with Fargo Moorhead of the Class C Northern League. At that time athletes could play professional sports and also participate in amateur sports. In the winter of 1942 he was sold to the New York Yankees and assigned to their AAA team, Kansas City, which sent him to Peoria in the Piedmont

Gene O'Brien, 1952

League. In July of 1943 Gene was hitting .299 for Norfolk. His teammate, Lawrence (Yogi) Berra was hitting .253. Berra became famous with the Yankees.

On July 23 Gene was activated by the Marines and sent to Paris Island, South Carolina to become an officer. "I was offered the opportunity to play with the Marine team, but I didn't because I had a strong commitment to the service, in the invasions, and to my friends from St. Thomas." Gene fought two and one-half years in the South Pacific. He and his college buddies led the charge on Okinawa.

Gene moved to Belle Plaine in 1946 and became the player-manager for the next eight years. In 1948 we lived in Gaylord and my grandpa lived in Belle Plaine. That year the Tigers led by Gene O'Brien played Winsted for the state championship in Shakopee. Grandpa Pete took me to the game, but it was so crowded we stood in left-center field behind a single rope barrier. The Tigers lost the game when an outfielder chased a ball into that crowd. If he had let the ball go and held up his hands, the hit would have been a ground-rule double. The Tigers also lost the championship game to Cannon Falls in 1953.

Year after year Gene was one of the most feared hitters in the league. When he took batting practice, he cracked line drives to all corners of the ballpark. Whack, whack, whack filled the night air. "How did you become such a great hitter?" I asked him.

"Back in '33 and '34 my brother Bob played in our backyard," Gene replied. "The bat was a broomstick handle and the ball was a bottle cap. We hit hundreds of bottle caps. We played all day long."

In Gene's final year of managing, I tried out for the Tigers. At that time playing for the town team was the dream of every kid who loved baseball. For years after the war, people flocked to the ballparks all over the state. It was the major leagues and at seventeen baseball was my life.

That spring many of the players from that wonderful 1953 team retired. During one of the first practices, Gene took me aside and said, "Tom, the pitching in this league is really tough. Give it all you've got all the time. Don't worry about your hitting. You're going to play."

I have never forgotten those words: "You're going to play." This spring, forty-four years later, I asked Gene how he could assure me that I was going to play.

"You've gotta participate," he said. "You've gotta get the chance. You've got to get in there and fail in order to win. That's life, of course, so I felt if I could spot the talent in young fellas, I wanted to get them in and experience what you've got to do along with the advice that I or others could give. Pretty soon those young guys start maturing and you've got a hell-of-a ballplayer. If you have the main ingredients like intensity and anticipation, if you show me these qualities, then I think I can guide you and coach you and make you a pretty good ballplayer."

I never learned to hit a twisting bottle cap. I never faced machine gun fire in the South Pacific. I never blistered line drives off the board fence, but I loved to play and I was blessed to have someone who gave me the chance. Four words can make a difference.

Mr. Humphrey

Steve Humphrey stood only an inch or two over five feet but he was a giant among men and I loved him.

Most of us called him Mr. Humphrey. The brightest and bravest called him Steve, especially the staunch Democrats. When he sat at his desk and lectured us about Camus, Flaubert, or sentence syntax, he struggled to control his nervous tick. He never won the battle. In one sweeping motion, he tucked his chin tightly against his clavicle and rolled his head to the left or right. The first person he saw as he was completing his question became his victim. Some days he would twist only to the left, other days only to the right. I tried to guess which direction he would twist and then I sat on the other side of the room. My plan seldom worked. On his worst days, he looked both left and right.

Mr. Humphrey

One day my classmate Jim Cesnik said, "Steve calls on me every time he rolls his head to the left because I'm the first person he sees. Last week he asked, 'What do you think of Madame Bovary's motives?' Then he turned to the left and finished his question with, 'Mr. Cesnik?'"

"I got tired being called on first," said Jim, "so I moved to the right side of the room. Yesterday Steve reversed his tick and rolled his head to the right. 'So,' he asked, 'what do you think about T. S. Eliot's wasteland imagery, Mr. Cesnik?'"

Five Words

On October 8, 1956, the New York Yankees were playing the Brooklyn Dodgers in the World Series. The rest of the baseball fanatics and I watched the game on the only TV set on campus, a tiny screen of flickering black and white dots—baseball played in an electronic snowstorm.

When the bell rang calling me to Mr. Humphrey's class, Don Larsen of the Yankees had not allowed a Dodger runner to reach first base for seven innings. A perfect game! I was transfixed. If the great Shakespeare himself had risen from the grave to give one final interview, I could not, would not, have left my chair.

In those days professors interrupted class to ask, "Why are you late?" They stopped us in the halls or at the ball game and asked, "What happened? Missed you in class yesterday." No one missed Mr. Humphrey's class, but I couldn't move. Larsen was perfect.

Larsen struck out Dale Mitchell for the final out, Yogi Berra jumped on Larsen, and I headed for Mr. Humphrey's class. Expecting the worst, I tried to slip in as inconspicuously as possible. The tick twisted my way. "Well," he asked, "did he do it?"

"Damn right he did it," I said and slid into my desk.

I never thought about his words at the time, but later when I began teaching, I played the scene over and over. "How could he know me that well?" I thought. "How could any teacher be that wise? How could a teacher whose passion was the great literature of the world know that at that time, at that moment in my life, baseball was more important than contemporary literature? Here I am looking at my students' faces. Will I ever know them that well?"

Whenever we played home games, Steve was somewhere in the crowd, rooting for me and his beloved Johnnies.

Three years later I invited him to our wedding. My wife and I were married on December 27th and it was twenty below zero that day. My bride and I sat facing the congregation. In the midst of our family and friends I saw the tick. I looked at Mr. Humphrey (Steve by this time) and smiled. He grinned and ticked a few times.

Years later I told him how those five words—"Well, did he do it?" had centered my teaching philosophy. I told him that he had inspired me to want to know my students as people, not just as bodies sitting in desks. I told him his inspiration had guided me throughout my career.

When Steve Humphrey died, I asked his sisters if I might have one of his books. They gave me his copy of *The Magic Mountain*.

Four words can indeed make a difference.

Mr. Chief

We all knew the school was his. An atmosphere of possessiveness hung throughout the building and we breathed it daily. We were temporary travelers on his ship and our journey might last anywhere from a one-year stay to retirement. We might have taught under the illusion that we were the masters of our classrooms. We learned quickly, however, who was in control, who was the superintendent.

Most of us called him Mister. A few called him Chief, a title he carried with great pride. One of the teachers said, "Nothing escaped him. He could smell that something wasn't right, even though it wasn't wrong." His office guarded the main entrance. He observed all comings and goings. In many ways he was Orwell's Big Brother, watching over us every moment. I am certain he also thought of himself as Machiavelli's Prince, the benign ruler who believes that power and expedience in the hands of someone who wants to "do good" is the most efficient way to govern.

Mr. Chief was hired to tend in a super manner and he did it his way, which was the "right way." A good school was a controlled school with clean blackboards, lined-up rows of desks, and polished, litter-free floors. He demanded that we turn off the lights at the end of the day and pull down the shades so they were even throughout the building. He didn't want to drive by his school and see one shade up and one shade down. He controlled the school board, the custodians, and the cooks.

To Mr. Chief a good student was a controlled student. He sent those garbed in leather jackets home to change. He sent longhaired hippies to the barbershop, where the clipping would "be taken care of" if the students claimed, "My parents can't afford this." He sent the unclean of body to physical education teachers with the directive, "Give this guy a shower." The leather jackets, long hair, and dirt soon disappeared.

To Mr. Chief a good teacher was a controlled teacher. A good teacher allowed no classroom turmoil. He sought to control the way we spoke, thought, taught, and dressed. Mr. Chief told us we could drink and socialize at one and only one club in town. Every other place was off limits.

I was the only teacher not hired by Mr. Chief. The principal hired me while I was teaching in Puerto Rico. Unfortunately the relationship between Mr. Chief and the principal was strained. Actually it was fractured. The feud had begun before I arrived and lasted long after I left. Sadly, we teachers were all caught in the middle of this power struggle. We walked a tightrope to keep from falling to our career deaths. Their feud played a major role in my decision to leave his school.

Mr. Chief could be kind and amiable one moment, vindictive and contentious the next. He had his favorites and woe to the unchosen. He praised some and humiliated others. Most of us felt intimidated and rarely taught with creative abandonment. Whether we liked him or took the first available train out of town, we all agreed that he was Mr. Chief.

THOSE WERE THE DAYS: A FEW OF US REMINISCE ABOUT MR. CHIEF

Mr. Science and later Mr. Principal: I had problems with swelling in my legs and ankles. I had been teaching in the district for four years. He came up to see me and brought me a carton of cigarettes, very nice. Before he left he said, "You won't be getting a raise next year because you didn't get your six continuing education credits. I went to talk with him when I got out of the hospital to see if I could get another year to take the credits. No way! He gave me cigarettes and told me he was going to cut my salary.

Later I became his principal. He was always in complete control. He went to Atlantic City in January for the Superintendents' Convention. I was sitting at home and he called. "You better close school for tomorrow (Monday)," he said.

"Why?" I asked.

"I just saw the news report," he said, "and you've got a big storm coming through."

"Are you serious?" I asked.

"Yes," he said, "close the school."

I went to the phone and cancelled school, and then I called all the teachers and we had a helluva big party. We got one inch of snow the next day.

I thought about applying for his superintendent's job when he retired, but the guys on the board said, "Don't even try for it."

Mr. Chief said, "Why don't you leave? There's a principal's job opening at my friend's school. He fired the principal for stealing money from the lunch fund."

He called his buddy, another Catholic superintendent, and said, "You still looking for a principal? Well, I got one here for you." Here I was sitting right there while this conversation was going on. I could tell by his answers what the questions were.

("Is he honest?")

"Oh, yes, he's honest.

("Does he owe any money?)

"I think he owes money on his house and car, but nothing other than that. You can trust him," said Mr. Chief.

("What's good about him?")

"He's faithful."

("What do I have to be careful of?")

"You've got to let him off for hunting and fishing," said Mr. Chief.

I went for an interview and the guy asked me the same questions he had asked Mr. Chief. I gave the same answers Mr. Chief had given. Then the chairman of the school board walked in and the superintendent asked him about my request to have off for hunting and fishing seasons. The board chairman and I talked about hunting and fishing the entire time. There was nothing said about the job or my honesty. I got the job and I got the hunting and fishing days off. It was all due to Mr. Chief. He gave me a great recommendation.

Mr. English: At times it was difficult to determine Mr. Chief's motives for recommending his teachers. One day Mr. Science Teacher, Mr. Chief, and I were sitting in a college cafeteria when one of Mr. Chief's superintending colleagues joined us for coffee. He said he was looking for a music teacher. "I've got one who wants to leave," said Mr. Chief. I was stunned. The "one who wants to leave" was my friend and he had said nothing to anyone about wanting to leave, not even to me.

Mr. Biology-Mr. Yearbook: When I started, I taught biology in a room with no electrical outlets. The switch was in the hall. Then we got a new lab. I went to Mr. Chief and said, "I need eighteen microscopes for the new lab."

"What do you need those for?" he snapped. I had to explain the whole process about using slides.

"Are you sure you need them?" he asked. "Are you going to use them?"

I got the microscopes, but I tell you, I made certain they were out because he expected to see them out when he walked around and he walked around every day.

Right after I started working as the timer for basketball games, Mr. Chief called me into his office and said, "You're going to be the timer for all the games."

I said, "Yes, I'd like to do that in lieu of chaperoning the bus to away games."

Then the he said, "Remember. It's an advantage to the home team and you're the one who will be doing the official timing." I was so nervous after that, nervous that I was going to do something wrong.

I never knew another person who could open and close a classroom door without anyone hearing him come in. You would turn around and there he was, standing somewhere in the room. If you did not teach for fifty-five minutes, he would call you down and say, "I hired you to teach for fifty-five minutes a period and I want you standing for fifty-five minutes. There will be no study hall at the end of the period." I didn't even need a chair in my room because I never sat. Nobody sat.

I was assigned five biology classes and the annual. I didn't know anything about publishing a yearbook. We didn't even have one at my high school. The first year the pages were just a photograph and a white page. The next year it was better. We put a thick red cover on it. The book was beautiful. I was standing in my room in early May. I knew the yearbooks were due to arrive. He came into my room and tapped me on the shoulder and said, "Look at this." He held out the yearbook.

Each year Mr. Chief wrote a letter to the students. It was printed at the front of the yearbook. He showed me the page. "Did you look at this?" he asked. "Didn't you proofread this? My name is spelled incorrectly."

I said, "These are seniors who should know how to spell your name."

"We can't have this," he said. "Send the books back."

My god, I thought I was going to faint. That was big-time money to have the books reprinted.

"We can't have this," he insisted. "My name is spelled incorrectly."

I said, "We can use a piece of paper and put it over the name and spell it correctly." We made that correction on every single yearbook.

Mr. Physical Education: I arrived at his office and told his secretary who I was and that I was there for an interview with Mr. ("incorrect pronunciation"), which I later discovered was a major faux pas. His secretary corrected me and said the name was Mr. ("corrected name,") and I'm Mrs. ("corrected name.") I figured I might just as well go home right then and there.

I don't think my interview lasted more than twenty minutes. I never saw his face that time or any other time I was in his office. He always sat behind his desk, turned, and looked out the window toward the street. It was just like going to confession. He smoked and looked out the window. The only time he turned toward me was to put his ashes into the ashtray.

I had phy. ed. first hour, health second hour, and then another phy. ed. class third hour. During the first week I met him in the hall on my way to health class. He tapped me on the shoulder and said, "Where are you going?"

I said, "I'm on my way to teach my health class."

"You're not dressed for teaching health," he said.

I said, " I just taught phy. ed. and as soon as this class is over, I've got to teach phy. ed. again. I didn't have time to change into my shirt and tie."

"When you are teaching here," he said, "you will always wear your coat and tie when you are in front of a regular class." From that time on I always wore a sport coat and tie. He also jumped me about walking with both hands in my pockets. He said something like, "That looks like hell. You don't do that." And I didn't.

Mr. Band: The man made my life miserable. One day I was teaching in the band room. There was no ventilation and the temperature outside was about ninety degrees. It was murder. I took my jacket off halfway through class and hung it over the back of a chair. Mr. Chief came in. He looked at me, he looked at my jacket, and then he looked back at me. I put on the jacket. He could make life miserable if he didn't like you.

The band had to play at every football and basketball game. For each football game we had to put on a different marching show. One night it was raining really hard, and the football coach came up to me and said, "Please don't take the team out on the field. It's slippery and I'm afraid someone will fall and get hurt." I said that was fine with me and we didn't go onto the field.

After the halftime Mr. Chief came walking toward me and said, "Why didn't you have the band out on the field?" I told him that the coach had asked me not to perform for fear that someone would get hurt.

He said, "The football coach doesn't run this school. I do, and unless I tell you not to, you will be on that football field." He never said a word to the coach, but he proceeded to make my life miserable because I talked back to him.

One day right in the middle of my seventh- and eighth-grade band class—there were seventy kids in the room—he stomped into the room as only he could do. He looked at me and hollered, "What's the matter with you? Don't you answer your phone any more?"

I knew better than to sass him back, so I turned and calmly said, "No, I don't. Don't you remember that you had it taken out six months ago?" He took the phone out just to get me. The school board had put it in because I used it for the summer band. It was dead quiet in the room. Those seventy kids never moved. He turned blue, turned around, stomped out of the room, and slammed the door. After he left, the kids all snickered. Later I was working in my room during my lunch period. He walked in and said, "Don't you ever talk to me like that again in front of students."

You could hear the click when he turned the intercom on to listen to what was going on in your class. Everyone knew he did it. The kids caught on fast. When they heard the click, they all pointed at the speaker and everything went dead quiet. When it clicked off, they started talking again. It was illegal, but nothing was illegal for Mr. Chief.

We won the Minnesota State Fair band trophy for the second time, something no other band had done at that time. Mr. Chief organized a big party at the American Legion Club. The band and all the band parents were there. He stood up and started praising people. First he praised the band kids, then the band parents, then the bus drivers, but he never said one word about me.

When I first came to the school, all the athletes were required to try out for the boys' glee club. They were good. Mr. Chief used to come in, sit down, and listen to those guys sing. He never stopped smiling. He loved to listen to them, but he never said a word to me about them.

I often thought about quitting teaching. I was a tool and die maker before I became a teacher. I could have made twice as much money there as I made teaching, but I loved teaching. There was a challenge every day, but working with this man made it difficult. I had a family to support. I knew that if I quit, he would give me such a poor recommendation that I would never teach again. It was hard to take.

Another teacher: You had a good band. Mr. Chief liked music and he liked to have the band out there at the football and basketball games. You did that for him although he never told you. He wanted you to stay because he liked that music.

Mr. Industrial Arts: I never knew what happened to the shop teacher who taught before I came or why the job opened.

Mr. Athletic Director: The reason there was a job opening was because the guy who was here before you was also the baseball coach. He made so many baseball bats on the lathe that Mr. Chief just couldn't handle it anymore.

Mr. Industrial Arts: That was the only shop job open in the state that year and I got it. I learned early that you had to be correct in anything you said to Mr. Chief and be able to back it up. One morning during my second year, I went to breakfast, and there was Mr. Chief sitting with one of his school board friends. Where else do you sit? They were talking about the shortage of industrial arts teachers. I said, "I just read an article in the *Minnesota Industrial Arts Newsletter* that said they expect an excess of twenty-two teachers this year and forty-five next year."

I went to school and got the article out and set it on the filing cabinet. Sure enough, Mr. Chief walked in about ten o'clock and wanted to know where I saw that information. I handed him the article, he looked at it, and handed it back to me. He walked out and never said a damn word. He could never be wrong.

Before I taught, I worked in a butcher shop, so I was familiar with sharpening knives. The butcher shop used a multi-stone, three stones that floated in oil. We sharpened knives, planes, and chisels. I ordered one. I think it cost about $36, a lot of money back then. It came in during the summer. The Ag. (agriculture) teacher was in the office the day it arrived.

"What's this?" asked Mr. Chief. "Are you starting a meat cutting class here." The Ag. teacher had no idea what it was. When he came back to the shop, he told me the sharpener had come, so I walked down to the office and said, "Oh, it finally came in." Mr. Chief said if he had known what it was he would have cancelled the order. A few months later he walked into the shop with three knives from home. He wanted me to sharpen them.

Mr. Athletic Director and Coach: There are many stories about Mr. Chief and food. He had to have his *vomacka* (potato soup). One of the cooks made it just for him and kept it in the refrigerator. He had it about three times a week.

During the Christmas vacations we had four metro teams down here for scrimmages and we fed them soup and sandwiches at noon. Mr. Chief made them tomato soup. Well, he forgot about the soup and burned it.

I said, "What are we going to feed them?"

"We're going to feed them the soup," he said. "We just won't get to the bottom."

Another incident happened when we upset our archrival in football. The following Monday the football team was fed T-bone steaks. They went through the lunch line first. Mr. Chief had bought a cow and had the T-bones cut for the players and the rest of the meat made into hamburger for the rest of the students.

Mr. Baseball: We won the district and went to the regional tournament. School was out. Mr. Chief called me into his office and said everything was arranged, and then he said, "You're driving the bus." He wouldn't hire a bus driver. I didn't have a license, but he gave me the directions and told me to drive. We played the first game and won. I asked for money to buy the kids a meal the next day because we were leaving early to play a late game. "Naw," he said, "you don't need that." I stopped at my wife's folks in St. Paul and they fed the kids sandwiches. He wouldn't pay for a bus driver or a meal.

Mr. Former Coach and Principal: An assistant coach at a Big Ten school came here twice to watch one of our players. The assistant coach said he could have a full ride for four years but the combination of his ACT scores wasn't high enough for him to qualify. The head football coach told me we could make a two-class ranking, one based on the grades in the required classes and one based on the electives, which was where the boy had the lower ranking. He would then be eligible because the class with the low grade was an elective.

I called Mr. Chief and the assistant coach explained the situation to him. After he hung up, I said, "This kid can get a full ride. He's a good kid. I think we should help him."

Mr. Chief went to see the counselor, and boy, the fur really flew! "You mean you are going to deny this kid a scholarship?" asked Mr. Chief.

"He doesn't qualify," said the counselor.

"Sit down," said Mr. Chief. I'm making a decision and it's not the football coach's decision. We're making two class ranks, one for the electives and one for the required courses. If you are going to turn someone in, you are going to turn me in, but that's what's going to happen and the boy is going to get his scholarship. (Mr. Chief was retiring that year.)

The counselor tried to object, but Mr. Chief barked, "YOU HEARD WHAT I SAID, DIDN'T YOU?"

The boy got his scholarship.

Author's Note: My wife and I were married in December during our second year of teaching in Mr. Chief's school. Both of us taught English. For our honeymoon we planned to go to Puerto Rico, where I had taught the year before. We discussed our plans with the principal. I agreed to pay for my substitute and he graciously agreed to teach my wife's classes. "You don't have to pay me," he said. "I'm happy to help you out."

The day we returned from Puerto Rico, my wife and I were summoned to Mr. Chief's office. He explained that the principal had no right to tell us he would cover my wife's classes and that she would be docked her full pay, not the amount paid for a substitute, which in this case was the principal who was paid nothing.

Mr. Chief intimidated me just like everyone else, but something snapped in me that day. "What," I said, "are you telling us that the principal's word means nothing and we will lose an entire week's pay? How can you do that? Do you think we would have made that arrangement if we had known you would do this? It's not fair."

"It's not school policy," he said, "but more than that it's a matter of principle. We can't set a precedent and cover classes when other people get married."

I fumed. We argued the same issue for an hour. Finally I said, "Don't you think we are smart enough that if we had known you would deduct full pay, we would have hired another substitute?" No matter how much I argued, his principle's commanded more power than my passion and righteous indignation.

I'm not exactly certain why that drama played out the way it did. Perhaps he refused to change because of his principles, but I had seen other principles disintegrate under similar conditions. Perhaps his feud with the principal was the cause of his actions. Perhaps he felt we needed to know who was in power. We left at the end of the school year.

When I think about those years, what strikes me most is that we were docile teachers who marched to our leader's music. There may have been different drumming banging away within us, but we marched Mr. Chief's march. Perhaps we had been conditioned to march in step. We started grade school in the '40s, completed high school and college in the '50s, and taught at the beginning of the '60s.

I stopped in to visit Mr. Chief a year before he died. I had seen him only once or twice in passing since the day I left, more than thirty years earlier. His wife had died. He sat in his easy chair, which held him with more ease than it had when he was a giant force. He was frail and his voice had withered to gentleness. I felt at ease calling him by his first name, something not even the most favored dared do when he was Mr. Chief.

We talked about the old days. He told me about his high school and college days. He reminisced about his years as county school superintendent, and he told me how he became a superintendent. He talked for an hour, and as I was getting ready to leave, he said, "I have always felt bad about that incident and your leaving." He didn't apologize, however, or admit that he may have made a mistake.

Before I left, I told him that of the seven superintendents I had worked for in my teaching career, he was the most committed to his students, school, and community. (He endowed scholarship money to the two schools he had served as superintendent.) I told him I didn't always agree with him, but that he had certainly influenced my life. No doubt about that!

Dr. MTL

"Find out all you can about your students," my professors said. "Become involved. Find our what their interests are, what school activities they participate in, and what their home lives are like. The more you know about them, the better teacher you will be. Check their cumulative folders. Check their test scores, especially their reading and math scores. At what level are they reading? Also check their Stanford-Benet I. Q. scores. The more information you gather, the better you can assess their needs. The better you can teach them."

During my first years of teaching I followed this advice religiously. I tried to read my students cum. folders during the first month of school. I jotted down the results of the Iowa Tests and whatever other information was available. I paid special attention to the discrepancies between their I. Q. scores and their grades. I applied the formulas passed down to me by the education seers who trained me: high I. Q. and high grades—right on track; high I. Q. scores and low grades—something's off kilter. Low I. Q. and high grades— an overachiever because I. Q. scores are infallible, (most of the time) and on and on. This foolishness ended the day I met Dr. Modern Theories of Language, (Dr. MTL).

I began graduate school at St. Thomas College (now St. Thomas University) in the summer of 1962. The English department offered a special seminar program along with the regular curriculum. Classes in the seminar met seven hours a day for three weeks. Classes in the regular curriculum met every day for six weeks. Enrollment in the seminar classes was limited and permission to take the classes was required from the chairman of the English department and the class instructors. For some reason unknown to me even today, I applied for admission to the seminars. Blame it on hubris.

Dr. MTL taught the first course. He interviewed me for a few minutes about my teaching and then he said, "Would you mind taking an I.Q. test?"

"Sure," I said, and he called in his secretary who administered the test. I should have screamed, "What the hell is the reason for this? Is this a class for Nobel scholars or geniuses?" But I was twenty-five and still naive as a garden slug about a college professor's motives. Wasn't I in graduate school and wasn't the program designed to help teachers? Weren't my professors in tune with secondary education? Naive as a garden slug!

I took the test and Dr. MTL discovered I was not the borderline genius he was hoping for. Of course I knew this. I had discovered that in grade school. Nevertheless, I was allowed to enter Dr. MTL's class, but he never showed much interest in me. He wanted Albert Einstein and he got me. He had opened my cum. folder and found me wanting.

Mr. Slusser

Herbert Slusser taught the second seminar, English 491, Reading Literature. The good professor had a reputation as a brilliant scholar and articulate lecturer. Rumor had it that he could be a garrulous, crotchety taskmaster, but I never saw that side of him.

Later that fall I took Mr. Slusser's course, English 485, The Novels of William Dean Howells and Henry James. We read *The Rise of Silas Lapham* by Howells and *The American, The Ambassadors,* and *The Golden Bowl* by James. Like all the other courses in my master's program, the works of Howells and James had nothing to do with our junior and senior high curriculum.

I knew that when I enrolled. I took the class because I wanted another course in The Life and Mind of Professor Herbert Slusser. On Thursday nights from 4:00 to 8:00, ten of us gathered to discuss the weekly novel and listen to Mr. Slusser, who knew the novels of Henry James better than I remembered the exploits of Dick and Jane.

Henry James did not believe in skipping any details or creating dialogue that sounded like the conversation between ordinary folks drinking ale at the local pub. Perhaps the most ponderous of his books is *The Golden Bowl*, approximately 500 pages, which narrates the story of seemingly genteel aristocrats.

Mr. Slusser had arranged the desks in a circle as usual. Most nights he began the class with a half-hour lecture, but that night he changed his format. "I want each of you to select one paragraph from the novel," he said, "and explain why you think that paragraph is typical of James's writing style and character development. Be as thorough as possible. Explain his use of metaphors and symbols. Each of you will be given five minutes to ten minutes to speak. Give the paragraph a scholarly analysis. I'll give you a few minutes to prepare."

My stomach knotted, my mouth dried, and my heart danced like a manic Fred Astaire. "This book has hundreds of paragraphs," I thought. "How the hell can I remember one lousy paragraph?" Fortunately I had written notes in the page margins and I chose the one paragraph I thought I could analyze.

"John, we'll begin with you and proceed clockwise around the circle," said Mr. Slusser. John sat on my left, and Ted sat on my right. John chose the fourth paragraph on page 415 (writer's license here). As he spoke, Ted frantically flipped pages, searching for a paragraph. He paid no attention to John's presentation. John finished his paragraph, and then I stumbled through my analysis. Mr. Slusser said, "Thank you," and nodded to Ted.

"I have selected the fourth paragraph on page 415," said Ted.

Heads snapped toward Ted. I froze. Mary gasped and covered her mouth. "My, god, I thought, "he's doing the same paragraph Ted analyzed." We looked at Mr. Slusser, who nodded and eased back in his chair.

Ted discussed the same symbols, metaphors, and writing style John had just analyzed. We looked at each other waiting for the volcano to erupt. Mr. Slusser never even wrinkled his forehead. He stared at Ted, who babbled on about James's skill in developing plot structure.

"Thank you, Ted," said Mr. Slusser. He folded hands under his chin like a man in prayer. "The lava is really bubbling now," I thought. I imagined what I would say to one of my students who had just laid such an egg. No instructor could let this infraction go unpunished. Mr. Slusser closed his eyes. Silence. We squirmed. Ted relaxed, his task accomplished. More silence. Slusser looked up and said, "Time for a break."

We swarmed around Ted in the hallway. "My god, Ted, do you know what you just did?" we asked and then revealed his blunder. Ted knew he was in trouble. Fifteen minutes later, ten timid graduate students returned to class, certain that the simmering lava would blow.

"Let's continue," said Mr. Slusser. "Ann, I think you are next."

"The man's a genius," I thought. "He let pour the lava".

Students battle the mythic monster SAT.
Drawing by Kelsey Mann, 1993

Leaning

Joseph Campbell said, "Find your center point and follow your bliss." My students' response was usually, "But I'm only sixteen. How do I know what my bliss is?"

"That's the reason for the hero's journey" was my usual response. "Being human means being out of sync with something, often many things. The hero's task is to find bliss, to live in this absurd world and discover one's center point, that which will allow the hero to live in balance with the spiritual, human, and natural worlds."

V-8 ran a series of commercials in the '90s, which featured a baseball player, businessman, and housewife leaning at a sixty-degree angle, completely out of sync with their worlds. While everyone else stood straight, smiled, and went about their tasks, these poor folks leaned. The solution—drink V-8, the magic elixir. Presto, a stand-up-straight hero. As easy as that.

I wrote to Campbell Soup and asked them if they would send me tapes of their commercials, so I could illustrate their mythology to my students. If Luke Skywalker needed help to stand up straight and find the hero within, how were the rest of us ordinary folks to find our bliss? Our mythology says that the answer will be bottled, frozen, tubed, or canned. Just a nip or bite of the magical food and drink will straighten us out. We all lean and we need help.

When I began teaching, I never realized some of my students were leaning or that I occasionally leaned as well. No college professor talked about leaning in our educational methods classes. I was much better prepared to diagram sentences than I was to figure out why my learners were so out of kilter. I swilled down my idealism and funneled gallons of British literature and classic grammar into the minds of my first-year seniors. Little did I realize that it's very difficult to swallow if one's neck is crooked from leaning too far. I was twenty-one and they were eighteen and we were leaning in many different directions.

As the years passed, I became better at identifying leaning students, and as more years passed, I could sometimes spot the shadow-leaning darkness within. Society as well as the gods of education demanded perception and action. Helping the leaners stand upright became as demanding as teaching them how to write. Although my college training gave me a few pointers about teaching writing, no one prepared me to straighten my Leaning Towers, pushed askew by poor self-esteem, drugs, depression, abuse, peer pressure as well as a plague of unidentifiable shadows.

Bell Telephone urged us "to reach out and touch someone," and we tried until touching was dangerous. From every voice, teachers heard the call—"Help them stand up straight. You can do it. Teach our children well. Don't let them lean and fall. Help them to stand straight. Nothing's too good for our kids. Forget all this new stuff. Do it the way they did it back then. They knew what was what. They had no idea what was what back then. Give 'em a good kick in the pants. No pain, no gain. Just do it. You and Coke must "teach the world to sing in perfect harmony". Reach out with helping hands. Plug in those "thousand points of light."

I pushed until I leaned. I looked at my colleagues. They were leaning, too. We were all leaning, but some of us never felt the tilt. If we did, we longed to feel the gentle touch that stood us straight. We were expected to be a blend of General Patton, Mother Theresa, Harry Houdini, soothsayers, and prophets. But we were just leaners helping leaners.

Where is the course about reaching out, about finding center points, about easing pain, about touching lives, about preventing us from drowning if we fall?

The Courage Center, Golden Valley, Minnesota

"Tom, you take Leland," said Nancy, the instructor for the strokers group.

"Do you think you can handle him? I think you will work out just fine. Just remember to keep your balance and your cool. Sometimes he can get pretty ornery."

"I think I'll be fine," I replied.

Leland sat in his wheelchair in his usual spot, surrounded by two or three other clients. Ed, a veteran volunteer, was giving Leland his daily dose of razzing. "Hey, Leland, when are you going to bring us some of that wall-eyed trout?"

Leland rolled his eyes and said, "Walleye—good. Son—game warden. Walleye—good." Leland's stroke had stolen all but a few often-repeated words and phrases from his vocabulary and paralyzed his left arm and left leg. He was perhaps five foot five and weighed well over two hundred pounds.

Beneath that weight lived a fierce fighting spirit. Leland had fought in Korea as well as Vietnam. The wounds from the shrapnel cuts in his scalp had healed, but we all knew why the scars were there. Of course I didn't know anything about Leland when I walked over to him that first day.

"Hello, Leland, my name is Tom and I'm going to be working with you today. Tom," I repeated, "my name is Tom."

He grabbed my right hand and squeezed. "Tom. Tom," he said and squeezed harder. My knuckles screamed as he rolled them into a neat little donut. I grabbed his fist with my left hand and pulled his fingers away from my hand.

"Tom—good," he grinned. I looked at his right hand. It was a sledge-hammer.

"Hey, Tom," yelled Ed, "we forgot to tell you that Ed boxed when he was in the army. Better be careful if you shake his hand."

"I bet you forgot," I laughed.

I wheeled Leland down the ramp backwards, so I could keep him from slipping out of my hands and zooming down the ramp. We eased down the ramp into the eighty-degree water. It crept up the sides of Leland's wheelchair until he was waist deep. I pushed him to the bench where the clients sat during the stretching routines.

I positioned his wheelchair carefully. He grabbed my left shoulder and I reached under his armpits. I braced my legs and grabbed him under the armpits. He tried to help me but he pushed so hard I lost my balance. We began to twist slowly. My right knee buckled. The muscles in my back began to tear. Leland was sliding out of my hands when Ed and Nancy grabbed him and spun him onto the bench.

"Leland, you almost took a dive there. You gotta take it easy on Tom," said Ed.

Leland smiled but his eyes said, "I'm not so sure about this guy. He damn near dropped me."

After the stretching exercises, Nancy yelled, "OK, straight to the bars for twenty pushups." The bar was really the top bar of the divider between the pool and the step entrance to our exercise area. Leland stood about three feet from the top bar and leaned forward. I placed the fingers on his left hand around the bar and held them there while I helped balance him with my right hand. One, two, three, four—the muscles in his arm and necked tightened like those of a world-class weightlifter. Eighteen, nineteen, twenty. He popped off those twenty one-armed pushups before the others had done three or four.

Nancy watched Leland and barked, "When you finish those, do twenty squats. Keep your legs and back straight. Way to go, Leland!"

He smiled at her and said, "Pretty." Leland loved the ladies.

To do the squats, Leland had to step up onto the wall, which held the bars. He couldn't place any weight on his left leg, so as I held him by the waist. He grabbed the bar with his good hand and hopped onto the ledge. Again I held his left hand on the bar for balance. Down, up, down up, six, seven, eight, nine ten. He bent his right knee, pulled, and shot out of the water—eighteen, nineteen, twenty. He was the champ and he knew it.

I stood behind him and grabbed him under the arms. He eased back and I floated him into deep water, about chest high. He again grabbed my left shoulder. I balanced his limp left arm on top of my right arm and grabbed his shoulders. The water seemed to lift his right foot as we hopped across the pool, practicing our walking exercises. Backwards, forwards, sideways, backwards, sideways, forwards, high-step marching, gliding, back and forth.

"Leland, step with that left foot," shouted Nancy. "You're leaning too hard on Tom. Put some pressure on your left foot." He tried but his leg dragged behind him and his foot caught against the back of his right heel. He leaned to the left and I struggled to keep him straight.

Each day I volunteered I learned more and more about Leland. One son was a game warden. "Son—game warden. Hunt. Fish. Walleyes—oooooh, walleyes," he said and smacked his lips. His other son was a businessman. "Oooooh—money," he exclaimed and rolled his eyes. "Money, money, money. Son—money."

I knew when Leland had been to the Veterans' Hospital to have his monthly heart examination. He slouched in his wheelchair and plodded through his exercises. but as soon as we started walking, he smiled and said, "Heart—OK. OK. Heart—OK." But the images of the guys at the Vets' haunted him. "Cancer—bad. Oooooh—cancer bad. Dying. Dying," he moaned.

At first I talked with him about what he had seen, but he became more and more depressed. Later, whenever he mentioned the Vets', I changed the subject, and nothing worked better than, "Leland, how about those— and then I would fill in the name of whichever team was playing.

He loved the Twins, Gophers, and Vikings, especially the Vikings. "How about that game last Sunday? Did you watch?" I asked.

Even on his worst days when he was feeling terrible and wanted to quit, he looked at me and grinned, "Black—OK," he said. "Black—OK. Moon—(Viking quarterback Warren Moon) OK. Moon—OK. He scrunched up his face and shouted, "MOON—OK!"

"What the heck is happening here?" I wondered. What arguments from the past had been silenced by his stroke? Leland clenched his teeth and glared at me, "BLACK—OK!"

"Right, right," I said. "Black—OK. Moon is a great player."

"Moon—OK," he grinned. "Go Vikings."

One day I asked him if he liked music. He stopped walking. His eyes lit up. "Ooooooh, boy—jazz! Jazz—OK." He squinted, puckered his mouth, and shuddered. "Frank—friend Frank—jazz. Oooooh, Frank—jazz."

"Did Frank play the trumpet?" I asked doing my best impersonation of Louis Armstrong. He shook his head and pumped his arm back and forth."

"The trombone," I said. "Frank played the trombone."

Leland closed his eyes and swayed his head to a melody from the past playing in his head. "Ooooooh—Frank—friend Frank!" he whispered. "Jazz—OK! Jazz—OK!"

Later Ed told me that Frank was an old Army buddy and that jazz meant big band music by Glen Miller, Tommy Dorsey, Harry James, and others from the 40s.

Leland hated the monotony of exercises, but he loved games. His favorite was Nancy's version of volleyball. Everyone made a big circle. We volunteers stood behind our clients and gave them as much support as we could. The object of the game was to punch, hit, or slap a huge beach ball and keep it from hitting the water. The ball seldom survived more than one punch, two at the most. Whenever that ball headed for Leland, I held him by the waist and dropped to my knees. He clenched his right fist, wound up, and walloped that poor beach ball. Everyone cheered when he landed his knock out punches.

From the moment we entered the pool, Leland kept his eyes on the clock. As we walked back and forth, he looked at the clock every four or five minutes. At 10:50 the strokers were free to float on their backs with the aid of two long banana tubes that were placed around their backs and under their arms. Leland had no time for floating.

At 10:45 he pointed at the clock and said, "Uh, uuuuuh, uuuuuuuh." Nancy looked at me and nodded. Leland held on to the side of the pool while I got his inner tube. He lifted his good arm and I slid the tube over his head and then eased the tube over his left arm and shoulder. I gently slid his left arm up and over the tube. Leland leaned forward and I pulled the tube snugly around his chest.

Back and forth we swam. With only his right arm and leg, Leland cruised the entire length of the pool. I swam on his left side, making certain I stayed away from his right leg. His kick was powerful.

Most of the time we swam in silence. Leland swam with primeval desperation. Often I swam under water to watch the power of his stroke. The muscles in his right leg bulged, driving each stroke, pulling his limp leg through the water.

One day I sang the Minnesota Rouser, "Minnesota hats off to thee—" but I didn't sing the words because I knew Leland couldn't say them. Instead, I sang, "Da, da, da, da, (Minn-a-so-ta) da, da, ta, dee (hats off to thee." He never missed a beat and we da daed across the pool. We da, daed the Vikings and Twins fight songs as well. I hit the first two or three notes and we were off.

We expanded our repertoire. I thought I would test Leland's love for jazz. "Daaa, dut, dut, daddle, da, la, dut, dut, daddle, da, la dut, dut, daddle da la dee," I sang out Glenn Miller's "American Patrol." He stopped dead in the water and we jammed. I mean we jammed. "Dut, dut, daddle" bounced off the ceiling and echoed throughout the pool. Glenn and the band would have been proud.

I had several big band discs and my mother's collection of Glenn Miller albums, so I taped them for Leland. That Wednesday, Leland had his back turned toward the locker room and did not see me walk in. I carried my tape player and headphones. I had set the tape on the first notes of "Chattanooga Choo-choo." I slipped the headphones on Leland's ears. He turned to see who was there, but when he heard "Pardon me boy, is that the Chattanooga, Choo Choo?" he shouted, "Jazz—oooooh jazz." He shut his eyes, made his monkey faces and swung his head to the music.

When Leland had a bad day, I had a bad day. Often he seemed depressed. Every exercise was drudgery. He hung his head and seldom smiled. He made little effort to help himself. The worse he felt, the heavier he got. He leaned on me when we walked, and we stumbled often. Not even Ed could lift his spirits. Leland loved to eat but not even the mention of his favorite, hamburgers and beer at the State Fair, made him smile. When he pointed to the door and wanted to quit before swimming, I knew he was having a terrible day.

When Leland was at the top of his game, the place was electric. No matter what Ed said, Leland talked back. Even when Ed taunted him about walleyed trout or barked, "Come on, Leland, put some zip into it," Leland laughed. We all laughed.

Ed talked like a drill sergeant, but he had a heart of gold. For years he and his wife Lillian had volunteered at the Center. Ed had struggled through open-heart surgery and he certainly knew more about courage and caring than I. Ed had worked with Mary, a young woman who had suffered from tumors. She had been through more than fifteen surgeries.

For five minutes at the end of each session, most of the group sat in the bubble bath. Not Leland. No bubble was going to cut into his swimming time. One Wednesday the group was having its usual bath. Leland was sitting in his chair and I was getting ready to push him up the ramp when Mary entered the pool with her aide. Ed stood and hollered, "Happy birthday, Mary."

We had no conductor but everyone in the pool—the volunteers, the aides, the lifeguard, the directors, and the clients who could speak—began to sing "Happy Birthday" to Mary. With the help of the pool acoustics, we sounded better than the Mormon Tabernacle Choir. Mary stood at the top of the ramp, smiled, and waved.

Leland and I waited at the bottom of the ramp as Mary struggled down to the water. At the bottom of the ramp, Mary stopped next to Leland to catch her balance. Two strangers passing. Leland reached out and took Mary's hand. He gently pressed it to his lips. "Nice," he said. "Nice."

From the moment I placed my hand on Leland's wheelchair until I pushed him out, it was my responsibility to take care of him, to encourage him, to assist him, to lift his spirits, but most importantly to keep him safe. The weight of his leaning was exhausting. He leaned and I braced myself by holding his arms.

When we swam, I often forgot his heaviness. He was such a powerful swimmer that it became routine for us to glide through the water face to face, lost in our own thoughts. One day while we were swimming in the deep end of the pool, there was a ruckus at the other end. I spun around for just a second. When I turned back, Leland was slipping through the inner tube. He pulled at the tube with his good hand. I grabbed his arm with one hand and pulled. I pushed the tube down and somehow managed to get both his arms over the tube. Then I pushed the tube under his armpits

I treaded water and Leland hung on to the tube. I grabbed his swimming suit and held his hand. His eyes were wild. My heart pounded. No one had seen us. Everyone had turned to the ruckus and the lifeguard ran to see what had happened. "Are you OK?" I asked.

"OK, OK," he said and we swam to the shallow water.

I volunteered at the Courage Center after I had retired from teaching. How I wish that experience had been required as part of my teacher training! I could have learned many lessons about my weaknesses and strengths. I could have learned valuable lessons about how fragile the body and spirit really are. I could have learned that no matter how grand my intentions or how hard I tried, I could not succeed alone. Sometime I helped people whose strokes had only slightly affected them, but most of the time, because I was bigger than many of the volunteers, I was assigned to taller, heavier men who had experienced severe strokes. Sometime it took all my strength to keep them from leaning, losing their balance, or falling. When it looked as if I could not keep my balance, other volunteers rushed to help.

Helping stroke patients to walk is not much different from teaching. It was more difficult, however, to know why my students were "leaning." I could determine quite easily that their writing and speaking skills were wobbly, but understanding why they were leaning was the real challenge. The "strokers," as they called themselves, acknowledged their infirmities and fought to stand alone. Many of my students could not tell they were leaning or falling, and if they did feel the tilt, they often refused help.

When I grabbed Leland's arms and tried to hold him upright, I helped him, but I could not cure his illness. I could not undo his stroke and I accepted that with no guilt. I tried equally as hard to keep my students from "slipping through the inner tube," but I fould it difficult to forgive myself when I failed. I'm proud, however, to belong to a profession that reaches out to help the "leaners" stand upright. I felt good being surrounded by so many "strokers" and students who found their center through courage.

7

Celebrities

IN THE LATE 1960s MY COLLEAGUE LEE TOPP AND I DECIDED to add some pizzazz to our autobiography-biography unit. For years we had followed the traditional read-a-book, write-a-paper, give-a-speech format. "Class," we announced to our social studies and English classes, "this year the assignment will be different. You must select someone who is alive and lives in the United States. In addition to reading about the person, writing a report, and giving a speech, we are going to try to interview your candidate by telephone."

After the students had read their books, we worked on writing the letters. I found the addresses in *Current Biography*. The students designed attention-grabbing envelopes. Sue Murphy glued her 8" X 10" glossy photo of Jack Lemmon to her envelope. Many of the students' candidates did not answer. Several wrote back but declined the interview, but a few agreed. Then everyone, especially the student doing the interview, shifted into high gear. The interviewer researched more information. We asked the class what questions they would like to ask.

The school rented a rotary-dial telephone and two large speakers from Bell Telephone. We conducted the interviews in the lecture theater. The student and I sat in front of the audience, which consisted of the student's grandparents, parents, friends, students, teachers, and administrators.

Once the call began the room became silent. The interviewer's heart beat faster and we all crossed our fingers. Most of the time things went smoothly. Once, however, we were not so lucky. Buddy Hackett told Warren Grover he would be delighted to be interviewed and agreed to the calling time. When the day arrived, the lecture theater was packed. Warren dialed and Buddy answered, "Yea, who is this and whaddya want?"

"This is Warren Grover calling, Mr. Hackett—"

"Ya," interrupted Buddy, "well go to hell," and he hung up.

"We were stunned. Warren was dumbfounded. "What the heck happened?" we asked. We're certainly were not going to call again to find out why!

Warren, the rest of the students, and I went back to class. At the end of the period, the bell rang and the students left for their next classes. Fifteen minutes later I received a call from the office that Buddy Hackett was on the line and wanted to speak to Warren. The secretary located Warren and transferred the call to a small conference room. Unfortunately, the telephone was not connected to a tape recorder, so we have no tape of the conversation. Buddy apologized for cutting Warren off and told him that his apartment had been burglarized and he had been up all night talking to the police. Warren and Buddy talked for an hour and Buddy paid for the call.

When I listened to these tapes, thirty years later, I felt I was again sitting next to the students. Most of them were very nervous. I could hear their voices tighten as they asked the first question. Once that was done they relaxed a bit, but they were so intent on asking the next question, they had a difficult time asking follow-up questions.

The student who called Pearl Buck knew *The Good Earth* better than a college scholar. She had researched Buck's life and compiled a list of insightful questions. About forty-five seconds into the interview she panicked and said, "I want to thank you for this interview," and hung up. At that moment I wished I had never thought of the "good idea" and put my student in such a stressful situation.

Gordon Parks, who wrote *A Choice of Weapons*, forgot about the interview and we woke him from a deep sleep. Several tapes were accidentally thrown away, so there are no transcrips of the interviews with Caesar Maniago, Minnesota North Stars goalie, Mary Wells, advertising executive who gained fame for her work with Braniff Airlines, and Senator Walter Mondale. I had never heard of Richard Buckminster Fuller, who was John Thompson's choice. They talked about Fuller's inventions, including the geodesic dome. That tape was also thrown away.

Most of the interviews were joyous events. A few are quite revealing if you read between the lines. I am certain most of these people had given hundreds of interviews and I admired the graciousness and patience with which they answered my student's questions. I remember the enthusiasm in Robin Selvig's voice as she and her hero, Wernher von Braun, speculated about whether we would ever walk on the moon or set up space stations. I can still hear Sandy Morris' giggle when Louis Armstrong asked, "Do you dig it, honey?" Paul Jager found Bart Starr's telephone number in the Green Bay phone book. I wonder how many NFL quarterbacks list their numbers today.

These were some my most precious teaching moments. Many people, including some of the students, said, "Where did you get that crazy idea?" and "Those people are too busy to talk to junior high students." I have enjoying contacting these students after all these years. Most remember the day as if it happened yesterday. The old cliche—"We are limited only by our imagination," speaks to us teachers.

The following are excerpts are taken from the original taped interviews.

Louis Armstrong

Louis Armstrong was interviewed by Sandy Morris
Sandy: Hello, Mr. Armstrong, I'd like to thank you for speaking with me. I consider it a great honor.

Armstrong: (Bad connection) I'm having some difficulty hearing you.
Sandy: Could you speak up a little, please? I'm having a difficult time hearing you.

Armstrong: I've got my chops right in the phone. What are you doing, writing a story?

Sandy: (Sandy could not hear the question.) In your book you describe the funeral marches in New Orleans. The class and I would appreciate hearing your description of those funeral marches.

Armstrong: Well, when someone died, they walked slowly to the cemetery. When they put the body in the ground, everybody came out happy and swinging. It's been a regular thing through life, through all the generations.

Sandy: How did the name Satchmo get stuck on you?

Armstrong: In England the editor asked the melody maker if my name was Satchel Mouth. Well, he shook my hand and said, "Hello, Satchmo." I asked my travel friend why he said "Satchmo," and he said the English brothers thought I had more mouth than satchel. So I was stuck with the name."

Sandy: Do you like the name?

Armstrong: I like it very much.

Sandy: I've heard so much about that famous salve of yours. Do you still use it?

Armstrong: Well, yes, since the '20s. You got to put something on your lips. In the olden days our lips would get dry. The spit would stick right in the middle like a pig's foot, ya know. So I learned to put some kind of grease, just a layer to keep it moist. It won't hinder you from blowing the trumpet. The salve is grease that helps protect the lips. I don't have no reason why I shouldn't use it, but the other trumpet players, that's their prerogative. I give them a little can and they thank me and all, but they don't look at it the way I do. We all have a little somethin' that we like and if you believe in it, you got to believe in a whole lot of things before they can do you some good. Understand? That's the way it is with me and my lip salve and my laxative. Do ya dig it?

Sandy: Ya, I dig it. Is there any group you played with, such as Armstrong's Hot Five, that you consider to be the best group you ever played with?

Armstrong: Well, you can't put it that way cuz they all had stuff on the ball, in their own way, ya know, from the Hot Five to the Hot Seven. I had different sets of Armstrongs starting out with Jack Teagarden. That was number one and as we went on certain ones dropped out. Then another one come in and take their place with the same mind and the same heart and the same feeling for the music, so I got to love all of 'em. I think they are all great, so special.

Sandy: I'm sure you've been asked this a hundred times, but I'd like to ask if there are any songs you have recorded that are your particular favorites.

Armstrong: "When It's Sleepy Time Down South." (Louis sings.) That's my theme song and that will be my favorite all my life, but I like the others, too. Don't get me wrong, ya know, but "Sleepy Time," that's me.

Every time you year that song you think of Satchmo. Any time that's played it's either Louis Armstrong playing it or somebody's thinkin' about him. That's his theme song. I'm known all over the world by that tune. When foreigners and everybody hears that tune, they think about Old Satchmo, Louis Armstrong.

Sandy: Most of the students my age enjoy several rock groups, especially the Beatles. What do you think of the Beatles' music?

Armstrong: I got all their records here. They like my music and I like theirs. It's got that same beat. I don't care who it is as long as it's got that beat and sense of phrasing and they sound good, I'm for them and what they did. I like 'em very much.

Sandy: Are there any popular groups you listen to?

Armstrong: All of 'em. I sit right here with the TV, relaxin' and I catch 'em all. I get their recordings anyway, cuz a lot of 'em still come in the office and they see that I get all the artists' recordings. So I get a chance to hear everybody play.

Sandy: I read that one of the turning points in your life was when you sang "Ain't Misbehavin'" in the Broadway Review *Hot Chocolate*.

Armstrong: You know how far back that was, 1929? There's been a lot of water under the bridge since then. I did sing "Ain't Misbehavin'" in *Hot Chocolate* in Broadway in 1929. Oh, boy, I've been all over the world in many shows, played a whole lot of one-night stands since then. I've had some beautiful times in my life like "Blueberry Hill," "Mack the Knife," and "Dolly."

Sandy: Of all the countries you visited in your tours, which did you enjoy the most?

Armstrong: Well, I like them all cuz I know how to ask for pork chops in all countries. I learn that first when I get off the plane. As long as I got some chops in every country, they dug it. That's why they go all out to show me a good time and they enjoy my music everywhere. Right now I'm sending my photographs all over the world cuz I get the letters here. I got a whole box of addresses from countries and from kids up the block, poor kids cuz they can't afford stamps and the pictures are going out to my fans.

When I was in the hospital, I had calls from the mayor, and they all wanted photographs. So that's what I'm tellin' you. All over the world it's just the same as right here on this block where I live, my neighbors, my friends, my fans. They're all waitin' for me. Every time they send a letter or card, they say, "Waitin' for you, Satch," and that makes me feel good, very good. It shows I'm still alive and in action. Ya know Cadillacs break down sometimes, so why can't I take a vacation?

Put a brand new engine in a Cadillac and you run again. That's what I did. I didn't get a new heart, but I had a good rest when I needed it. That's the same, ya know. My Lucille is one of the finest nurses you ever heard of cuz she saw to it that I had my medicine and my food and other nice things that I should have had. Ya know what I mean? Beautiful! Now I'm ready to go back on the mound again, gradually until I'm good.

Sandy: A few weeks ago another student in class interviewed Gordon Parks (*Choice of Weapons*). He said he used his many art forms such as novels, photography, and film as weapons against poverty and prejudice. Have you ever thought of your trumpet or music as a weapon?

Armstrong: Well, no. Where I came from, honey, we were lucky to get an instrument to play on. We were so glad to play music. I didn't go into all them deep things like that. You take a lot of boys and they got a swell education and they go to college and think up some big words. All we did was play the music. I hope I don't be a disappointment about that answer, but it don't move me to even talk about it.

All I want to do is play music, sing, and please my public, and they appreciate me and that's all I've done all my life anyhow. The people around me here, they all play and we don't put on airs. I don't want to put on no more than is necessary, so long as I can play my horn and sing and treat my fellow man right, respect my public, and they respect me. That's all then. If you are gonna write a story, my quotation is all plain down to earth— "Don't expect me to do a whole lot of fancy words that are gonna bust my brains or nothin' like that. I need my brains so I can concentrate on them notes." Ya dig it?

Sandy: I can't remember whether you or your mother said, "If you can't do it, the hell with it. Don't worry about what the other fella has."

Armstrong: That's right and I still say that. Like the song 'The Bare Necessities,' at the end of it, it says, (Louis sings) "Don't spend your time just lookin' around for something you want that can't be found. You'll find out you can live without and go along not thinkin' about it. It tells you something true and the bare necessities of life will come to you." Understand? Now you get that recording and you listen to those lyrics. That's the kind of quotation I like to give.

Sandy: Would you please tell us what it was like to play in Fate Marabell's band as you traveled up and down the Mississippi in 1919?

Armstrong: It was an education for me. I was only nineteen years old and that was my big band. I got in with all the old timers cuz I was the hot kid on the trumpet. That was the first big band that read music that I played with. When we got up to St. Louis and they took a load up to Davenport, Iowa, that's where I met that kid that played so much horn called Bix Beiderbecke. He was just a teenager like myself. How old are you?

Sandy: I'm fourteen.

Armstrong: Fourteen? Well, Bix was around fifteen years old when I first met him and he was playin' beautiful cornet, ya know. My experience with Fate Maribel was beautiful and every time I go to St. Louis I make it my business to go down to the boat and make it my business to see the family that owns these boats. It makes Old Louis feel like a kid.

Bix was fifteen and I was nineteen. That's so many years ago and I still remember. I'll never forget the first goin' down the levee there in those honkytonks. We could go up there, and all the bad characters, shootin' and cuttin' and everything. It didn't bother me. Don't come near me blowin' that quail. They didn't know what a cornet was. "What ya call that quail?" they asked. "I like the way you play that quail." It was a beautiful life in those early days with Fate Maribel's band. We used to take excursions from St. Louis twice a day. We'd go up the river, up to Illinois, play, and come on back and have supper. The night crew'd come on about 8:30 and we'd cruise up and down the river until about 11 or 12 o'clock. It was just like a dance hall.

Sandy: I have one more question to ask you. Would you mind giving me one of your typical Armstrong "oh, yeahs"?

Armstrong: Give you what, baby?

Sandy: Would you give us one of your typical Armstrong "oh, yeahs"?

Armstrong: Oh, yeah? (Louis sings.) "Ba, ba, da, do, bee, ay, ohh, yeaaaaaa." (Louis sings an octave higher.) Ba, ba, Boo, Dee, da, pop, oh, yeaaaaaaaaaaaaa.

Sandy: That sounds great. I want to thank you again for this honor.

Armstrong: You send me your name and address and I'll send you a nice photograph. You put that over your interview.

Sandy: Thank you.

Armstrong: You gonna send me your address and name?

Sandy: Sure.

Armstrong: OK, baby. Bye, bye.

Bart Starr

Bart Starr was interviewed by Paul Jaeger

Paul Jaeger, grade 9, 1969

Paul: What does it take to make it as a pro quarterback?

Starr: It takes a lot of experience. You don't just step right into this league and burn it up. You're playing with people who have had a lot of experience—great talent. The competition is much keener than it is in college. It just takes a long time to fit into the picture.

You don't make it overnight. You might play a few brilliant games because of individual effort, but you're not going to step in there in the first season and take your team to a championship. You just don't do it. It takes awhile to get acclimated.

Paul: Do you really enjoy playing pro football or do you just do it to make a living?

Starr: I enjoy doing it a great deal. I think I can answer that question by saying anything you don't enjoy doing, you wouldn't have a part of it regardless of what the remuneration involved might be. We feel the same way about pro football. It's a great life but no amount of money would have you play it if you really didn't enjoy the game.

Paul: What do you think makes Mr. Lombardi such a good coach?

Starr: First of all, he's an inspirational man. He can motivate you. I think today you have to be able to motivate people who are under you. If you can't motivate people who are working for you, you are in real trouble. He can handle men extremely well. He's a great psychologist. He is tough, hard-nosed, and a real disciplinarian.

When you saw what he demanded, you had an inner feeling that he wasn't demanding anything that he had not done somewhere in his life, so you had a great respect for this. He also was a great teacher.

I think in order to coach well you have to be able to teach well because coaching is teaching and teaching is coaching. These are some of the things that have made him a great man, plus the fact that he's obviously a perfectionist and he strives for perfection."

Paul: I'd like to thank you for the time and consideration you have given us to make our project a great success. Since I'm alone in this class of Viking fans, I want to say I strongly believe that the Pack will be back.

Starr: Thank you, Paul. We will be.

Wernher von Braun

Wernher von Braun was interviewed by Robin Selvig
Wernher von Braun developed the German V-2 rocket sign bomb. He surrendered to the 44th US Division. He was naturalized in 1955 and acclaimed for the major share of America's first earth satellite, Explorer I.

Robin: When you were working on the V-2 rocket, did you foresee the rapid development of rockets and missiles?

Photograph of Wernher von Braun from the National Archives

von Braun: I went into this rocket business because I was interested in astronomy, and I had always been dreaming about flying equipment and people to the moon. I considered all the other things that went on before this as steps to a rocket to the moon. So the answer is "yes."

Robin: How long did it take you to develop the V-2 rocket

von Braun: That took about four years. Now the thing was that there was a smaller version of it and before that there was an even smaller one. I started in rocketry in earnest in 1932 and the V-2 flew 10 years later, but the V-2 itself, a rocket this size, was started in 1938.

Robin Selvig, grade 9, 1969

Robin: What has been most satisfying about your scientific career?

von Braun: I would say our recent flight around the moon was undoubtedly most satisfactory. It was in a way the culmination of many of my plans and it was highly gratifying to see how successful the precise precision with which the thing really came out.

Robin: After looking at pictures of the moon, it all looks very different. What about purposely trying to land there?

von Braun: We have already identified quite a number of locations on the moon that are of very great scientific interest. The moon has no atmosphere and as a result, it never had erosion caused by wind and by waves and so the moon is almost like a photographic image that needs a precise record of anything that ever happened on it for millions of years past. Every meteor that ever hit it or any moonquake that ever shook up the moon left its imprint on the face of the moon and no erosion has ever washed out the traces. As a result the moon can teach us a lot of things that the earth cannot. Now there are some very specific intriguing questions.

Let me give you just one example: Many people believe that there will be permafrost on the moon, which means you drill a hole into the lunar soil down a few feet deep you may hit ice, just like in the arctic regions, permafrost, ice that is continuously frozen there and that doesn't even melt in the lunar days in the shelter of insulating properties of the soil that covers it up. Now this ice may be on top of liquid water on the moon and in fact, there are some indications that every now and then when a meteorite hits the lunar service, it may locally fragment this permafrost and the water from underneath comes gushing out and runs down a little river maybe a mile long, evaporating all the time because there is no atmosphere and what it leaves behind is a dry river bed, what they call an arroyo in California. There are some such dry riverbeds on the moon. Nobody can explain them at the moment, but many people believe that this may be what causes them, impacts of meteorites under the permafrost.

Robin: Do you feel we really are in a space race with Russia?

von Braun: The Russians are not racing us, but they are surely moving at a pretty good clip and I wonder how fast it will be running if we start racing? I suppose we are racing them.

Robin: In what ways do you feel Russia is ahead of the United States?

von Braun: It's a little hard to tell. We just flew around the moon. The Russians just had four men up in an earth orbit to build a space station, so we both have very ambitious programs. They may not be aimed in precisely the same direction all the time. We seem to be ahead of them in some fields and they are ahead of us in other fields. You cannot necessarily say who is ahead of whom if the objectives are not exactly alike.

Robin: Considering the immensity of Saturn 5, how much larger will rockets get?

von Braun: We don't know, really. To us it still looks awfully big and for the time being, we have a tremendous payload hauling capability there in the Saturn 5. On our last flight we carried 142 tons of payload fully loaded of fuel and passengers, just the payload, and are still busy filling this payload capability with meaningful scientific missions.

Robin: How much larger do you think they will have to get for interplanetary travel?

von Braun: For interplanetary travel you could do something else. That is what we are presently planning. We would fly a number of Saturn 5's into an earth orbit, each carrying a part of an interplanetary rocket ship into earth orbit and there we would assemble these vehicles that fly on say to the planet Mars from payloads that were carried up by several of these Saturn 5 rockets. This way you can start with a pretty big rocket in earth orbit already where you have already the orbiter speed and it can carry substantial payloads to Mars.

Robin: Do you think we will ever be able to reuse rockets?

von Braun: Yes. this is one of the most exciting programs we are presently working on. It is absolutely necessary that with reusable rockets we will be able to cut the costs to about ten percent of what it is now.

Robin: I'd like to thank you. This has all been very interesting.

von Braun: Thank you very much, Miss Selvig, and please greet your class for me. I really enjoyed this.

Jack Lemmon

Jack Lemmon was interviewed by Sue Murphy.

Sue Murphy
grade 9, 1969

Lemmon: Hello?

Sue: Hello.

Lemmon: Hello. How are you, Sue?

Sue: Fine. How are you?

Lemmon: I'm terrible. I've got a bad cold but I'm up and around. I don't know if I may be getting sick, but I'm up and around.

Sue: I've got a few questions jotted down. You have made a great many movies. Which one did you enjoy making the most and gave you the most satisfaction?

Lemmon: Actually, not any single one. Not one and for several reasons. I think there's a tendency among actors when they have a good part that this part right now is the best part they've ever been in and then suddenly when the next good one comes along, you drop the curtain on the one before. Your involvement is at such a high emotional level that you feel the same way again and you are convinced that each time you get a good part that this is the best one until another one comes along.

Also, I think that different kinds of parts can appeal. I couldn't pick a definite one. I enjoyed *Days of Wine and Roses* and I enjoyed *Some Like It Hot*, yet they are widely diverse types of parts. Again, I think *Mr. Roberts* and also *The Apartment* and *Odd Fellows*. I would say I like *Days of Wine and Roses* and *Some Like It Hot* as much as anything I've ever done and the last one is called the *The Out of Towners*, which isn't released yet.

Sue: Of all the people you've worked with, who did you enjoy the most?

Lemmon: I think Walter Matthau. I think he's the best all-around actor I've ever acted with, and also personally because we hit it off so well.

Sue: How many movies have you made with him?

Lemmon: With Walter, I've made two. The first was called *The Fortune Cookie* and then *The Odd Couple*. Hopefully we'll be able to find something again.

Sue: In *Days of Wine and Roses* you played a dramatic part. Do you enjoy playing this type of part or comedy?

Lemmon: I don't have any preference for drama over comedy or comedy over drama. It depends on the appeal of the part itself, not the part. If it's a well-written part and strangely enough, if I feel that when I first read a script and I don't know how to play it, I am more excited about doing it than if I have done it. If it's challenging, if I am a little worried about whether or not I can do it and how I do the part, it will probably stretch me and I'll be a better actor.

Sue: After all the comedy roles you've played, do you think you're stereotyped as a comedian?

Lemmon: Yes, to a certain extent. Eighty percent of the scripts, just to pick a figure that I receive are comedies purely because people think of me from all the comedies that I have done.

Sue: Every one who knows anything about movies knows that you are the number one actor in film today. Who, in your opinion, are the other great stars today?

Lemmon: Oh, that depends on—that's very flattering—but according to different polls I wouldn't be number one right now, but five months from now, well, those crazy things all depend on what film happened to click at what time.

Theater owners look over the films and say, "Well, gee, Jack Lemmon's films are our biggest gross and, therefore, he's the number one fellow," but I think the polls all vary. I think Paul Newman and Steve McQueen are very big and popular today. Dustin Hoffman is becoming enormously successful and I think he deserves it. I think he's a fine actor. I imagine Jon Voight will become quite popular after his success in *Midnight Cowboy*. I think also that he is a very fine young actor.

Sue: In your biography I noticed that Billy Wilder directed several of your movies. Who is your favorite director?

Lemmon: I would have to say Billy. Again, as I said about Walter, not alone for the talent, which is so immense—as a matter of fact, I think Billy is one of the best teachers because he is one of a handful of producer, writer, and directors. He's not only a brilliant writer, he's also a very fine director, and it's difficult to find both talents in one person.

The only other one that comes to mind is Fellini with as much consistency and success. Personally, Wilder and I are so close. If you hit it off personally, you have a tendency to say, "He's my favorite director," because that does affect your work a great deal, the enjoyment of the personal relationship.

Sue: How much influence does the movie-goer have on the kinds of movies being made?

Lemmon: I think they have a very big influence, but strangely, I don't think they will use it as much as they could. They have an enormous influence on whatever the public picks and makes extremely popular than anyone sitting in a studio in Hollywood thinks. A movie is made and the public likes it. "Well, gee, whiz," say the Hollywood people, "that's the type of movie I have to make.

Take *Easy Rider*. It was unique. Suddenly it becomes a hit and nobody expected it to be. So now everybody in Hollywood is desperately running around trying to make another *Easy Rider*-type picture and they don't know what it is. What happens is you get an awful lot of carbon copies of the original that are never as good. That's why there are so many bad movies. I don't think that if the public sat down and wrote letters that those letters would affect the studios. If the stayed away in droves, they would have an effect. The films to be made are only affected by box office.

Sue: Have you modeled your acting after anyone else?

Lemmon: I never have. I am still surprised when someone says, "It's a Jack Lemmon-like part." I never really know what that means. I try to approach each part as a separate entity and try to create a different character.

Sue: Thanks very much for calling me and giving us your time.

Lemmon: You're very welcome. I enjoyed it and I wish you and everybody else who's out there a Happy New Year and peace to all.

Dear Sue:

    Just a brief note to thank you so very much for your very sweet letter. I am delighted that you felt the phone call went well and I can only tell you that I enjoyed it immensely. I find it's always rather awkward to have a prolonged telephone conversation with someone I've never met -- and, when you say that I made you feel at ease, I must say that you made me feel the same way. You were charming, intelligent, and you couldn't have handled it better.

    Once again, my many thanks for the call, your letter, and your picture. I appreciate them.

Most sincerely,

Jack Lemmon

Jack Lemmon

John H. Glenn Jr.

John H. Glenn Jr. was interviewed by Steve Flaten
On February 20, 1962, John Glenn flew the first United States manned orbital mission on board Mercury-6, Friendship 7. Glenn orbited the earth three times, flying a distance of 75,679 miles.

Photograph of John Glenn from the National Archives

Steve: We are very interested in having you describe firsthand your impressions of liftoff, orbit, and re-entry.

Steve Flaten
grade 9, 1969

Glenn: That's a big order to describe in a few minutes. I think there's a false impression that people have of what it's like at liftoff. I think many people have seen *Star Trek* too many times on TV or *Captain Video* because they think at liftoff you're squashed back in the seat and practically unconscious. It's quite the opposite because at liftoff you barely have enough thrust on the booster and you just overcome the weight of the whole booster and you lift off very quietly. On a couple of flights, the people have not really been sure whether they had lifted off the launch pad and were underway or not. Once you get up almost in orbit is when you have the most force involved on the astro because by that time the fuel has been burned down, and you're up to eight G's, eight times gravity at time of insertion into orbit.

The weightless period while you're in flight is a very comfortable time. The main thing is learning how to handle equipment in a weightless state, where things just float about in air or float in the oxygen in front of you if you let go of them. During re-entry once again you get up to seven and one half or eight G's. This is a very busy time and it's probably the most critical time of most flights because that's when the most force is working on the spacecraft. You have the highest G level, the highest shaking or resonance, the highest number of varying forces are all set up there at that same time, so if you're going to have any trouble with the structure of the spacecraft, that's probably when it would occur.

"Re-entry is the most spectacular time because that's when you're enveloped in a whole fireball. When you're looking out the window, it can be the most interesting time of the whole flight."

Steve: Please describe what the earth looked like from space.

Glenn: On my flight we were much more limited in our view because it was the first of the orbital flights, and we were up about 110 to 160 miles altitude. The colors back toward the earth looked much the same as they do flying in a jet plane at high altitude. In space you see blackness even on the daylight side of the earth. You don't have the blue sky up there because we don't have any atmosphere for the light to be refracted.

Steve: Another student talked with Wernher von Braun, who thought space exploration was very important. How do you feel about this?

Glenn: We don't know what the benefits might be, but it's like any exploration or any research. You can't pinpoint the benefit in advance. We know its value. Our progress is largely dependent on the fact that we are a curious people. We've been willing to spend money on research and exploration. It's almost a way of life in this country for businesses and individuals. Many businesses have devoted huge staffs and a lot of time and effort to research programs. The government has devoted a lot of time and effort.

Of course we have the political implications of our space race with Russia, which I think have been overdone, but we can't ignore that facet of the program. Sixty-three countries have come into their present national identities since World War I. They are naturally going to follow a technological leader, many of them, anyway. We don't want to be second best in this area either, but the long term implications of space research and exploration are more important for the long run of mankind than just these political considerations of our progress versus the Russian program.

The new principles that may come from the space program that we can't see at the onset could be illustrated by some of the Van Allen Radiation Belt studies. Before the space program no one had any idea that there were even radiation belts up there. Then probes went up and found the Van Allen Belts. Later probes better defined them. This was just an interesting scientific curiosity, but then later on we found that the solar winds actually hit the Van Allen Radiation Belts and flow around the earth. They are deflected and flow around the earth in a big teardrop-shape pattern, like bow waves around a ship.

This is academic and not of much importance until times of high solar activity. When most of this deflection is occurring, the heating of our upper atmosphere is changed, and when that heating changes, it changes the jet stream in the atmosphere and high altitude. Then we find that when the jet streams change, our weather patterns here on earth change.

We can begin to see a pattern here that may someday help us know how we can control them. Perhaps we end up with some means of weather control here on earth in various patterns, but maybe someday it will give us the opportunity to put more moisture by weather control into desert areas or something like that. None of this could be seen at the beginning of the space program, and we don't know yet what benefits may come of this, but it's the type of thing I'm talking about where we encounter new principles or new information that becomes very, very valuable and later provides the information for a whole new area of progress we could not foresee before the explorations were conducted.

CHARLES M. SCHULZ
2162 COFFEE LANE
SEBASTOPOL, CALIFORNIA 95472

Dec. 13, 1968

Connie Gustafson
10905 London Dr.
Burnsville, Minn. 55378

Dear Connie:

Thank you for your kind letter. It would
be a pleasure for me to talk with you and
your class.

January 10 will be fine with me. My
number is   . I will be looking
forward to talking with you then.

Kindest regards.

Sincerely yours,

Charles M. Schulz

© 1950 United Feature Syndicate

Charles Schultz

Charles Schultz was interviewed by Connie Gustafson

Connie Gustafson
grade 9, 1969

Connie: I'm wondering why you don't include adults in your comic strip.

Schultz: Oh, because it's funnier this way. There have been comic strips about adults and kids for years, and this was a new form. That was all. I just think it gave it a new angle.

Connie: Do you have any favorite characters and a favorite cartoon?

Schultz: I suppose that I like not just one favorite character. I like Linus, Charlie Brown and Snoopy the best, and I can't really pick out one cartoon that would be my favorite.

Connie: Do you find cartooning an enjoyable career?

Schultz: I think it's the best career in the world.

Connie: Are your characters fashioned after real people?

Schultz: No! No! No!

Connie: Where do you get most of your ideas?

Schultz: I just sit here in my room and think of them.

Connie: Are you planning any new characters?

Schultz: I have no plans for any. I always have hopes that I'll think of something, but I never plan that far ahead. I have to get something in the mail all the time. I just work for day to day.

Connie: From my research I found that you don't like naming your comic strip *Peanuts*.

Schultz: No, it's a terrible name.

Connie: Why don't you change it?

Schultz: It's a very complicated business. You see the strip is owned by United Feature Syndicate, and there are a lot of people involved in this and you just can't do things at a whim that way, but maybe I'll change it some-day.

Connie: Why did you change the style of your drawings?

Schultz: You're not aware of that. This is not something you do delib-erately. Every day you draw the strip I think you change styles, but you're not aware of it. You just keep drawing it from day to day, and each day you draw it the best you can and gradually the characters do change.

This happens to all comic strips. Mine just seemed to be a little more extreme than others but it happens to all drawings. If you look back upon any comic strips which were drawn ten to twenty years ago, you'll see there was a considerable change in style.

Connie: Do you have any advice for people considering cartooning as a career?

Schultz: You have to be dedicated. I know of very few who are not completely dedicated because it's such a tremendously competitive field. I wanted to be nothing but a cartoonist ever since I was about six years old. It's not the sort of thing you can just go into halfheartedly. You have to know how to draw pretty well. You have to have quite an imagination and be reasonably sensitive to things that happen around you.

Connie: Mr. Schultz, thank you very, very much.

Schultz: Well, thank you. I appreciate your calling.

Connie: Good-bye.

Schultz: Bye.

Connie Gustafson interviewing
Charles Schultz

Vice President Hubert H. Humphrey

Vice President Hubert H. Humphrey was interviewed by Randy Nurenberg

Randy Nurenberg
grade 9, 1969

Randy: What have been some of the high points and low points of your career?

Vice President Humphrey: Oh, you ask tough questions don't you. My career started in 1945 when I was mayor of Minneapolis. I feel it was a good beginning—the program of law enforcement we gave to that community, improving the recreational and welfare services. I think that was one of the better things that I've been able to make a contribution to.

Here in the Senate, serving for sixteen years, the high point was to be the Majority Whip, which I had as a position for four years, a position of great responsibility. To manage the passage of the Civil Rights Bill of 1964 took eighty-three days of debate. It was the first time in the history of the Senate we were able to break a filibuster. We were able to overcome that and pass the legislation. I would say that those were the high points.

Of course, to be elected the Vice President was the greatest honor of my life. To have the opportunity to run for President was the greatest challenge of my life and it was a great honor.

What were the disappointments? That I didn't do better. The greatest disappointment was not winning the Presidency, but having said that, I hope that in my campaign I conducted myself in a way that people thought was honorable and decent and worthy of my trust and faith.

Randy: What are some of the major contributions you have made while serving as a senator and vice president?

Vice President Humphrey: I was the author of the Peace Corps legislation, which provided for sending young Americans who volunteered for service to help other people in other lands, to teach them and help them with their programs of agriculture and education and community development. I was the author of the Defense Education Act, which provided aid for our schools, one of the big education programs.

I was also the author of the Nuclear Test Ban Treaty Resolution. That was a resolution by Congress, asking the President of the United States to negotiate with the Soviet Union a treaty to prevent further testing of nuclear weapons in the atmosphere. I went to Moscow to sign that treaty for our government in 1963. I had many other things such as the Job Corps in the Poverty Program of which I was the author.

I would say my most interesting work was to be chairman of the Space Council. We coordinated all of the space activities such as Apollo 8. That program was my responsibility and to be chairman of the Marine Council, to work with government and industry in the exploration of the seas and oceans. My work with young people as the chairman of the Youth Opportunity Council. We were able to provide over a million jobs for teenagers, students, young men and women, young people that were poor, who needed a job. We had millions of young men and women in organized athletics.

Randy: What were some of your thoughts as you watched President Johnson close his political career last night?

Vice President Humphrey: I thought of the days he served here, dramatic days, through World War II and all the years since then. What turmoil our country has gone through! What change! I couldn't help think about how much has been done as he reviewed last night in his State of the Union message what programs were now on the law books and what we were now doing. I felt a great sense of pride to have had a little share in getting this done.

Many of the programs we have today, I helped author as the Vice President. I know President Johnson must have felt a great sense of pride, humble pride, to know that despite all of our troubles, that our country today is the richest country in the world, growing richer everyday, strongest in the world, but more importantly, more people, just plain ordinary people are getting a good chance, better than any place else in the world.

The President must have had a great feeling of pride and joy knowing that he had such an important part in developing all this. And as vice-president and senator, I couldn't help but feel as the President said, "We tried." I think that we not only tried, but speaking for the President, I think we not only tried, I think he's done very, very well, and I think history will judge him as one of the truly great Presidents of the United States.

Randy: Do you think the system of choosing the President should be changed?

Vice President Humphrey: Yes, I do. I think there should be direct election of the President. I think the electoral system is obsolete and designed for a century ago, and it could cause a very great constitutional crisis in this country. I have long believed and advocated it whenever I have the chance.

Eddie Rickenbacker

Eddie Rickenbacker was interviewed by Craig Drake.
Edward Vernon Rickenbacker enlisted in the United States Army, became a fighter pilot and was given the command of the 94th Aero Squadron. He received the Distinguished Service Cross, the French *Croix de Guerre*, and the Congressional Medal of Honor.

Photograph of Eddie Rickenbacher from the National Archives

Craig: What one thing in your life are you most proud of?

Rickenbacker: The one thing that I'm most proud of is that I've learned to be a good American citizen. I've been able to pay back my debts which are the blessings that I'm enjoying and have enjoyed in my lifetime by being a good citizen and having the prestige of a real American.

Craig: What was it like being in a dogfight in World War I?

Rickenbacker: Number one was, Craig, you had an adversary up there that was equipped with a machine gun or two. If you didn't want to get shot down, because that's what he was there to do, you tried to shoot him down first to save your own life. When you've got an adversary trying to kill you, you've got to kill him first.

Craig: Do you think it's important to beat Russia to the moon?

Rickenbacker: Oh, definitely. It's very vital. The key to that is to get power enough in the boosters to put platforms into orbit which will act as a service station around Mother Earth where you can shuttle crews back and forth and actually use the platform as a service station to refuel.

Craig Drake
grade 9, 1969

Craig: If you were in the White House, how would you handle the Vietnam War?

Rickenbacker: I wouldn't handle it. I would have handled it. You can't win a war without winning. You can't win a war without trying. The only way we'll ever get out of Vietnam is by fighting our way out.

Craig: Why is it that you never ran for a political office?

Rickenbacker: I was never interested in politics. You can't always be honest with yourself if you are a politician.

Craig: What do you think of America's young people today?

Rickenbacker: There are a great many more fine and able youngsters than there are what I'd call "hippies," "beatniks," or "stupid card burners."

I was just out to the Air Force Academy over the weekend. They have around 3100 students, finest young men you ever laid your eyes on. All someday are going to be leaders in our military service, one way or another. That training they can never get anywhere else in the world. For that reason they are outstanding. I didn't see one longhaired boy there out of those 3100. I didn't see one with long sideburns hanging down to his chin. They all looked like American boys.

Craig: For my vocation I have chosen to be an airline pilot. Are there any tips you can give me in fulfilling this desire?

Rickenbacker: You better learn everything you can from the ground up. First, learn to be a good student. If you want to be a pilot, you ought to go to the Academy or become a cadet in the U.S. Air Force. You can't get better training anywhere in the world, but you better know a lot of things before you get to that point. Do you understand?

Craig: Thank you very much for letting us do this interview.

Rickenbacker: I'm delighted to have a chance to talk to you, Craig. Send me a copy of the tape, and I'll make the corrections and send it back.

The Adventures of Isaac Asimov and Mr. Chips

Seemed Like a Good Idea at the Time

Final Note from Mr. Chips: After reflecting on this incident for thirty-one years, I would like to apologize posthumously to Mr. Asimov. In my enthusiasm to help Philip interview his hero, I did indeed, push too hard. I asked to have the interview held at 7:00 A.M. because that was when our class met. We canceled the interview because Philip and I had other classes at 9:00. I would like to apologize, also, Mr. Asimov, for badgering and being curt and imposing. I'm disappointed I never had the opportunity to meet the real Isaac Asimov and that he never got to meet the real Mr. Chips.

Mr. Tom Melchior
John Metcalf Junior High School
County Road 30 and Highway 13
Burnsville, Minnesota, 55378

Dear Mr. Metcalf,

Your undated letter cancelling the telephone interview with your student Philip Short has been received. The interview is indeed cancelled.

Despite your perfunctory apologies, I suspect you haven't the slightest idea of how (to use a mild word) irritating you have been.

Mr. Short sent me a letter (with your encouragement no doubt) asking me to tape the answers to some questions for him:

1) He did not send the tape

2) If he had, it would have done no good since I do not have a tape-recorder and I don't know why it should be assumed I do.

3) Every mail brings me requests from young people all over the world. I have no secretary and I try to answer as many requests as I can---but to devote the necessary thirty-six hours a day to answering all of them is obviously impossible

I answered, therefore, that I could not accede to the request and, in response, I received a badgering phone call from you. I honestly think you expected I ought to be glad to engage in a telephoned interview at 7:30 A.M. and were annoyed to have me suggest 9:30 A.M. instead.

Then, after I agreed, with some visible reluctance, you send me the current curt letter which is clearly intended to make me feel guilty. Sir, if you see yourself in the role of Mr. Chips, that is your business, but please have some consideration for the people on whom you attempt to impose.

Yours,

Isaac Asimov

Isaac Asimov

8

Guest Storyteller

T HIS FINAL CHAPTER IS AN INVITATION TO YOU TO TELL
your stories. It is important that we teachers tell our stories. How
else will we discover who we are? How else will the public discover the magic that goes on behind the walls of their schools?

Don Glover taught K-12 adapted physical education in the White Bear Lake school system. Don was named Minnesota Teacher of the Year in 1981.

Eric

I HAD COACHED AND TAUGHT FOR TWENTY-SEVEN YEARS.
Most of my experience during that time was in the mainstream elementary and secondary physical education classroom. In the spring of 1979, our district started an adapted physical education program and asked if I would teach it.

Don and Eric

I didn't have much of a background working with disabled youngsters, but I thought it would be a welcome change, so decided to try it. Back then special licensure training for eventual licensure was "on the job experience." One of my first students was Eric. He had had a stroke when he was in the second grade, and as a result, the stroke left him very unstable and quite weak. When I started with Eric, he was a ninth grader. Eric was very small, about four feet, ten inches tall and quite heavy for his height, about one hundred fifty pounds. He also had very poor balance and a lot of difficulty walking and running. But Eric had a terrific spirit and a wonderful sense of humor. In the fall of 1980 in what was the first adapted physical education class of my career, I asked Eric what type of activity he would like to try. "Football," he said.

I said, "Well, Eric, how about croquet or bocce ball or archery?" My main concern was keeping Eric safe. The last thing on my mind was football.

He persisted. So did I. I won. We didn't play football. Oh, we practiced plays, we threw passes, and we tried pass routes. We knew all the positions and all the rules, but we never played the game. How could we? There were only two of us.

We had a great ninth grade year. We attempted many sports and activities, all safe with little risk involved. The only close call we had that year was when I took Eric in his wheelchair into the bathroom. We got in all right, but we couldn't get out. The wheelchair wedged between the door and the toilet stool. We were trapped. We simply could not get out. We started laughing so hard we would have fallen, but we couldn't because there was no room.

In the fall of Eric's sophomore year, he again informed me that he would like to play football. Eric's condition had deteriorated, and he was even more unstable, but again he persisted saying, "Mr. Glover, I want to play the game of football." Again we practiced plays, ran pass routes, studied positions and rules, but I was very cautious about letting him play in an actual game.

Finally one day Eric got upset. I had never seen him that angry, so it made me realize just how much he wanted to play the game. So I said, "Eric, I promise on Friday we will play a game of football." That gave me just two days to find some kids that I could get out of study hall to play with us.

On Friday morning I walked into the first hour study hall, and lo and behold, the study hall was full of football players. The varsity team had a game that night, and all the players were wearing their game jerseys.

When I met Eric on the practice field with eight real football players, his eyes got wide and his hands got shaky. I could tell he was excited and thrilled.

After I had explained to the players that this class was for Eric's success and not theirs, and after going over some special rules, such as only walking allowed, and after cautioning the players not to be rough, our game got underway.

I was the quarterback on Eric's team. I always put him at wide receiver and ran the ball or threw it away from his position. "Remember, Don," I kept telling myself, "keep Eric safe. Don't let him get too involved."

Eric was getting frustrated. He was playing the game but at the same time he wasn't really playing. I may as well have made him a cheerleader. Finally he came to the huddle and said, "Mr. Glover, can I run the ball?"

Eric could not run and I was very nervous about him carrying the ball. But after cautioning the other players about touching and bumping him, we made up a play just for him. When I called "Blue 22," Eric would start in motion from his wide receiver position. On the signal "hut two," the ball would be snapped and I would give it to Eric. The guards would pull out and block for Eric so he could score a touchdown.

"Ready, break," I yelled. "Blue 22. Hut one! Hut two!" Eric got the ball and started walking as fast as he could around end. The defense was opening up. The offense yelled, "Go, Eric! Go!"

Eric was getting closer to the goal line. He was going faster than his balance would allow and down he went. He fell forward and landed on his face and chest. He did not let go of the ball nor did his other arm get forward to break his fall. He plowed a furrow into the dirt with his nose.

The football players grew suddenly silent. I rushed over to pick him up. His glasses were cockeyed, his noise was bleeding, and blood and tears mixed with dirt streaked down his face.

I was devastated. I wanted him to have fun. I didn't want him killed. I wanted him safe!

Once he stopped sobbing, we walked back to our huddle. I was determined to get through the rest of the hour and keep Eric out of the game and as safe as possible. I was about to call another play when Eric said, "Mr. Glover," sob, choke, sob, "can I carry the ball again?"

I looked at the faces of our teammates, and they looked as dumbfounded as I did. I agreed to let him try for the touchdown again.

"Ready, break," I hollered. "Blue 22." Eric went in motion. "Hut one! Hut two!" I handed him the ball. He started around end again, this time keeping his balance. He crossed the goal line, spiked the ball, and threw up his arms.

His teammates mobbed him and gave him high fives.

Eric's touchdown did more for my teaching than any license preparation courses ever could have. Eric and his touchdown taught me this about the human spirit: No matter what kind of body the spirit is encased in, it will win if it perseveres.

The Joy of Running

Her name was Leah and she was blind. Leah was in the seventh grade when I taught her how to run. She grabbed one end of a shuffleboard pole, a golf club, or a hockey stick. She grabbed the stick with one hand and I grabbed the other end and we ran on the track.

Don Glover

As long as Leah had something to hang on to, she was fine. When I led, she would trot or run at a faster pace. But if I had her run by herself, her hands went immediately into the high guard position, up close to her face and out in front of her because she was afraid of hitting something.

Leah was totally blind and had been since birth. She was also legally deaf, but she could hear with her earphones when I used a microphone and a transmitter. This projected my voice to her electronically and she could hear quite well that way. She used this device in the classroom also.

After a year of running with me as her guide, I started having her run by herself. We started with very short distances. We went to a flat area such as a football field. I'd say, "OK, Leah, you can hear my voice. I'm standing about twenty yards in front of you. I want you to run to my voice."

She always ran at a slow trot, keeping her hands at the high guard position. We did that over and over. I tried to get her to trust enough to let her hands down along her sides.

Can you imagine being totally blind and running fast? Leah had to trust me implicitly to do that. We worked and worked on running freely that fall. She got to be pretty good at it, and so me moved into the gym during the winter. First we tried it in half the gym. Knowing that we were in the gym, she trusted me enough to begin drop her arms and pump them. She started to run more freely.

That spring I thought she was ready to run fast. One day we were not on the track but on a flat field. The school was about one hundred meters away. The field was very flat. We practiced there every day because it was quite a trek to get to the football field, almost a block away.

Leah got better and better and better and I got lazier and lazier and lazier. We didn't run with the pole. I said, "Go," into the microphone and she ran. When I said, "Stop," she stopped on a dime and her hands would go up. She got more confidence in herself. She ran with her arms at her side. She ran faster. I didn't run with her because I had a lot of confidence in the transmitter. All I had to do was say, "Leah, stop," and she would stop. Then I said, "OK, now turn around and run back to me. Ready. Go." When she was close to me, I said, "Stop," and she stopped.

One beautiful spring morning, everything clicked for her. I said, "OK, let's try it one more time. Ready. Go." She took off and when she was twenty yards away, I yelled, "Leah, stop." But she didn't stop. Her running was beautiful. She was now using her arms and running with speed. She was landing on the balls of her feet and I thought, "Gee, she's really into this."

I yelled again, "Leah, stop." She was thirty yards away well within the range of my transmitter, but she didn't stop. She kept going, running toward the side of the junior high school. If she didn't stop running, she was going to run into the side of that brick building. Her hands were not up in the high guard position. She would hit the building with her head. All the trust she had placed in me for the past two years would be lost in one shattering blow.

Momentarily paralyzed and still trusting the transmitter, I screamed, "LEAH, STOP!" She didn't stop. She was into her running. I thought she would anyway because she had gone twice as far as she had ever gone before.

I knew I had precious little time to catch her before she hit the building. I used to be a sprinter in high school, but now I was forty years old, and I didn't know if I had had any sprint left in my legs. I yelled once more, but she didn't stop. She was in the zone and heading for the wall.

I took off. I was moving. I couldn't run and yell into the transmitter at the same time, so I let the transmitter hang from my neck and I ran. I grabbed her by the back of her jacket and pulled. When I stopped Leah, she was less than six inches from the wall. Her hands flew up into the high guard position.

"Leah," I said, "I yelled, 'Stop.' Why didn't you stop?"

"I didn't hear you," she said. "I was running."

The rites of passage take us through the doors of the unknown where we will dance the dance of life whether or not we can name the tune. I hope those of you who passed through this door with me enjoyed the music.

These stairs and the bannister were just a few steps from my first-grade classroom On the first day of school, the teacher commanded, "No sliding down the bannister," but few of us could resist the temptation to whiz down the polished oak? Once I began the journey as a student and teacher, it lasted forty-seven years. What a grand adventure it was!   *Gaylord Public School,*